OXFORD STUDIES
IN MODERN EUROPEAN HISTORY

General Editors
SIMON DIXON, MARK MAZOWER,
and
JAMES RETALLACK

States of Division

*Border and Boundary Formation
in Cold War Rural Germany*

SAGI SCHAEFER

OXFORD
UNIVERSITY PRESS

OXFORD
UNIVERSITY PRESS

Great Clarendon Street, Oxford, OX2 6DP,
United Kingdom

Oxford University Press is a department of the University of Oxford.
It furthers the University's objective of excellence in research, scholarship,
and education by publishing worldwide. Oxford is a registered trade mark of
Oxford University Press in the UK and in certain other countries

First Edition published in 2014

Impression: 2

Published in the United States of America by Oxford University Press
198 Madison Avenue, New York, NY 10016, United States of America

British Library Cataloguing in Publication Data
Data available

Library of Congress Control Number: 2014936191

ISBN 978–0–19–967238–7

Printed and bound by
CPI Group (UK) Ltd, Croydon, CR0 4YY

To Tali, Aviv and Gil

Acknowledgments

This book has its roots in a dissertation, which I began working on more than seven years ago. The contributions of many friends, colleagues, and teachers left indelible marks on this work. I have not included or accepted all the good comments and suggestions I received, but all of them challenged me to think and in many other ways improved my work.

I cannot imagine a better, more knowledgeable, or generous advisor than Volker Berghahn. From its earliest moments, as a vague amalgam of ideas, this book grew in a series of conversations with Volker. He has been unwavering in his support, while flowing with insightful comments and incisive questions. Even as I delved into the minutiae of daily life in the Eichsfeld, Volker never tired of reminding me what should be at stake with this project. Volker is my model of excellent mentoring—seeing students foremost as people and supporting their efforts to break their own paths. Volker's and Marion's home became a sort of home-away-from-home for us in New York and we are indebted to them for much more than just academic mentoring.

Karen Barkey opened her office and home to me during my years in New York and I am deeply thankful for both. The consummate teacher that she is, Karen spent long hours acquainting me with relevant scholarship and sharpening my academic tools. She encouraged me to apply a more theoretical thinking, to clarify, and to organize coherently. Her attention to overall arguments and systematic presentation improved my work tremendously.

I was fortunate to arrive at Columbia the same year as Mark Mazower. As a teacher, a writer, and a reader, Mark's scholarship has influenced my work immensely. Mark has the gift of seeing the importance of local, social, economic, and political conditions in the framework of broad, global, and continental historical currents, which I can only hope to emulate. His reading of my work was always the catalyst for crucial improvements.

I first contacted Frank Biess when I was formulating early dissertation ideas and saw in his dissertation a model for a successful project. Ever since, he commented patiently on countless drafts, helping me make sense of history as a profession. At Göttingen, Frank and Uli offered great food for soul and body, many nights on their sofa, and most valuably—their friendship. Frank's deep understanding of the dynamics of postwar German history and his careful reading and advice helped me figure out how to contribute meaningfully to this well-populated field.

Gil Eyal's contribution to my thinking has changed the final shape of the book crucially. He made concise, pointed, and thoughtful comments on every chapter, often opening my eyes to the potentials and limitations of my arguments. Gil's keen eye for the important and meaningful argument helped untangle many threads in my analysis.

Michael Gordin and Erika Milam have become my guides for the beginning historian, providing sage advice and helping me navigate the exciting territory of a young academic career. With their different emphases on content, style, and depth of argument, Erika and Michael helped me shape the framework of the book in important ways, teaching me much in the process about what it is that makes a text into a good book.

George Gavrilis's name was on the lips of almost everyone I told about my ideas early on, and rightfully so. George's writing supplied an important inspiration for my project. George also commented on a chapter draft and taught me much about concise and readable writing. Atina Grossmann agreed to read the full dissertation as the external reader and added several important dimensions to the conversation. Istvan Deak shared parts of his infinite treasure of knowledge about European history, commented on papers and was always ready to call my bluff. Istvan and Gloria opened their home to me and provided perspective and encouragement.

I first came across Edith Sheffer's name reading the programme of the GSA conference in 2006. Having single-handedly carved a viable field of research of the inter-German border with incredible footwork, sharp senses, and a true gift for meaningful interpretation, Edith was very generous towards the newcomer conveniently treading the path she had so laboriously cleared. Her work never fails to challenge and inspire me, setting high standards, and at the same time supplying the groundwork to build upon.

Astrid Eckert was already forming her own project about the inter-German border and its role in the history of the 'old federal republic' at the time I began my research. She offered insightful advice and shared with me materials and references she uncovered in her own work.

Brad Abrams, Gadi Algazi, Muriel Blaive, Jose Brunner, Jörg Echternkamp, Carole Fink, Christina Goldmann, Victoria de Grazia, Thomas Lindenberger, Anna Lipphardt, Berthold Molden, Sam Moyn, Libora Oates-Indruchová, Jan Palmowski, Susan Pedersen, Andrew Port, Oded Rabinovitch, Iris Rachamimov, Miriam Rürup, David Sabean, the late Charles Tilly, Adelheid von Saldern, Gerhard Sälter, Bernd Weisbrod, and Yfaat Weiss have all answered questions, shared information, and offered advice when I needed it.

Quite a few friends and colleagues supported my project—and my survival in general—throughout the work on this book. Giuliana Chamedes was my first friend at Columbia. Giuliana's insightful comments, curiosity, and humour were a great resource, keeping me sane and my work on course. Her comments on several drafts along the way made me engage bigger and more meaningful questions. Sara Doskow has offered an invaluable support for me and my work. She read patiently, repeatedly, drafts upon drafts, thoughtfully editing content, structure, and style.

Chris Barthel, Brandon County, Reto Hofmann, Dani Lainer-Voss, Daniel Mahla, Bill McAllister, Harel Shapira, Uri Shwed, Mari Webel, and Steve Wills all read drafts and helped improve my chapters, offering constructive critique and useful suggestions. The participants of the European History Seminar and the ISERP Graduate Fellow Colloquium at Columbia have contributed helpful comments and suggestions, as have the members of the inter-university borders research group in Israel.

The careful reading and suggestions offered by the three anonymous readers for OUP have been tremendously helpful. I thank Christopher Wheeler and Cathryn Steele at OUP for patiently walking me through this process.

The first time I saw the word 'Eichsfeld' was in the late Daphne Berdahl's *Where the World Ended*, the book which in many ways started me on this journey. It seemed like a potentially suitable region to study, but not until Georg Wamhof shared his Eichsfeld reading list with me, had I realized how interesting and rewarding it could be. Petra Behrens's long acquaintance with the region and its history were an invaluable resource for me during research in Germany.

Quite a few Eichsfelder generously aided my searches and inquiries. Dieter Wagner, manager of the relevant archives in Duderstadt and Göttingen, found time to offer a guided tour of the border, complete with stories about growing up in Fuhrbach. Ben Thustek, an Eichsfelder by choice and the educational manager of the Border Museum in Teistungen, opened the museum's archives and connections to me and assembled valuable materials. He also introduced me to Agnes Ekhardt, a true daughter of the borderlands and a great fountain of knowledge. I thank Herbert Koch and Siegfried Schmidt in Duderstadt, Herr Spiegel in the border Museum Shifflersgrund, and many others who spoke to me, hosted me and fed me during my travels in the Eichsfeld.

I was fortunate to find many patient, knowledgeable, and welcoming archivists, who enabled me to assemble the materials I needed. Regina Huschenbeth and the entire team of the *Kreisarchiv Eichsfeld* in Heiligenstadt went out of their way—and beyond their opening hours—to indulge my interest. Dr. Reinhard Buthmann of the BStU Erfurt branch creatively and patiently dug relevant materials out of the infinite well of Stasi files. Herr Franz and Frau Rössler, from the Bundesarchiv in Koblenz, Eveline Bock at the main Thuringian archive in Weimar, Kirsten Hoffmann at the main Lower Saxon archive in Hanover, Anne Severin at the Heiligenstadt town archive, and many other archivists spent patient hours assisting me in my searches.

The work for this book was supported by the Institute for Social and Economic Research and Policy (ISERP) at Columbia University, the Center for Metropolitan Studies at the Technical University in Berlin, the Graduate School of Arts and Sciences at Columbia University, the German Academic Exchange Service (DAAD), the Whiting Foundation, Howard and Natalie Shawn, the German Historical Institute in Washington DC, the Lady Davis Foundation, and the Franz Rosenzweig Minerva Center at the Hebrew University in Jerusalem. I finished this book while working at Tel Aviv University. I thank my colleagues and students at the history department for their support and inspiration during this work.

Working on this book has been quite a journey, one that I embarked on with Tali and probably would never have done so without her. Tali is the first, second, and third reader of every text I produce, my best commentator and critic. I have learned my most important lessons about research and writing from Tali, watching her pursue her own work, and talking to her endlessly about our and other people's research. Throughout this period, pursuing a doctoral project of her own, Tali never lost her confidence in me and my work, and in crucial moments her confidence and love held me and this project together. I am deeply indebted to Tali for this book and for so much more and am full of joy at the thought of accruing further debts and repaying them, day after day.

Tel Aviv, January 2014

Contents

Abbreviations

BGS	West German Federal Border Guard (*Bundesgrenzschutz*)
EEC	European Economic Community (*Europäische Wirtschaftsgemeinschaft*)
EU	European Union
FRG	Federal Republic of Germany (West Germany)
GDR	German Democratic Republic (East Germany)
GIP	Border Information Points (*Grenzinformationspunkte*)
GNV	border area traffic (*Grenznahverkehr*), 1973–89
Grepo/GP	East German Border Police (*Grenzpolizei*)
HO	Official government trade stores in East Germany (*Handelsorganization*)
KGV	Little Border Traffic (*Kleine Grenzverkehr*), 1946–52
LPG	Agricultural collective (*Landwirtschaftliche Produktionsgenossenschaft*)
MdF	Ministry or Minister of Finance (*Ministerium der Finanzen*)
MdI	Minister or Ministry of the Interior (*Ministerium des Innern*)
MfgF	West German Ministry for All-German Affairs (*Bundesministerium für Gesamtdetusche Fragen*)
MTS	Machine and Tractor Stations (*Maschinen-Traktoren Stationen*)
NVA	National People's Army (*Nationale Volksarmee*), East German army
PoW	Prisoner of War
SED	Socialist Unity Party (*Sozialistische Einheitspartei Deutschland*), East German ruling party
SMAD	Soviet Military Administration
SBZ	Soviet Occupation Zone (*Sovietische Besatzungszone*)
SPD	Social Democratic Party
VEB	People's Enterprise (*Volkseigene Betrieb*), nationalized factories, businesses and other enterprises in East Germany
VP	People's Police (*Volkspolizei*), East German police
ZGD/ZGS	Customs Service/Customs Guard (*Zollgrenzdienst/Zollgrenzschutz*), West German Customs Service
ZRG	Zonal Border Area (*Zonenrandgebiet*), the West German term for the area along the border with East Germany

ARCHIVES

BArch-B	Federal Archive, Berlin
BArch-K	Federal Archive, Koblenz
BArch-M	Federal Military Archive, Freiburg
BStU	Archives of the Federal Commissioner for the Stasi Files (several locations)
HeHStAW	Main Hessian State Archive, Wiesbaden
HeStAM	Hessian State Archive, Marburg
KrAGö	District Archive, Rural District of Göttingen, Lower Saxony
KrAEich	Eichsfeld District Archive, Heiligenstadt, Thuringia
NARA	United States National Archives, College Park, Maryland

NLA-HStAH	Main Lower Saxon State Archive, Hanover
NLA-StAW	Lower Saxon State Archive, Wolfenbüttel
StADud	Duderstadt Municipal Archive, Lower Saxony
StAGö	Göttingen Municipal Archive, Lower Saxony
StAHig	Heiligenstadt Municipal Archive, Thuringia
StAWitz	Witzenhausen Municipal Archive, Hessen
ThHStAW	Main Thuringian State Archive, Weimar

PRIVATE COLLECTIONS

The majority of documents used in this work are from the above named archives. I thank Ben Thustek and the Grenzlandmuseum Eichsfeld in Teistungen for helping me get in touch with several Eichsfelder, some of whom have shared some private documents with me. In the book, documents have been used from three private collections. Two of the owners requested to remain anonymous. The third is Siegfried Schmidt from Duderstadt, a long-time official, now retired, of the district of Duderstadt.

List of Figures and Tables

Introduction

A border's function and meaning are the sum total of decisions and actions of people; they cannot be deduced from maps and treaties. The border between East and West Germany effected considerable changes, most significantly the emergence of deep-set social boundaries in Germany. This book analyses bordering processes in postwar Germany to show that interactions between individuals, organizations, and communities determined this outcome. It focuses on practices, and examines what people and organizations did when faced with new lines on the map and on the ground. Communities, families, and organizations in Germany were initially unconstrained by the borders arbitrarily set between occupation zones. At the outset, the inter-German border was a bustling place where West and East met regularly, worked together, traded, and celebrated common traditions; where local authorities cooperated as a matter of routine. Fluidity and cooperation were not undone by diplomatic fiat or by the early development of the Cold War. Rather, border formation only gradually wove demarcation lines into the social and political fabric of imagined and experienced communities. This book tells the story of the four-decade-long voyage between two *States of Division*: the indefinite, unruly one and the well-defined, disciplined one.

Two parallel projects of state building in East and West Germany partnered in constructing the border to attain power and recognition, and relied on separation for legitimacy and mobilization. To achieve this, state organizations were forced into difficult conflicts and negotiations with frontier society. Intensive interaction *within* the divided territorial polities east and west of the border limited the possibility of interaction *across* the divide. Prolonged negotiations altered border policy on both sides and reoriented frontier economy and politics towards the separate centres in Bonn and East Berlin. The arbitrary partition thus gradually turned into a meaningful boundary. Western policy was as pivotal in creating the inter-German divide as the more infamous Eastern initiatives of physical division.

The process of division was long and complicated partly because it took place primarily in a rural environment. Forested hills, open expanses of snow and frost in winter, painted brown, and then green in spring, crisscrossed by field roads and streams, and dotted by villages and small towns: this was the landscape of the Iron Curtain. Frontier farmers became protagonists in the drama of border formation and state building when state agents ventured to regulate and control the borderlands. Land, and its centrality in rural society's economy and tradition, became the crux of drawn-out struggles between frontier communities and state agencies. The parameters of the rural borderlands, such as private land ownership and the breadth of open space, were at least as important in the development of German division as the policies made in Washington, Moscow, Berlin, and Bonn.[1] *States of Division* is the first book to analyse the impact of rural conditions on the manner in which temporary political demarcations turned into stable social boundaries along the Iron Curtain.

In this process, East and West Germany, indeed *The East* and *The West*, were produced and reproduced in the German borderlands. This book foregrounds interactions between individuals and organizations as the source of the transform-ations that produced separate East and West German communities. For example, when in 1952 the East German regime deported thousands of residents from the borderlands and declared new regulations for the restricted zone, thousands of frontier residents fled to the West. This unforeseen reaction confronted the regime with a significant drop in agricultural production. To avoid further depletion of workforce at the frontier, East German state agencies adopted a policy of leniency towards frontier residents and attempted to accommodate their needs. The result was a compromise, whereby East German frontier farmers were given land east of the border and were allowed to quietly keep their ownership over land west of the border. In return, they cooperated in excluding Western frontier farmers from ownership rights east of the border. The interwoven processes of state building and border formation thus fuelled the division of German society. Focusing on inter-actions offers a way out of a dichotomous interpretation of agency in border formation. This method emphasizes neither the state agents' role in division nor that of the 'ordinary people'. Instead, it shows how different state and civil organizations, communities, and individuals created division by interacting with the ever-changing border and among each other.

This book underscores the reactive, multi-actor dynamics of border and bound-ary formation. Division was absorbed in Germans' perceptions of space and sense of belonging because they practised it over time. Rather than concentrating on the exceptional, the violent, and the outstanding, I emphasize the routine and the repeated, the acts that occupied the largest proportion of frontier residents' and state agents' time and attention.

Division as a stable reality materialized through experience rather than impos-ition. Economic motives drove the earliest incursions of state agencies into the routine practice of frontier communities and networks. Prioritizing state building through economic stabilization and growth, Western state agencies initiated an escalation of border control in the years 1948–52. Supervision of border crossing goods was dramatically tightened as part of an effort to combat black marketeering. Border-crossing trade was crucial to frontier economy at that time, and in an attempt to curb it, state agencies increasingly restricted the economic opportunities of individuals and communities in the borderlands.

In May 1952, East German state building changed gear and moved forward, taking the initiative from the West in pushing division deeper into the experience

---

[1] See George Last, *After the 'Socialist Spring': Collectivisation and Economic Transformation in the GDR* (New York: Berghahn, 2009), xxiv and FN 13 for a similar argument.

and daily lives of Germans. The Socialist Unity Party (SED) regime declared the former zonal demarcation 'State Border West', and ventured to uphold strict discipline around it. The newly established state agencies were no match for this enormous task, but their declarations were not empty. Violent deportations and mass flight to the West marked the early stages of this operation. When the dust settled, it turned out that on the ground the new regulations stood in the way of relatively few daily practices. The most dramatic transformation brought by this regulation was in agriculture, at that time still a mainstay of frontier economy and an important anchor of identification for many frontier residents. The following two decades saw bitter struggles over land between frontier farmers and state agencies on both sides of the border. When border formation engaged the land it disturbed deeply rooted land-based practices, interests, and identifications. The ensuing conflicts gave rise to new orientations and loyalties. Such changes served as a foundation for boundaries, which emerged within previously cohesive networks, communities, and families; that was the process of German division. As it evolved, land along the border was gradually taken over by state agencies. Cultivated land diminished on the frontier and barren, enclosed plots replaced it. The 'green border', as the belt of parks along the border came to be called in the 1990s, originated in this no man's land.

Along the inter-German border, regional communities and administrations struggled to keep valued traditions and coordination on pragmatic issues alive in the face of the emerging separation. The biggest hurdle before them was the West German campaign against recognition of the GDR, especially from 1955. This diplomatic tenet of the Federal Government dictated strict supervision by East and West German state agencies over every border-crossing contact. Enforcing symbolic political priorities on regional coordination initiatives, state agencies eventually deprived such contacts of value and by 1960 these initiatives had all died out. Border-crossing regional networks and communities were thus severed before the construction of the wall in Berlin. Under Willy Brandt, the West German government changed direction, and in 1972 reached a historical compromise with its East German neighbour. The Basic Treaty they signed transformed the denied border into an openly negotiated one and instituted permanent state-level coordination in the Border Committee. After long years of complete separation, however, local and regional coordination proved unresuscitable.

The inter-German compromise also increased the opportunities for border-crossing travel, with new checkpoints and a special permit for Western frontier residents. Travel and interaction across the border increased, leading to a partial re-emergence of personal and kinship networks. It also confronted Germans with the differences that had developed between them over decades of separation. Travel served as the bookend issue for this period. Division appeared in the lives of Germans through travel limitations imposed in the spring and summer of 1945, and it was through the undoing of travel limitations that division most palpably ended in 1989, as the inter-German border opened for free crossing for all. In contrast to the dramatic events of 1945 and 1989, though, most inter-German travel between those years was quite unimpressive. The trajectory of border-crossing travel shows that the opening of the inter-German border should be seen as a gradual development unfolding from the mid-1980s.

Through four decades of state building and border formation, frontier residents on both sides of an arbitrary line reoriented themselves towards state agencies' regulations. Despite their rivalry, state agencies on both sides of the border shared an interest in a clear demarcation of jurisdictions. The official compromise between the two governments in 1972 was crucial for the final cementing of division along the border. Interacting with divergent sets of expectations and rules, members of two parts of the German national community learned to think of themselves as different from each other.

BRINGING THE RURAL BACK IN

The rural nature of the inter-German border has been masked by an overrepresentation in literature of urban environments. Berlin has always attracted more attention than any other part of the border. The divided metropolis, severed by an ominous wall, provided captivating imagery. Berlin was the most important icon of the Cold War,[2] and the 'fall' of the Berlin Wall remains the most dramatic marker of its end. Little wonder, then, that scholars have studied Berlin more extensively than any other part of the inter-German border.[3]

Since 1990, and especially during the past decade, scholars have turned their attention to other areas, realizing that Berlin, an enclave within the German Democratic Republic (GDR), was highly unrepresentative. The emerging new history of the inter-German border relies on an exploration of other parts of the inter-German border between Lübeck in the north and Hof in the south.[4]

---

[2] Patrick Major makes a similar point in his recent book. See Patrick Major, *Behind the Berlin Wall: East Germany and the Frontiers of Power* (Oxford: Oxford University Press, 2010), 1.

[3] The list of studies of divided Berlin and the different aspects of city life leading to or emanating from the building of the Wall is too long to recount here. Some examples from recent years include: Frank Roggenbuch, *Das Berliner Grenzgängerproblem* (Berlin: Walter de Gruyter, 2008); Hope M. Harrison, *Driving the Soviets up the Wall: Soviet–East German Relations, 1953–1961* (Princeton: Princeton University Press, 2003); Pertti Ahonen, *Death at the Berlin Wall* (Oxford: Oxford University Press, 2011); Hans-Hermann Hertle, Konrad H. Jarausch and Christoph Kleßmann (eds), *Mauerbau und Mauerfall: Ursachen—Verlauf—Auswirkungen* (Berlin: Links, 2002); Edgar Wolfrum, *Die Mauer: Geschichte einer Teilung* (Munich: C. H. Beck, 2009).

[4] For some recent examples, see: Maren Ullrich, *Geteilte Ansichten: Erinnerungslandschaft deutsch-deutsche Grenze* (Berlin: Aufbau Verlag, 2006); Edith Sheffer, *Burned Bridge: How East and West Germans Made the Iron Curtain* (Oxford: Oxford University Press, 2011). See also Edith Sheffer, 'On Edge: Building the Border in East and West Germany', *Central European History* 40 (2007): 307–39. Astrid M. Eckert is preparing a book under the working title, 'West Germany and the Iron Curtain'. She began this project with an investigation of border tourism in the Federal Republic of Germany (FRG). See Astrid Eckert, '"Greetings from the Zonal Border": Tourism to the Iron Curtain in West Germany', *Zeithistorische Forschung/Studies in Contemporary History* 8 (2011): 9–36. Jason Johnson wrote a dissertation about the division of a village on the Bavarian–Thuringian border. See Jason B. Johnson, 'Dividing Mödlareuth: The Incorporation of Half a German Village into the GDR Regime, 1945–1989' (PhD diss., Evanston, IL: Northwestern University, 2011). These projects, and my own, owe a great deal to the late Daphne Berdahl's fascinating anthropological analysis of an East German frontier village following the unification of Germany in 1990. See Daphne Berdahl,

I build on this developing body of research to push the analysis further by focusing on rural conditions, often a hidden variable in the history of twentieth-century Europe. The majority of Europeans no longer made their living off the land; the power of the great estate owners had been broken under both socialist and capitalist systems. Industry, commerce, services, finance, and media—all urban enterprises—became the primary engines of economic expansion and agricultural lobbies lost much of their power. Residents of rural areas leave far less behind in material and written sources than do urban dwellers, and so relatively few historians today pay attention to people and areas largely perceived as objects of the modernization process.

Urban and rural spaces differ on many parameters crucial for border formation. Constructing and supervising urban borders typically requires only minor conflicts with private property, whereas establishing rural borders invariably means large-scale land appropriation and negotiation with private owners. Urban space is dense and narrow, giving rise to intense interaction with state agents and regulations. In most villages along the inter-German border, state presence prior to the emergence of the border was minimal; in 1945 many of them did not even have a school, a post office, or a police station. To understand how the border took on a certain shape, and how division itself shaped society, one has to account for these conditions.

Border formation in rural areas necessitated a transformation of the relations between frontier residents and the borderlands. For the borderlands to become arenas for the manifestation of state authority—a central function of any modern border—these lands had to become more the states' and less the farmers' land. Relationship to the land was fundamental to frontier residents' self-perception and a key marker of social-economic status. Adding these elements to the story changes the understanding of agency in the process of border formation and clarifies the challenges it faced. In East Germany, collectivization and the physical build-up of barriers both played major roles in transforming border residents' relationship with the land, especially during the 1960s and 70s. In the West, emigration and integration in the European market led to similar results during the same period—fewer people worked the land along the border and larger portions of the borderland lay fallow or were taken up, or at least supervised, by state organizations.

AGENCY: MAKING THE IRON CURTAIN 'FROM ABOVE' AND 'FROM BELOW'

Border formation brings state power to the fore and easily lends itself to 'top-down' analyses. Instruments of power directed by state organizations (e.g., war and

Where the World Ended: Re-Unification and Identity in the German Borderland (Berkeley, CA: University of California Press, 1999). See also a recent volume, which accompanied an exhibition, featuring short articles by some of the above-mentioned people and many others: Thomas Schwark et al. (eds), *Grenzziehungen—Grenzerfahrungen—Grenzüberschreitungen: Die innerdeutsche Grenze 1945–1990* (Darmstadt: WBG, 2011).

occupation, tariffs, roadblocks, and fences) are highly visible and command attention. As a consequence, scholars tend to perceive frontier populations as passive
objects of border formation.[5] Peter Sahlins' analysis of the development of
the border between France and Spain showed that frontier populations can have
considerable agency in border formation and in shaping national identifications.[6]

Assigning agency for the development of the Iron Curtain has been a contested
practice in German history, especially in the past two decades. The inter-German
border severed families, deprived many thousands of home and work, and claimed
the health and lives of thousands more. The issue of agency carries implications of
responsibility for these consequences. This partially explains the relatively long
dominance of 'top-down' approaches to this border. During the Cold War, writing
about the inter-German border was mostly undertaken by journalists and Western
government branches. Both kinds of publications assigned primary responsibility
for the division and the construction of the border to Soviet and East German state
and party organizations.[7] Since the 1980s, this one-sided story has been challenged
by several scholars, who argued that decisions and policies of the Western Allies and
West German governments contributed to the division of Germany.[8] These critics
share the view that the division of Germany came from the top, disputing only
which state organizations carried what part of the responsibility for bringing it
about.

Following the collapse of the GDR, a flurry of personal narratives with or by
frontier residents and border guards were published, largely supporting the view of
border construction and division as having been imposed from above. The border is
portrayed in these texts as something that *happened* to frontier residents. The stories

---

[5] James Anderson and Liam O'Dowd, 'Borders, Border Regions and Territoriality: Contradictory
Meanings, Changing Significance', *Regional Studies* 33 (1999): 595–6.

[6] Peter Sahlins, *Boundaries: The Making of France and Spain in the Pyrenees* (Berkeley, CA: University
of California Press, 1989), 7–9, 285–6. See also Thomas Lindenberger, ' "Zonenrand", "Sperrgebiet"
und "Westberlin": Deutschland als Grenzregion des Kalten Kriegs,' in *Teilung und Integration: die
doppelte deutsche Nachkriegsgeschichte als wissenschaftliches und didaktisches Problem*, edited by Christoph
Kleßmann and Peter Lautzas (Bonn: BpB, 2005), 98; Caitlin E. Murdock, ' "The Leaky Boundaries of
Man-Made States": National Identity, State Policy and Everyday Life in the Saxon-Bohemian Border
Lands 1870–1938' (PhD diss., Stanford, CA: Stanford University, 2003), 2–3.

[7] Bundesministerium für Gesamtdeutsche Fragen (ed.), *Im Schatten der Zonengrenze* (Bonn, 1956);
Bundesministerium für innerdeutsche Beziehungen (ed.), *Die innerdeutsche Grenze* (Bonn:
Gesamtdeutsches Institut, 1987); Bundesminister des Innern (ed.), *6 Jahre Grenzkommission mit der
DDR* (Bonn, 1979); Gesamtdeutsches Institut, Bundesanstalt für gesamtdeutsche Aufgaben (ed.), *Wo
Deutschland geteilt ist: Beiderseits der innerdeutschen Grenze* (Bonn, 1985), David Shears, *The Ugly
Frontier* (New York: Knopf, 1970), Josef Hans Sauer (ed.), *Die Rhön: Grenzland im Herzen Deutschland*
(Fulda: Verlag Parzeller and Co., 1967). I thank Astrid M. Eckert for sharing with me copies of some of
these publications.

[8] Rolf Steininger, *Eine Vertane Chance: Die Stalin-Note Vom 10. März 1952 Und Die
Wiedervereinigung* (Berlin: J. H. W. Dietz Nachf., 1985); Gerhard Wettig, 'Stalin and German
Reunification: Archival Evidence on Soviet Foreign Policy in Spring 1952', *Historical Journal* 37
(1994): 411–19; Wilfried Loth, *Die Sowjetunion und die deutsche Frage* (Göttingen: Vandenhoeck and
Ruprecht, 2007); Bruce Kuklick, *American Policy and the Division of Germany: The Clash with Russia
over Reparations* (Ithaca, NY: Cornell University Press, 1972); Carolyn W. Eisenberg, *Drawing the
Line: The American Decision to Divide Germany, 1944–1949* (Cambridge: Cambridge University Press,
1996).

they tell emphasize frontier residents' powerlessness in the face of these processes.[9] Since the late 1990s, studies of the inter-German border have challenged the passivity attributed to 'ordinary Germans' in general and to residents of frontier areas in particular. The works of Daphne Berdahl and especially Edith Sheffer have carved out considerable room for manoeuvring for these frontier residents, showing that their choices and interests affected division and border formation importantly.[10]

Building on these efforts, *States of Division* establishes a new balance in the question of agency in the creation of the inter-German border. It lends further support to the claim that the Iron Curtain was not simply imposed from above and that frontier residents had an important role in producing the division of Germany. At the same time, it suggests that this role should be interpreted carefully. Individual choices and practices interacted with those of state organizations, acting on and reacting to them in this process. This book rejects both the 'from above' approach to agency and the reduction of the role of state organizations to just one of many agents in this process. Borders are sites of extreme significance for state organizations, and crucial elements of state building are at stake in border formation. The book explores the gradual concentration of power in the hands of state organizations as both a cause and a consequence of the solidification of the border, demonstrating the interconnectedness of state building and border formation. The actions and choices of frontier residents and administrators played a pivotal role in the creation of the Iron Curtain in Germany, but did so within limits determined in constant interaction with state agencies. Individual agency diminished over the decades, both paralleling and attesting to the progress of state building.

Frontier residents made sense of their choices in the context of their own interests and goals and acted accordingly. Their behaviours are best interpreted as representing their *Eigen-Sinn* (literally own-sense, translated also as self-will or obstinacy).[11] *Eigen-Sinn* connotes a broad variety of choices and practices, including those which aided ('collaboration') and others that stood in the way of ('resistance') to state organizations' intentions.[12] Such a framework highlights the reasoning of

[9] Cornelia Röhlke (ed.), *Erzählunge von der deutsch-deutsche Grenze* (Erfurt: Sutton Verlag, 2001), 7. For other collections of interviews, stories and memoirs see: Alois Buckler, *Grenzgänger. Erlebnisse aus den Jahren 1947–1961 an der inner-deutschen Grenze* (Leipzig: Thomas Verlag, 1991); Roman Grafe (ed.), *Die Grenze durch Deutschland: Eine Chronik von 1945 bis 1990* (Berlin: Siedler, 2002); Jürgen Kleindienst (ed.), *Von hier nach drüben: Grenzgänge, Fluchten und Reisen im kalten Krieg 1945–1961* (Berlin: Zeitgut Verlag, 2001); Joachim S. Hohmann and Gerhard Grischok (eds), *Grenzland Rhön: Geschichten und Bilder aus der Zeit der Teilung* (Hünfeld: Rhön Verlag, 1997); Andreas Hartmann and Sabine Doering-Manteuffel (eds), *Grenzgeschichten: Berichte Aus Dem Deutschen Niemandsland* (Frankfurt am Main: S. Fischer, 1990).

[10] Berdahl, *Where the World Ended*; Sheffer, *Burned Bridge*.

[11] The term *Eigen-Sinn* was first introduced by Alf Lüdtke in the early 1990s and has become a staple in the study of everyday life history in Germany. See Alf Lüdtke, *Eigen-Sinn: Fabrikalltag, Arbeitserfahrungen und Politik vom Kaiserreich bis in den Faschismus* (Hamburg: Ergebnisse Verlag, 1993).

[12] As elaborated by Thomas Lindenberger, the historical application of 'resistance', 'collaboration', and similar labels makes sense only in relatively rare cases. Thomas Lindenberger, 'Die Diktatur der Grenzen', in *Herrschaft und Eigen-Sinn in der Diktatur*, edited by Thomas Lindenberger (Colougne, Weimar and Vienna: Böhlau Verlag, 1999), 23–6.

individuals and the way they absorbed their decisions and actions into their self-perceptions.

The kinds of historical question raised here are best answered through unpacking the meanings implicit in interactions between individuals, organizations, and groups. Charles Tilly called this approach 'relational', claiming that it is in interaction with other persons and groups that identities and dispositions are formed, and that it is there that they exist.[13] The book therefore looks at interactions between state and non-state organizations and individuals as arenas in which changes in perceptions and dispositions were tied to the separate, emerging statehoods. The rubbing against each other of state and non-state interests was often most visible within state organizations themselves. Bureaucrats and administrators functioned in specific social contexts. Frontier administrators play a significant role in the book because they often embodied the points of conflict between state and non-state goals.

MULTI-LAYERED REGIONAL FOCUS: THE EICHSFELD

The Eichsfeld region in Central Germany is especially suitable for the study of border formation in rural Germany. It is an overwhelmingly rural-agricultural region with a centuries-old regional identification founded on shared faith. Following a long tradition of plot division through inheritance, the Eichsfeld was a region of primarily small and medium landholders. Consequently, border formation affected early and deeply the lives and livelihoods of thousands of frontier residents in the region who owned, rented, or worked plots along the border.

The defining characteristics and the boundaries of the region were tied to the power of the bishopric of Mainz. From a modest holding in Heiligenstadt in the eleventh century, the Mainzer Eichsfeld had grown to encompass a region of almost 600 square miles by the fifteenth century, defining the borders of the Eichsfeld for centuries to come. During the first half of the sixteenth century, the region was swept up in the Lutheran Reformation until in 1574 the Mainz Bishop ushered in the counter-reformation of his domain. The Peace of Westphalia in 1648 ended decades of indecision with a clear Catholic victory in the Eichsfeld, while all the other principalities of the region remained Lutheran. Ever since, the Eichsfeld has existed as a Catholic enclave in a Protestant-dominated region.[14] Catholicism became the major marker of belonging in the Eichsfeld, further cemented over centuries of endogamous marriage of Catholics in the region which gave rise to thick kinship networks. The distance from the bishopric's centre induced the development of regional institutions in the Eichsfeld, contributing to a

---

[13] Charles Tilly, *Identities, Boundaries, and Social Ties* (Boulder, CO: Paradigm Publishers, 2005), 6–9.

[14] Peter Aufgebauer, 'Geschichte einer Grenzlandschaft', in *Das Eichsfeld: Ein deutscher Grenzraum*, edited by Peter Aufgebauer et al. (Duderstadt: Mecke, 2002), 66–74; Petra Behrens, *Regionale Identität und Regional kulture im Demokratie und Diktatur* (Baden-Baden: Nomos, 2012), 35–6.

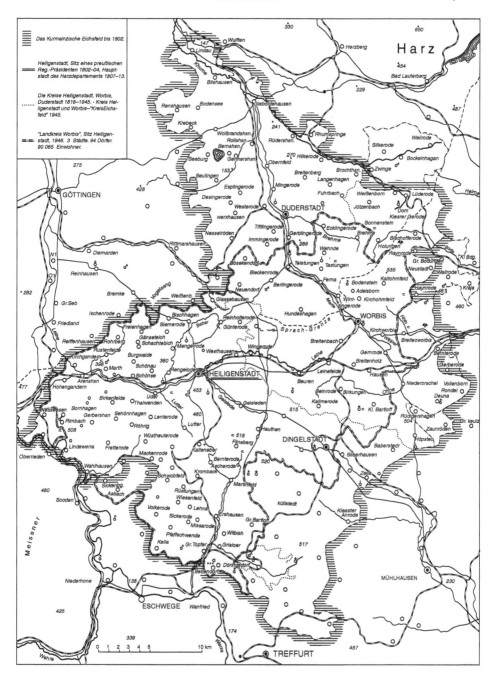

Fig. I.1. Map of the Eichsfeld around 1900 with district borders. The district of Duderstadt is the part that fell to Hanover in the post-Napoleonic order and later to the British zone. The rest of the Eichsfeld went to Prussia in 1815 and to the Soviet zone in 1945.

Source: H. Leineweber, Das Buch vom Eichsfelde, Heiligenstadt 1900. Downloaded from Wikimedia Commons (commons. wikimedia.org).

consciousness of regional belonging. The meshing of confessional-regional loyalties was further cemented during Bismarck's Culture War (*Kulturkampf*) against Catholics in the 1870s and 80s.[15]

In the post-Napoleonic order, the Eichsfeld was divided between Prussia and Hanover. Prussia got the larger, mountainous part around Heiligenstadt and Worbis, also known as Upper Eichsfeld (*Obereichsfeld*), which became part of its province of Saxony. Hanover received the smaller, more fertile, plain area around Duderstadt, known as the Lower Eichsfeld (*Untereichsfeld*). In 1866, Hanover fought against Prussia and after its defeat was reduced to a Prussian province. The border between the two parts of the Eichsfeld thus turned into an internal border between Prussian provinces of the German Empire. The borderline drawn in 1815 remained on the maps and was adopted in 1945 as the dividing line between the Soviet, British, and American zones (see Figure I.1).[16] This historical development makes the Eichsfeld an especially intriguing test-case for the history of border and boundary formation: a stable regional community divided by a modern border. The Eichsfeld is also large enough to include several socio-economic settings, with four small towns accounting for about a quarter of the total population. Its territory spanned three occupation zones and diverse terrains. At the same time it was cohesive enough to maintain elaborate regional traditions, organizations, and face-to-face networks. Honing in on a limited geographic unit to investigate the complex and wide-ranging processes of border formation and state building allows for a rich analysis of interactions in and between the various layers of state organizations and frontier society over three decades.

WHEN WAS GERMANY DIVIDED?

The crucial stages in the interrelated processes of spatial and social division in Germany took place between the currency reform of June 1948 and 1978, when representatives of the two German states finished marking and regulating the border between them. The lion's share of the book is devoted to developments during these three decades. The first chapter begins at the end of the Second World War, and devotes considerable space to the important stages in the division of occupied Germany before 1949. The final chapter continues the story of division beyond 1978 and until the border collapsed in 1989.

So far, scholarship has highlighted the importance of three major turning points in the history of this border: the end of the war and the emergence of the zonal demarcation lines (1944–5); the East German announcement of a strict border regime, including the deportation of thousands from the East German borderlands and the construction of the first fence along the demarcation line (spring–summer 1952); and the construction of the Berlin Wall, followed by additional deportations

---

[15] Behrens, *Regionale Identität*, 38–9.

[16] Behrens, *Regionale Identität*, 36; Peter Aufgebauer, 'Geschichte einer Grenzlandschaft', 74–6. For more details about 'the first division of the Eichsfeld' in 1815–16 see Ulrich Hussong, 'Die Teilung des Eichsfeldes im Jahre 1815', *Eichsfeld Jahrbuch* (1993): 5–92.

and the gradual emergence of the 'modern border' (summer–fall 1961). *States of Division* adds two key points of reference: the year following the currency reform in June 1948, including the Berlin Blockade and the Western counter-blockade and the creation of two parallel state apparatuses; and the Basic Treaty (*Grundvertrag*), marking the FRG's willingness to recognize the GDR (December 1972) and leading to the establishment of a joint border committee which over the next six years settled the many border disputes between the two states. Mutual recognition and consensual border regulation stamped division with a mark of finality.

Compromise, and growing measures of coordination between West and East German governments and border guards, transformed the dynamics of division. State agencies acquired new confidence in making and enforcing border policies based on their newly established understanding. From the mid-1970s, frontier residents' leverage diminished markedly in negotiations with state agencies.

But the tendency to focus on prominent events and dramatic years is misleading. While certain events affected border construction and state building importantly, crucial elements in the division of German society were gradual, protracted processes. They developed unevenly, progressing faster in some areas than others and were sometimes temporarily halted or even reversed. They were affected by such factors as personnel and regulation of border guards, international alliances and treaties, and availability of transportation connections.

Concentrating on processes of change between turning points, I show that neither 1952 nor 1961 were wholly transformative. Rather, border build-up—through the assignment of a growing number of state agents and restrictive regulations—preceded 1952. Indeed, in 1949–52 even physical barriers, such as ditches and earth piles, were constructed along the border. In August 1961, the Berlin Wall immediately affected reality in Berlin, and drastically reduced the options for border crossing for all Germans. However, along the rural border, cross-border communities and networks had already been severely undermined in the preceding decade, making the wall only one link in a long chain of action and reaction, a big step down a path already chosen.[17] In addition, the physical transformation of the border from a single low fence to a system of sophisticated, deadly barriers, identified in research as part of the 1961 transformation, progressed slowly in rural provinces, and was only completed during the 1970s.

The notion of 'the border' as a uniform, stable entity falls apart in the study of individual and group experiences. For example, frontier residents experienced the border differently from people for whom its development was an item in the newspaper. As a result, any uniform chronology of the emergence of this border would be misleading. Foregrounding the rural character of the borderlands, the account below follows a chronology roughly reflecting the experience of farmers. Many frontier farmers were immediately affected by the drawing of zonal

---

[17] Corey Ross has also argued that the transformation of state–society relations some scholars assume for 1961 is overemphasized. See Corey Ross, 'East Germans and the Berlin Wall: Popular Opinion and Social Change before and after the Border Closure of August 1961', *Journal of Contemporary History* 39 (2004), 25–43.

demarcation lines in 1945, as access to their fields was denied. Tilling the land became possible again in the fall of 1946, before access was completely eliminated in May 1952. For many other farmers east of the border, division became real when they gave up private for collective ownership, in most cases only during the 1960s.

A focus on practice reveals the centrality of economic considerations in border formation. Analysing the interaction of national economy and trade balance with local and communal economic interests, the book discusses the implications of centrally devised economic policies on the economy of frontier areas. The currency reform of June 1948 in the Western occupation zones, for example, started a chain reaction that eventually redefined as criminal many established practices of frontier economy because they relied on border-crossing trade. Investment in public transportation and heavy industry in East Germany sent working-age men and women away from frontier villages and undermined agricultural production. Studies that have addressed economic aspects of German division have done so either from a macro-perspective of overall trade balances or from a micro-perspective of individual and communal interests.[18] This book links the two perspectives, analysing the conflicts between them, the ways these conflicts played out, and their implications for the process of border formation.

THEORETICAL UNDERPINNINGS AND TERMINOLOGY: BORDERS AND STATES

In the modern world, borders are perceived first and foremost as markers of state authority. They are manifestations of state power, asserting a state's prerogative to enforce certain rules and policies within the territory they delimit. Any analysis of borders must therefore adopt a certain concept of the state. This book relies on Timothy Mitchell's understanding of the state as neither a clearly bounded set of organizations, nor a completely indistinguishable part of society.[19] The state is rather what he terms 'a structural effect'. Following Michel Foucault, Mitchell argues that disciplinary techniques transformed over generations the appearance of institutions such as the army, the law, and the bureaucracy. These institutions came to be perceived as independent of any individual or group. They appear not as part of society, but as if existing outside it—or hovering above it—representing an entity with a separate set of interests and rules: 'the state'. This effect depends on constant

---

[18] Good examples of the macro-level studies are Werner Abelshauser's works about the economic history of West Germany in which he accounts for the effects of division and inter-German trade. See Werner Abelshauser, *Wirtschaftsgeschichte der Bundesrepublik Deutschland, 1945–1980* (Frankfurt am Main: Suhrkamp, 1983). The best micro-level analysis of economic interests and their significance in the process of border formation is in Edith Sheffer's dissertation and book. See, for example, Sheffer, *Burned Bridge*, 50–71.

[19] Timothy Mitchell, 'The Limits of the State: Beyond Statist Approaches and Their Critics', *American Political Science Review* 85 (1991): 77–96.

reproduction.[20] This is not to say that the distinction of state and society is not real or important. The effect of state is crucial for the working of power.[21] Mitchell's approach enables the study of state organizations while allowing for incoherence in goals, policies, and practices. Because people and organizations which share in the effect of state are part of society, there is no clear line between state and society.[22]

Not surprisingly, Mitchell uses state borders to demonstrate his argument. Officials stationed at the frontier apply practices such as passport control and customs checks to people and goods seeking to move across the border, and use symbols such as uniforms and stamps. These practices and symbols create the effect of a state—a coherent entity, clearly demarcated from society and from other states—directing all these actions. In reality, power exercised through these people and practices serves specific groups, organizations, or individuals anchored in specific social contexts. Seen this way, borders are quintessential sites for delimiting 'state' from 'society' and from 'other states', thus producing the effect of state.

In accordance with this understanding, the text below avoids referring to 'the state', and discusses instead specific people and organizations. The terms 'state organizations', 'state agencies', and 'state agents' denote people and organizations which were perceived as parts of that state. 'West Germany/FRG/Bonn' and 'East Germany/GDR/East Berlin' are shorthand for the East and West German governments.

State organizations depend on the solidity of the effect of state for the legitimacy of their actions, critical, for example, in the extraction from society of resources (e.g., money and soldiers). Such resources help reproduce the effect of state and extract additional resources (e.g., enlarging bureaucracies, equipping armies). The growth in the power of state organizations vis-à-vis other elements in society, also referred to as centralization, is the process of *state building*.[23]

This book explores the interrelations between political division, physical demarcation, and dynamics of social exclusion. To avoid confusion in a discussion of different modes of division, a brief definition of the terms used is in order. Border scholars have developed elaborate sets of distinctions, but a stable, inter-disciplinary terminology has yet to be established.[24] I employ the following distinctions:

---

[20] Mitchell, 'The Limits of the State', 89–94. See also Gil Eyal, *The Disenchantment of the Orient: Expertise in Arab Affairs and the Israeli State* (Stanford, CA: Stanford University Press, 2006), 12.

[21] Without popular and international acceptance of the state as an autonomous entity—that is without the effect of state—state organizations' actions would not be perceived as legitimate and would not be able to achieve their goals. See Eyal, *Disenchantment*, 12.

[22] Mitchell, 'The Limits of the State', 95.

[23] Because of the central role of borders in producing the effect of state, projects of state building and border formation are closely tied expressions of the same powers and interests. Mitchell, 'The Limits of the State', 94–5; Eyal, *Disenchantment*, 108–19.

[24] See David Newman, 'Borders and Bordering: Towards an Interdisciplinary Dialogue', *European Journal of Social Theory* 9 (2006), 171–86. And see also the different uses and discussions of terminology in studying borders by some scholars in the field: Berdahl, *Where the World Ended*, 4–9; Thomas M. Wilson and Hastings Donnan, 'Nation, State and Identity at International Borders', in *Border Identities: Nation and State at International Frontiers*, edited by Thomas M. Wilson and Hastings Donnan (Cambridge: Cambridge University Press, 1998), 9; Anderson and O'Dowd, 'Borders, Border Regions and Territoriality', 594–5; Joel S. Migdal (ed.), *Boundaries and Belonging:*

Borders are political institutions marking the territorial limit of jurisdiction of state organizations and the beginning of the jurisdiction of organizations representing another state. Borders usually develop in connection with *borderlines*, but are not confined to—or spatially defined by—these lines. The common assumption that borderlines exist and that crossing them bears consequences lies at the heart of a border's function. Borders stretch along borderlines, as state organizations station their agents (e.g., police, customs services, military, and other administrations), construct facilities (e.g., barracks, refugee camps, checkpoints, and barriers), and implement policies and regulations.

Boundaries, as used here, are markers separating groups of people from each other, mechanisms of exclusion and inclusion. Boundaries could be based on religion, class, language, or other perceived group characteristics. In other words, boundaries are the imaginary lines people draw around communities to which they belong, the lines between 'us' and 'them'. Boundaries fluctuate in response to circumstances. They exist irrespective of borders, between groups enclosed within a certain set of borders, or straddling many borders.[25] The idea of the nation-state as a political unit encompassing a unified national community idealizes a complete overlap of borders and boundaries, which is never the case in reality.

Frontiers/Borderlands/Border zones are broad, loosely defined areas that are affected by the proximity of borders. Their character may be shaped by policies and practices of state institutions—such as the granting of benefits or the circumscription of movement—or through other interactions with the border, such as accessibility of smuggled goods. The term may be applied to a geographic area, for example, the area that falls within the range of 'the enemy's' artillery; or according to characteristics of population, such as the concentration of members of a minority group. The term 'frontier' particularly connotes a sense of lawlessness and openness that derives from its prevalence in writing about the European colonization of the North-American 'West'.

SCOPE AND STRUCTURE OF THE BOOK

This book investigates the division of German society by analysing processes that took place primarily in border areas. The protagonists in the text are those people and organizations that interacted with or were affected by the development of the border: residents of those borderlands (usually referred to as 'frontier residents') and state officials and agencies. This methodological decision stands on two legs: analytical and quantitative. As the previous section made clear, the analytical

---

States and Societies in the Struggle to Shape Identities and Local Practices (Cambridge: Cambridge University Press, 2004), 5–12; Caitlin E. Murdock, *Changing Places: Society, Culture and Territory in the Saxon-Bohemian Borderlands, 1870–1946* (Ann Arbor, MI: University of Michigan Press, 2010), 7–11; Malcolm Anderson, *Frontiers: Territory and State Formation in the Modern World* (Cambridge: Polity Press, 1996), 1–9.

[25] Anderson and O'Dowd, 'Borders, Border Regions and Territoriality', 594–5, Migdal, *Boundaries and Belonging*, 5–12.

justification for this focus is the understanding of borders as privileged sites for the production of identification and nation-state effects. The quantitative leg leans on the length of the inter-German border and the size of the population that came into direct interaction with its development. This divide, 1,393km in length, grew through intensive social interactions with a population that made up over 10 per cent of the entire population of East and West Germany. So there is very good reason to view processes in the inter-German borderlands as key for the division of German society in its entirety.

The narrative attempted here of such broad processes over four decades inevitably entails a degree of omission. The influx of refugees from bombed cities and from the former German-ruled territories in East-Central Europe is largely excluded from this book.[26] Refugees' influence on the relations of frontier residents with both postwar states was not very significant, and in the conflicts of border formation they rarely had a separate voice. Moreover, since the book concentrates on rural areas it has little to say about war damages, population decline, casualties, prisoners of war, and the consequent gender imbalance. Wartime damages were not as massive in rural Germany as they were in urban areas. The small communities that were characteristic of rural areas were less susceptible than urban areas to openly changing gender roles. Formal, public positions of power remained in men's hands; men represented and headed communities and committees and spoke at public events well into the 1970s in the Eichsfeld. Communist party-governed hierarchies in the GDR changed this picture, appointing women to leadership roles. But at least in the rural area I studied, civil society and local organizations did not adopt this trend.

Two important background factors receive relatively little attention in this book: Catholicism and the Third Reich. Eichsfeld scholars and enthusiasts will probably find much less discussion of Catholic rites, routines, hierarchies, and networks than they expect. In addition, the book treats Catholicism as a relatively stable social and political infrastructure. It does not address the Catholic faith directly because the challenges and developments in that area were only marginally related to the processes of border formation and division. While the Third Reich and the Second World War formed the immediate historical background of the period covered in the book, I consciously chose to keep them in the background. Clearly, German division would not have come to be (or not in this particular manner) had the Second World War not taken place. And yet, while events and processes of the postwar period developed in the context of the war and Nazi-ruled Europe, the former cannot be deduced directly from the latter.

The first chapter argues that fragile and temporary demarcation lines between the zones of occupation in Germany began to solidify between 1948 and 1952, showing that Western economic reconstruction was the most powerful motor of

---

[26] Many refugees and expellees initially settled in rural frontier areas. Being the least rooted, these newcomers were the first to leave when work and opportunities opened in the Western industrial and commercial centres. Those who stayed in the rural borderlands rarely made it into positions of influence.

division in those years. When East German forces began constructing the first fence along these lines in 1952, crucial steps had already been taken in both policy and practice on the road to German division. Following the currency reform of the summer of 1948, state organizations attempted to control more closely the movement of goods across zonal borders. Both sides increased the number of guards for this purpose. The guards' function in facilitating and/or curbing border-crossing economic activity was crucial to the development of the early border.

The second chapter analyses the transformation of the inter-German border in 1952–3 from the novel perspective of land use and property ownership. In May 1952, the government of the GDR announced an overhaul of border policy, officially sealing its western border. Hidden behind the violent and visible aspects of this policy was the chaos it created in frontier agriculture. The chapter compares the reactions to the new situation of three groups of frontier farmers, showing that they perceived the new policy foremost as an economic challenge and tried to further their economic interests. Farmers usurped land and fought to retain ownership, all within boundaries set by state regulations, their own social networks, and the resources they could marshal. Their choices propelled them headlong into conflict with other farmers and with state agencies. Early border formation thus translated official policy into economic preferences and practices of frontier farmers; these practices, in turn, dug the foundations of division deeper into the social terrain of the Eichsfeld.

The third chapter discusses a contradiction at the heart of the West German state-building project. Paradoxically, the West German claim to exclusive representation of the German people fuelled division. West German policy reflected a denial of the GDR and, claiming to represent all Germans, worked to isolate the GDR diplomatically. This policy contributed to, rather than obstructed, East German state building. By dictating the priorities of state agencies on both sides of the border, the Western non-recognition strategy led to the undermining of cross-border communities and networks. Frontier residents, organizations, and administrators tried to preserve cross-border communities and networks, but their efforts ran into the wall of non-recognition. By the time the Berlin Wall was built in 1961, these earlier walls had already given rise to the dynamics of separation.

The fourth chapter argues that the transformation of frontier agriculture turned the land itself into an instrument and an exemplar of German division. The chapter investigates the interrelatedness of struggles over land ownership and usage, and the development of German division in the years 1953–69. It shows that through intensive struggles with state agencies during the 1950s, Eastern and Western frontier farmers learned to operate within the separate legal and institutional frameworks created on both sides of the border, thus practising and enforcing division. With the resulting solidification of the de facto division, state agencies and frontier residents were able in the 1960s to reach compromises that further solidified boundaries between the two states and societies. Collectivization and the massive construction of barriers in the East and investments in industry and the restructuring of agriculture in both West and East all but eliminated farmers' attachment to their land as an obstacle to border formation in the 1960s.

The fifth chapter begins at the watershed marked by *Ostpolitik*, and the historical compromise reached between the governments of East and West Germany. The about-face in West German policy transformed the inter-German border into a negotiated political division, institutionalized in the joint Border Committee. The chapter argues that the altered international climate worked to solidify the inter-German border in the short term, but also contributed to its undermining in the longer term. Newly gained legitimacy allowed the GDR to complete the construction of barriers and related installations and to make the border almost impenetrable for illegal crossing. At the same time, the Basic Treaty of 1972 changed freedom of travel from an aspiration to a demand for East Germans. It also allowed it to become so central an issue in state–society conflicts that it gradually unsettled the regime. The treaty also established new channels for border-crossing coordination, but, in stark contrast with the early stages of division, regional and local administrations were not involved. Regional coordination only re-emerged along the inter-German border following the border's collapse in November 1989. The fifth chapter reflects in source and argument the stark change in the dynamics of state–society relations brought about by the Basic Treaty. Inter-state channels eliminated state organizations' dependence on frontier populations. Frontier residents' room for negotiation shrunk significantly as they faced a stable division and state agencies much more secure in their positions. Consequently, frontier residents and authorities had no special role in the late 1980s' crumbling of the GDR's ability to contain emigration; in fact, they lagged behind the major centres of the hinterland in pressuring the regime for greater mobility.

A border is what a border does. The inter-German border was a set of interactive processes of political, spatial, and social division. These processes progressed through interactions of state-building organizations with individuals and communities. Rehearsed over decades, these interactions gave rise to deep-seated attitudes and orientations. When the border collapsed in 1989, and especially after the GDR was consumed by unification a year later, the inter-German border was stricken off the map. Many reasoned during the early euphoric years, when the momentum of unification seemed inexorable, that all aspects of division would soon vanish. But more than two decades later, the inter-German border still marks viable lines of separation in the unified country. The multi-level analysis of the process of division offered in this book, taking into account transformations of space, policy, practice, and orientation, suggests that undoing division will be as laborious a process as its creation.

I

DMark-ation

The Division of German Economy and the Emergence of the Inter-German Border 1945–52

In June of 1952, as part of a wide-ranging reform of border regime,[1] East German police forces deported hundreds of frontier residents from the Eichsfeld to the GDR hinterland. Among them was the blacksmith Gerhard Schäfer from the village of Rohrberg. Three months after his 'evacuation', representatives of the community, including communist political figures, pleaded in a letter to the district council that the state authorities reinstate their blacksmith.[2] Party activists included the blacksmith in the deportation list because he had smuggled unauthorized materials from the West. The authors of the letter stated that he did so for the good of the entire community and not for his own profit. This letter demonstrates the importance of cross-border networks and the unofficial economy that relied on such networks for the frontier rural economy.

Blacksmith services were crucial for agricultural communities, and the smithy in Rohrberg served several villages in the area. Some of the materials essential to the smith's work were difficult to come by in the Soviet zone of occupation and later in the GDR. To support effectively the work of frontier farmers, the smith turned to his son, who lived in Göttingen in the British zone. At his father's commission, the son purchased the required materials and smuggled them to Rohrberg. This continued for a number of years. In their letter, the village representatives argued that this should be counted not against the smith but rather in his favour. The smith's ingenuity served to enable and improve farming in their villages under difficult conditions. The smith's absence since June was threatening routine agricultural work in the area.

This episode highlights the clash of two different systems of reasoning—that of frontier residents and that of state agencies—regarding the interaction of the inter-German border with economic activity. The blacksmith's immediate family network stretched across the new inter-German border, like the family networks of many other frontier residents. After 1945, border-crossing exchanges assumed growing importance in the lives of frontier residents. Their vicinity to the border,

---

[1] This reform and its consequences are the subject of Chapter II.
[2] 'Umsiedlung des Betriebes Schmiedemeisters', September 1952, KrAEich, EA HIG, Nr. 192. As in all cases in the book, names of people mentioned in the text who were not holding official positions were changed to protect their privacy.

and the ease with which they routinely crossed it, gave them access to opportunities, materials, and markets that were rare or unavailable to others. State organizations defined these economic activities as illegal and thus pushed them into the unofficial sector of frontier economy. Consequently, such activities became as important as official ones, if not more so.

Decision makers in Bonn and East Berlin regarded controlling the movement and dissemination of goods as a prerogative of state agencies. Border formation in its earliest stages saw a process by which state agencies tried to increase their ability to supervise border-crossing economic activity. This chapter tells the story of Western and Eastern state agencies' efforts to impose their priorities on frontier economy and bind it according to their territorial jurisdictions. It leads up to 1952, showing that the violent actions of East German state organizations during that year, which will be discussed in Chapter II, were another step in the gradual process of division.

THE EMERGENCE OF THE INTER-GERMAN BORDER

Long before the overhaul of the Central European map following the Second World War, internal and external borders across the broad areas in Europe populated by German speakers were contested, shifted, and regularly redrawn. By 1945, most of the internal borders in (the reduced territory of) occupied Germany had been nearly invisible for at least three-quarters of a century. During the war, the Allies had drafted and debated different ideas regarding the dismemberment and rule of postwar Germany.[3] The border-lines between the occupation zones they created were taken from existing maps, but some had been long inactive or insignificant (see Figure 1.1).

The border between East and West first began to emerge in Germany during the last year of the war, as projected zonal demarcation lines became significant for many of the millions of refugees in Central Europe.[4] Despite this, the division of Germany into occupation zones was established and treated as temporary by both the Allies and their German subjects. The Allies' agreed-upon goal, reaffirmed in the postwar Potsdam Conference, was to work together toward a future unified German state.[5] But the impermanence of the border was gradually eroded. This chapter shows that the first steps in this gradual erosion were taken through economic policy and practice, which turned demarcation into 'DMark-ation'.

[3] J. K. Sowden, *The German Question 1945–1975* (London: Bradford University Press, 1975), 45–73; Ina Dietzsch, *Grenzen Überschreiben: Deutsch-deutsche Briefwechsel 1948–1989* (Cologne: Böhlau, 2004), 118–19. For the relevant wartime decisions of the Allies see Peter März, 'Protokol über die Besatzungszonen in Deutschland und die Verwaltung von Groß-Berlin (Londoner Protokoll) vom 12. September 1944', in *Dokumente zu Deutschland 1944–1994*, edited by Peter März (Munich: Olzog, 1996), 63–4, and in the same volume also 'Abkommen über Kontrolleinrichtungen in Deutschland – Londoner Erklärung der Alliierten vom 14. November 1944' (65–6) and 'Erklärung der Alliierten von Jalta (Auszug) vom 11. Februar 1945' (67–8).
[4] Lindenberger, 'Deutschland als Grenzregion', 98–101.
[5] See Peter März, 'Potsdammer Abkommen', in *Dokumente zu Deutschalnd*, 75–7.

Fig. 1.1. A map prepared in October 1944 by the US foreign economic administration. The Allies adopted existing administrative and state borders in designing their occupation zones.[6]

Initially, it was the economic function of the new inter-German border that most strongly impacted the lives of Germans. From its earliest days as a zonal demarcation line, the border affected many routine economic practices. Border regulations and their enforcement bounded many aspects of legal or official trade. In the early years, however, state agencies were largely powerless to apply these regulations to unofficial or illegal trade.[7] The emergence of the border created many opportunities and channelled much capital into the unofficial economy. During the occupation years, the Allies' economic policies were decisive in shaping differences between occupation zones and between the experiences of those living in them. Economic concerns, plans, and interests became primary drivers of border

---

[6] The map in Figure 1.1 was copied from the Lehman Library Map Collection at Columbia University. I thank Jeremiah Trinidad-Christensen for his help in obtaining the copy.

[7] Throughout this chapter, I use the term 'official economy' to refer to all activities which were (as a matter of choice or in absence of alternatives) pursued within the regulations imposed by state agencies. 'Unofficial economy' denotes all economic activity outside this supervision, either by design or out of ignorance of the regulations. Determining legality was a prerogative of state organizations. Analysing the process by which these organizations' power to shape perceptions grew, I chose not to adopt a priori their definition of the situation. I employ the labels 'legal' or 'illegal' only when they denote state organizations' positions.

construction, and coloured the earliest steps in the long road to the division of German society. While the Cold War was still assuming its early contours—before the threat of nuclear war or the Korean War, and when German unified independence was still expected and generally hoped for—economic policy and practice gave rise to a dynamic of division.

The wartime Allies initially conceived of occupied Germany as a single economic unit ruled by three (and then four) cooperating territorial administrations. In 1945, all four occupation administrations faced grave economic problems, including large-scale destruction of infrastructure and housing, mass dislocation of populations, depressed production and unemployment, and scarcity of food. But the growing discord between the Allies dictated radically divergent economic reconstructions in the different parts of divided Germany. Disputes between the Allies repeatedly undermined economic coordination between their zonal administrations. The currency reform in the Western zones of occupation that took place on 18 June 1948 and in Berlin three days later, officially buried the idea of a unified German economy. As in many other parts of postwar Europe, it became clear, after a relatively brief period, that there would be no place for a 'third way' between socialism and capitalism.

Social divisions along the inter-German border both created and resulted from developments in frontier and border-crossing economic practices. The two emerging economic systems engaged each other along the German borderlands. Occupying this space were people, communities, and organizations. Directly exposed to both systems, they experienced the clash between them in daily, practical ways. Frontier and border-crossing economic activity was transformed by the parallel reconstruction projects, growing into new niches created through their interaction or the lack thereof and shrinking from areas they eliminated or constricted. But this transformation was not restricted to, and cannot be summarized in terms of, economic values alone.

The study of economic practices reveals how interests and actions of individuals and communities interacted with policies and priorities enforced by state agencies to shape the development of the border. Edith Sheffer showed how significant the initiative of frontier residents was in establishing economic division following the currency reform.[8] My study of the frontier and the cross-border economy in the Eichsfeld and other rural areas contextualizes residents' initiative and demonstrates that they reacted to state policies and state agents' practices at least as much as they acted upon them. Their economic interests were closely aligned with material assets, particularly with land. Their economic practices were deeply embedded within stable, cross-border social networks and were therefore less flexible and slower in reacting to changing economic conditions than those of commercially or industrially oriented populations. The dynamic of economic separation in rural border areas was consequently different from the one described by Sheffer—in rural

---

[8] Sheffer, *Burned Bridge*, 53–8.

border areas, most local actors were either hesitant when state and federal offices pushed for steps of separation or tended to object to such policies.

The emergence of economic barriers between occupation zones in Germany posed a severe threat to existing economic practices and interests. Intra-German interdependencies were of vital importance to many branches of the economy. In most cases, zonal borders adopted preexisting provincial and state borders that had previously not hindered economic exchange. Many well-established patterns of exchange were put at risk by the progress of economic division along the inter-German border.

In the Eichsfeld, the structural dependency of the Eastern part on cross-border economy was decidedly greater than that of the Western part. The prospect of economic division was more ominous for residents of the Eastern Eichsfeld for many reasons. Topography contributed to a dependence of Eastern frontier villages on Western towns. The Eichsfeld's economy had depended for generations on work migration to the West, especially to the industrial centres of northwestern Germany. Cities such as Göttingen, Kassel, Hanover, Wolfsburg—all within a hundred miles of Duderstadt—could offer significantly greater industrial and commercial opportunities than their parallels in the East (Nordhausen, Erfurt, Weimar, Eisenach). The heart of Germany's industry, the Ruhr area, was not too far either (approximately 150 miles). This asymmetry increased when West Germany's economy boomed from the early 1950s.[9]

No activity better demonstrates the significance of creating an economic border than smuggling. Smuggling was created by the emergence of the inter-German border and became a central battleground of state and society along it. State organizations redefined routine economic activities as illegal, while opportunities created by the border brought new economic networks and interests into existence.[10] Businesses and individuals with cross-border economic interests and markets developed and maintained regulation-circumventing channels. State agencies in turn laboured to block these channels in order to enforce new parameters and rules of economic practice.

Examining this conflict underscores the relations between frontier residents and border-guarding forces. The former were the most active agents of unofficial cross-border economy. Their knowledge of the terrain, their cross-border networks, and their own economic interests made many frontier residents the best smugglers of both people and goods. On both sides of the border, occupation forces and the new German states instructed border-guarding forces to prevent activities they defined

[9] Markus Krüsemann, 'Struktur und Entwicklung der regionalen Wirtschaft seit dem Zweiten Weltkrieg', in *Das Eichsfeld: Ein deutscher Grenzraum*, edited by Peter Aufgebauer and Dietrich Denecke (Duderstadt: Mecke, 2002), 84–7.

[10] This was of course not unique to the inter-German borderlands. For other examples see Joshua M. Smith, *Borderland Smuggling: Patriots, Loyalists, and Illicit Trade in the Northeast, 1783–1820* (Gainsville, FL: University Press of Florida, 2006); Murdock, *Changing Places*, 95–7, 122–4; George Gavrilis, 'The Greek-Ottoman Boundary as Institution, Locality, and Process (1832–1882)' (paper presented at the Rethymno Conference in honour of Charles Tilly, University of Crete, Greece, 17–18 October 2003); Luk Joossens and Martin Raw, 'Smuggling and Cross Border Shopping of Tobacco in Europe', *British Medical Journal* 310, (1995), 1393–7.

as illegal. State agencies tried to ensure that the men charged with enforcing policies along the border were able and willing to do so. In practice, many guards and units were well integrated in unofficial border-crossing exchange, as enablers or as active agents. In the late 1940s and early 1950s, state agencies in both East and West expended much effort on turning border guards into enforcers of state policies. The overall trend was a gradual growth of state organizations' power over border guards, and a consequent distancing of guarding organizations from the unofficial frontier economy. In both East and West, the changing role played by border guards reflected efforts to establish the effects of state and the different chronologies of Eastern and Western state-building.

This chapter analyses the emergence of economic division in Germany as the first act in the protracted process of border formation and the division of Germany. It begins with a review of the interests and policies of the occupying Allies that led to the emergence of opposing economic systems in East and West Germany. The chapter then examines the importance of border-crossing transactions in the economic practice of frontier residents and the difficulties state agencies encountered while trying to control them. Finally, the chapter shows that the efforts of Eastern and Western state agencies to curb unofficial border-crossing economic activity were more successful in producing the effects of state than they were in actually reducing smuggling.

An economic imbalance existed between the parts of prewar Germany that eventually became the FRG and those that became the GDR. The former had almost four times as many residents, a considerably larger territory, better-developed industry and infrastructure, greater concentration of capital, and access to more lucrative markets.[11] This imbalance was heightened during the occupation years by the different resources, priorities, and policies of the occupying Allies. The divergent ideologies and resources of the Allies resulted in starkly different approaches to economic planning in their occupation zones and meant that zonal borders played different roles in economic planning in each of the zones. The three wartime Allies had all originally intended to manage occupied Germany as a single economic unit.[12] But their respective priorities, together with France's refusal to submit to the understandings reached at Potsdam, made these intentions impracticable. As economic policies and practices diverged, demarcation lines between the zones assumed growing significance.

DIVISION OF INTEREST: ALLIED ECONOMIC POLICIES

The USSR had suffered immense destruction during four years of total war with Germany. It had emerged from this war as a victorious and proud military superpower, ruling half of the European continent. After the German surrender,

---

[11] See data in Abelshauser, *Wirtschaftsgeschichte*, 13–14.
[12] Alan Kramer, *The West German Economy, 1945–1955* (New York: Berg, 1991), 33–60; Eisenberg, *Drawing the Line*, 14–120.

the Soviet Union was finally able to turn its resources toward the overwhelming task of reconstruction. Occupied Germany played an important role in the Soviet plans to achieve this goal. The Soviets set the sum of 10 billion dollars as the minimum goal for reparations from Germany. It was often difficult to differentiate between exacting revenge and extracting reparations, especially as both were accompanied by sheer opportunism, particularly in the first few months of occupation.[13]

Zonal divisions were a hindrance in the Soviets' effort to achieve their economic goals in occupied Germany. The Soviets had expected to extract reparations from the entire territory of occupied Germany and especially from the industrial centre of the Ruhr area in the British zone. The Soviets therefore had an interest in an economically unified occupied Germany.[14] The Western Allies refused to allow the amount and type of reparations demanded by the Soviets from their zones. They were powerless to prevent dismantling and extraction in the Soviet zone, but they feared the consequences of this policy for the German economy in general and sought to protect their own zones from its implications.[15]

Like the Soviet Union, Britain also expected to exact extensive reparations from defeated Germany. War damages in Britain were not nearly as great as in the Soviet Union, but domestic economic concerns were quite grave in postwar London, requiring food rationing and growing dependence on the US. Under these conditions, British policymakers, responsible for the densely populated, industrialized northwestern occupation zone, were eager to avoid having to feed yesterday's enemies with food taken from British citizens' mouths. They wanted to use German production and export, first to feed Germans and then to obtain reparations. Dismantling, removals, and sequestering were therefore kept to a minimum in the British zone. To make this plan work, the British became increasingly dependent on American food surpluses and had to align their economic planning with the United States'.[16]

In the US, several government branches developed competing plans for occupied Germany during the final years of the war. The conflict between the Treasury Department's punitive approach and the State Department's reconstruction-oriented plan was finally decided in favour of the latter when Truman replaced the deceased Roosevelt. Dismantling and limiting economic growth remained part of official US occupation policy, written into the guidelines for the occupation, but these same guidelines included many escape hatches that allowed the occupation

---

[13] Kramer, *The West German Economy*, 34; Norman Naimark, *The Russians in Germany: A History of the Soviet Zone of Occupation, 1945–1949* (Cambridge, MA: Belknap Press, 1995), 166–9; André Steiner, 'Wirtschaftsgeschichte der DDR', in *Bilanz und Perspektiven der DDR-Forschung*, edited by Rainer Eppelmann, Bernd Faulenbach, and Ulrich Mählert (Paderborn: Ferdinand Schöningh, 2003), 229–31.

[14] Kramer, *The West German Economy*, 35–9.

[15] Kramer, *The West German Economy*, 39–40.

[16] John E. Farquharson, *The Western Allies and the Politics of Food: Agrarian Management in Postwar Germany* (Leamington Spa: Berg, 1985), here especially chapters 3–6; Kramer, *The West German Economy*, 49–51; Lucius D. Clay, *Decision in Germany* (Garden City, NY: Doubleday and Company, 1950).

administration much room to manoeuvre.[17] General Lucius D. Clay, the military governor of the US zone, used these clauses to neutralize the restrictive articles. Under his command, occupation administrators on the ground saw their role mainly in assisting the reconstruction of Germany. This was considered crucial for the reconstruction of the struggling economies of other Western European states as well, and by extension, for the realization of the goal of multilateral 'Open Door' economic trade policies as envisioned by Washington.[18] By the summer of 1945, Truman and Churchill jointly ordered the occupation administration to maximize German coal production for export in order to fuel the efforts of reconstruction in Western Europe as a whole.[19] In September 1946, the US Secretary of State, James Byrnes, gave a speech in Stuttgart, considered by many to mark the definitive adoption in Washington of a reconstruction and reconciliation policy towards Germany.[20]

But US and British policymakers, interested in reconstructing the German economy and eager to use German coal and industrial production for revitalizing the European economy, also feared that by encouraging West German production they might play into Soviet hands. Should the Soviets have their way on the question of reparations, any investments in German industry and any increase in German production might end up flowing all the way to Moscow.[21] To avoid this risk, US negotiators insisted that German exports must first be used to pay for 'necessary imports' prior to any reparation payments. This US argument was termed 'the first charge principle'. In practical terms, applying this priority of paying for imports over paying reparations meant funnelling German exports to the US instead of to the Soviet Union, because necessary imports were clearly to come primarily from the US, the most dynamic economic power of the time and the only one of the wartime Allies to come out of the war with industrial and agricultural surplus. This principle, then, was not only favourable to German economic reconstruction but also to the creation of a US-dominated multilateral trade market in Europe.[22] While planning the European Recovery Program (better known as the Marshall Plan), US policymakers wanted to ensure the protection of their investments in West Germany from Soviet reparation demands. In the conference of foreign ministers in London at the end of 1947, State Secretary George C. Marshall was determined to block all possible channels for Soviet reparations from West Germany.[23]

---

[17] Eisenberg, *Drawing the Line*, 14–70; Kuklick, *American Policy*. For the decision in favour of the state and war departments' position following Roosevelt's death, see 114–20.

[18] Clay, *Decision in Germany*, 185–226.

[19] Abelshauser, 15–17; Kramer, *The West German Economy*, 42–7.

[20] This famous speech has been reprinted many times. See 'Stuttgart Speech by J. F. Byrnes, United States Secretary of State: Restatement of Policy on Germany', in Beate Ruhm von Oppen, *Documents on Germany under Occupation, 1945–1954* (London: Oxford University Press, 1955), 152–60, here especially 154–6.

[21] Eisenberg, *Drawing the Line*, 277–317; Kuklick, *American Policy*, 123–40.

[22] Kuklick, *American Policy*, 134–8; Eisenberg, *Drawing the Line*, 314–16.

[23] Eisenberg, *Drawing the Line*, 354–62.

The conflicting economic plans and priorities of the occupying Allies in Germany prevented effective economic cooperation between them. The British (and eventually the French) were persuaded to come closer to American positions, facilitating an economic and political merger of the Western zones. But the extreme incongruence of Soviet and US–British economic planning stood in the way of even minimal economic coordination. Each of the superpowers gradually gave up hopes of effecting an economic policy for the whole occupied territory and resorted to protecting its own zone's economy from interference by the others.

Western economic interests relied more heavily than Soviet interests on constructing an economic border. Because the Soviets and the Western Allies preferred different economic systems, protection of zonal economy carried different implications for economic cooperation across zonal lines. The Soviet military government worked to acquire direct control over East German material assets and economic activity through nationalization, confiscation, and centralization and through the establishment of Communist Party control of key positions. Such means enabled the Soviets to ensure their extraction priorities within their occupation zone with minimal concern about external influence. The American economic vision for Germany had not included such measures. Quite the contrary, it was that of a liberal-capitalist decentralized economy, suited for integration in a multi-lateral global trade system. Such a scheme left their zone vulnerable to influences of centrally directed planned economy in the Soviet zone, unless an effective barrier was put into place to stave off these influences. To achieve growth and reconstruction in West Germany on their terms, the Western Allies depended on formal measures to isolate the West German economy from the East German economy.

Nothing made the division of occupied Germany into two different economic systems more tangible than the currency reform of 18 June 1948. In the US–British zone, the new Western Deutsche Mark (DM) replaced the old Reichsmark (RM). In principle the ratio was 1:1, but this only applied for the 60 marks which the law allowed every citizen to draw in the new currency (and to stocks). Savings, etc. were exchanged in a ratio of 1:10 up to a maximal sum. The overall effect was to reduce the quantity of marks in the market by 93.5 per cent. The reform was not accompanied by a redistribution of non-monetary capital.[24] The Western decision to opt for a separate currency for the Western zones of occupation brought the French zone into the Anglo-American Bi-zonal system and marked more clearly than before the significance of the border between this unified economic space and the Soviet zone.

Currency reform had been on the agenda of the Allied Control Committee for a long time. Progress towards a resolution was very slow, however. The Western Allies' decision to opt for a separate currency served as a statement that the Western Allies prioritized economic reconstruction and the growth of their combined zones over the diminishing prospect of a unified Germany. By then, the formation of

---

[24] The details of the currency reform itself have been studied and analysed by many scholars. For a short review see Abelshauser, *Wirtschaftsgeschichte*, 46–54.

German state agencies was well underway in the Soviet zone and in the Bi-zone. The currency reform was an important step in West German economic reconstruction. Disagreements regarding its actual contribution to economic growth and overall production notwithstanding, the currency reform effected a dramatic shift from unofficial to official economy. It also increased the availability of goods in stores and allowed for better state regulation and control of economic activity.[25]

The chain of reactions and counter-reactions spurred by the currency reform led to the Berlin Blockade. The blockade eventually played into the hands of the United States. The airlift publicly demonstrated US military superiority, while at the same time presenting the Soviet Union as the aggressive, divisive power and the US as the benevolent one. The blockade also gave the Western Allies an opportunity to impose even stricter economic division through a counter-blockade and a reorganization of border guarding along the entire length of the inter-German border.[26]

CENTRALIZATION AND BORDER CONTROL IN EARLY POSTWAR GERMANY

Besides seeing their zone as a source of needed materials and goods, the Soviets (and German communists) planned and pushed for wide-ranging socio-economic restructuring in their zone. Along with real and alleged Nazi war criminals, owners of landed estates and of large factories and businesses were dispossessed. Within two years, 30 per cent of the industrial capacity not dismantled by the Soviets was placed in government hands. By the early 1950s, almost 80 per cent of the industrial production in the GDR was in the hands of state organizations dominated by the SED.[27]

Socialization of the means of production was a staple of socialist ideology. Since the 1920s in the Soviet Union, and throughout Soviet-occupied Europe after the Second World War, it was common practice for the Communist Party to assume all crucial positions of power in the state. The East German party-bureaucratic dictatorship developed according to these general patterns, seeking to direct and

[25] Abelshauser, *Wirtschaftsgeschichte*, 32–62; Eisenberg, *Drawing the Line*, 363–410; Matthias Uhl, *Die Teilung Deutschlands: Niederlage, Ost-West-Spaltung Und Wiederaufbau 1945–49* (Berlin: be.bra, 2009), 135–40, 165–8; Kramer, *The West German Economy*, 134–9; Christoph Kleßmeann, *Die Doppelte Staatsgründung: Deutsche Geschichte 1945–1955* (Göttingen: Vandenhoeck und Ruprecht, 1982), 185–92. See also Sheffer, *Burned Bridge*, 53–5 on the experience of the currency reform in the border towns of Neustadt bei Coburg (Bavaria) and Sonneberg (Thuringia). For personal accounts of the immediate changes brought about by the currency reform see Christoph Kleßmann and Georg Wagner (eds), *Das Gespaltene Land* (Munich: C. H. Beck, 1993), 174–9.

[26] Eisenberg, *Drawing the Line*, 411–59; Paul Steege, *Black Market, Cold War: Everyday Life in Berlin, 1946–1949* (Cambridge: Cambridge University Press, 2007), 195–200; Uhl, *Die Teilung Deutschlands*, 169–74; Clay, *Decision in Germany*, 358–92.

[27] Naimark, *The Russians in Germany*, 170–3; Matthias Judt, 'Aufstieg und Niedergang der "Trabi-Wirtschaft"', in *DDR—Geschichte in Dokumenten*, edited by Matthias Judt (Berlin: Links, 1997), 90–1.

control all areas of life through the tight grip of the party while keeping the mirage of multi-party democracy. The transformation of industrial and agricultural ownership went along with the establishment of communist dominance in politics as the first phase of GDR state building.[28] However, party efforts to penetrate and control society were not fully successful and the party's rule continued to depend on the Soviet Union and the presence of the Red Army, as demonstrated by the strike-turned-popular-uprising of June 1953.

Central direction and control by the party also applied, of course, to the instruments of order and security. Initially, only Soviet forces guarded the demarcation lines with neighbouring occupation zones. In the fall of 1946, the Soviets ordered the German administrations in their zone to establish border police forces. This was in accordance with the Allied Control Committee's agreement to found border police forces on the *Länder* (federated states of Germany), not zonal, level, which the Western Allies also did at the same time. But the Soviets only paid lip service to this agreement. In practice, their border police was established as a zonal force from day one. Like other police forces, it was under Soviet command, though also subject to the growing influence of and political direction by the SED. In August 1947, the border police was officially joined to the German Administration of the Interior (*Deutsche Verwaltung des Innern*, a zonal administration dominated by the SED). Under this administration, policing in general and border policing in particular was gradually removed from the control of the federated states and directed centrally from Berlin. This process was completed in early 1951 with the official subordination of all state police forces to GDR ministries in Berlin.[29]

Centralization was much more controversial in the Western occupation zones, especially centralization of the armed forces. All allied governments opposed the idea of a national German army, but US and British occupation administrations also opposed the idea of a centralized police force and initially defined border guarding as a police matter. Based on their domestic traditions, they established German police forces on a local basis with no central administration. The federal states bordering on the Soviet zone assigned police units to the border initially not as part of an overall approach to border guarding but because the border was part of their territory. Before 1949, then, there was no central organization coordinating border guarding in the Bi-zone.[30] British and American forces cooperated to a large

[28] Ralph Jessen, 'Partei, Staat und "Bündnispartner": Die Herrschaftsmechanismen der SED-Diktatur', in *DDR—Geschichte in Dokumenten*, edited by Matthias Judt (Berlin: Links, 1997), 27–43. Hope Harrison considers Ulbricht's personal role in creating this structure as crucial. See Harrison, *Driving the Soviets*, 16–19.

[29] Peter Joachim Lapp, *Gefechtsdienst im Frieden—das Grenzregime der DDR* (Bonn: Bernard and Grafe, 1999), 10–12; Naimark, *The Russians in Germany*, 357–9; Gerhard Sälter, *Grenzpolizisten: Konformität, Verweigrung und Repression in der Volkspolizei und den Grenztruppen der DDR 1952 bis 1961* (Berlin: Links, 2009), 61–8.

[30] Ludwig Dierske, *Der Bundesgrenzschutz* (Regensburg: Walhalla- und Praetoria-Verlag, 1967), 25–8.

extent and shared some information with German police forces in the four border states, but there was no single connective hierarchy. During the occupation period, German administrators and politicians repeatedly tried to persuade the occupiers that the German perception of policing was different and required central direction.

When it did finally occur, the move to centralize border guarding in the West was initially propelled by economic considerations. The Western Allies began to change their views regarding centralization of border guarding when the border assumed a greater economic significance following the currency reform and the Berlin Blockade.[31] The inter-German border was not yet, at that time, a major security concern for the Allies, as its ineffective guarding testifies. But in early 1949 the Western Allies decided to station a zonal customs service (later the Federal Customs Service, *Zollgrenzdienst*) along the border with the Soviet zone. Ultimately, the border became one of the most important engines of economic division in Germany. It is a testimony to the Western Allies' recognition of the border's growing economic significance that the first federal force assigned to the border from the West was there primarily to supervise the movement of goods. Only two years later did the Western Allies allow the FRG to assign to the inter-German Border a federal force dedicated to security.

After the establishment of the FRG in the summer of 1949, its government tried repeatedly to gain Allied approval for a national border guarding force. As the Cold War frontline gradually came to be perceived as the potential front of the next war in the early 1950s, the Allies found it more difficult to oppose German arguments. Finally, after the war in Korea produced scenarios of invasions for the European Cold War border as well, the Federal Border Guard (*Bundesgrenzschutz*, henceforth BGS) Act was approved by the Western Allies and passed swiftly through the Bundestag. Beginning in the summer of 1951, the first 10,000 recruits of the BGS were stationed at the border area. Ten thousand more joined within two years.

During its early years, the inter-German border affected very different developments in the official and unofficial sectors of the economy. The official economy was quickly reined in by border regulations and the economic policy of occupation administrations. Each territorial administration tried to harness all available resources to the effort of feeding the population and stabilizing the economy within its territorial jurisdiction. This also translated into trying to pull frontier supplies and demands away from the borderlands and towards the hinterland. Frontier residents' economic activity, based on many border-crossing transactions, was severely affected by this policy. This was especially true for activities that were difficult to transfer to the unofficial sector. Unofficial economic activity blossomed around the zonal demarcation lines in the postwar years. The emerging divide in economic regulation and conditions created a host of new opportunities of which frontier residents were well equipped to take advantage.

[31] Dierske, *Der Bundesgrenzschutz*, 30–8.

THE POSTWAR BOOM IN UNOFFICIAL ECONOMY

During the early postwar years, official inter-zonal economic transactions necessitated complicated inter-Allied agreements and permits. Combined with massive population movements, high unemployment, widespread hunger, and uncertainty, this difficulty in official trade made the unofficial sector of the economy, beyond the reach of central supervision, as important (if not more so) as the official one. Werner Abelshauser estimated that the volume of illegal trade between the bi-zone and the Soviet and French zones in 1946 was twice as large as the legal trade.[32] Frontier residents were in an especially privileged position to improve their economic situation through unofficial economic activity. Black market trade was available throughout Germany, but frontier residents had the best access to markets in both West and East. This not only gave them a superior position in manoeuvring between prices and different supply and demand structures but also enabled them to profit from smuggling goods and people across the border in the service of others. The development of the frontier economy is to a large extent a story of state organizations' efforts to curb the unofficial sector and control the flow of goods and people across their borders. Through these efforts, state agencies forced their way into cross-border economic networks and markets and redefined them as illegal. Frontier residents in turn defended their sources of income to the best of their ability, mostly by concealing them from state agents. In the case of Monika Albers, a mere coincidence revealed to unsuspecting state agents the hidden trails of border-crossing economic activity. Under police pressure to account for the presence of unregistered and illegal goods, one head of household from a frontier village detailed her postwar economic networks. Mapping her contacts reveals that the demarcation line did not limit her economic options but rather created many opportunities for those who could, like her, cross it at will.

In the fall of 1948, the Thuringian People's Police raided a few houses near the demarcation line of the Soviet with the British zone of occupation in search of illegal arms used in recent robberies in the area. Searching the house of Berthold and Monika Albers in the village of Ecklingerode (Soviet zone), policemen found no concealed arms. Instead they found surprising quantities of forbidden or rationed wares, far exceeding the officially approved quantities for a single household. Among other things, the list of goods confiscated from the Albers that day included 2,618 cigars, 35 cans of meat, various other meat products, two unregistered pigs and several unregistered chickens, four cameras, three new pairs of shoes, and large quantities of bottled brandy and cigarettes. In her deposition following the raid, which she amended twice in the following days, Monika Albers gave elaborate explanations as to the origins of these goods, revealing an interesting picture of frontier economy in the early postwar years.[33]

---

[32] Abelshauser, *Wirtschaftsgeschichte*, 27–32.
[33] ThHStAW, LBdVP Thüringen, Nr. 405, 102–5.

In the difficult times of rationing, occupation, and the emergence of the inter-German border, Monika Albers' husband fell ill. She had to fend for the family using the assets of a guesthouse, a bakery, and a modest farmland in the frontier village of Ecklingerode. Relying on her thick networks in the region and her knowledge of the terrain, she did quite well in those years. Six distinct unofficial channels of economic activity can be deduced from her depositions, listed here in order of importance for her household and reflecting roughly a more general pattern in the Eichsfeld.

a. *Capitalizing on border-crossing kinship networks*: Monika was born and raised on the Paterhof estate near the Western frontier village of Fuhrbach (West Germany; when she was born it was still Hanover, part of Prussia). During the interwar years, she married a man from the neighbouring village of Ecklingerode, just east of the border in Thuringia. Her brother still managed the family estate, and its resources (for example, an oil presser, meat products, and vegetables) were important in supporting Monika's household. She kept up an active exchange with her brother's estate, supplying and especially acquiring agricultural goods, in what under occupation became illegal acts of smuggling.

b. *Black market on both sides of the border*: by her own admission, Monika traded in the black market in both the British and the Soviet zones, using cigarettes, tobacco, brandy, and Western money. Of the products seized in her house, she admitted to having bought in the black market fabric for clothing, coffee beans, leather for shoes, and thermos bottles.

c. *Smuggling people and goods*: Monika admitted to illegally helping a number of people cross the border to the West, and most probably helped more than she admitted to. She stored furniture and carted it across the border for a company from the Ruhr. The company owner left her a carpet as partial payment. She acquired a typewriter and a camera in the same way. The Western money she was in possession of most probably came into her hands in that way too—money that she claimed she held in order to pay the tuition for her son's school in Duderstadt (British zone). In the Soviet zone in 1948, it was still legal to cross the border in order to go to school.

d. *Private farming in excess of quota*: the Albers had planted mostly canola on their land, and produced more than the quota they supplied to state requisition agencies. The quantity they had left was turned into oil using an oil presser, which they obtained illegally from Monika's brother in the British zone. They also kept unreported farm animals (seven hens and two pigs more than registered). When they did not receive slaughter permits, they illegally took a pig across the border to Monika's brother who slaughtered the pig in the British zone for them (without the permit which was required there as well) and supplied them with canned and other meat products at a reduced price.

e. *Money into goods to counter monetary fluctuation*: when the currency reform was imminent, the Albers invested in goods that would withstand the transition better than cash. They bought a large quantity of brandy, to sell once the currency stabilized. This was the only product seized in the house, which Monika stated that she went outside the Eichsfeld (to Nordhausen) to buy.

f. *War and defeat windfall:* toward the war's end, many people were on the move and needed to get rid of all sorts of equipment and goods quickly. Sedentary residents who had some saved cash or could offer transportation, food, or guidance could thus strike good bargains. The Albers collected deserted military equipment and police uniforms belonging to the village police sergeant who escaped the advancing occupation forces. They also bought cheaply a bicycle from a Russian forced labourer who went home.

Neither the zonal border nor the border of the Eichsfeld limited Monika's movements and economic transactions, but both played roles in shaping her networks

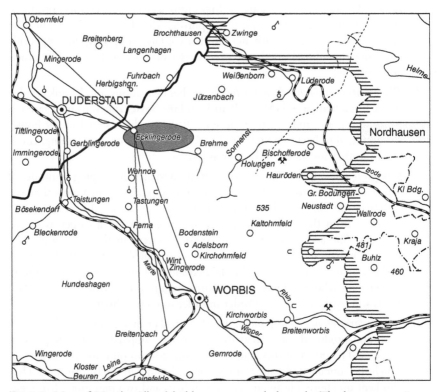

Fig. 1.2. Map of Monika Albers' hidden sources and channels. The lines converging at Ecklingerode mark her economic network, which clearly traversed the inter-German border (black line) but was mostly contained within the boundaries of the Eichsfeld (broad striped line).[34]

---

[34] The map in Figure 1.2 was cut and edited from 'Das Eichsfeld und der Kreis Worbis' (no name of cartographer), 1947, BArch-B, DE 1, 5295, 8.

(see Figure 1.2). The zonal border created opportunities and gave her freedom of action, keeping the Soviet zone police away from and unaware of her dealings in the West and vice versa. The Eichsfeld border clearly marked her contact network and with it the limits of her manoeuvring ability. She crossed that line only once, to get a large quantity of brandy, not an Eichsfeld staple. Note also that cross-border contacts in Figure 1.2, including with the regional centre of Duderstadt, were closer to Ecklingerode than the ones inside the Soviet zone, including the regional centre of Worbis. Duderstadt also lies at roughly the same elevation as Ecklingerode, whereas Worbis is approximately 1,000 feet higher. This geography underlay the centuries-old connections between the towns and villages of the plain, which the new border threatened to sever.

OFFICIAL ECONOMY: FROM BORDER-CROSSING TO BORDER-BOUND

Many aspects of frontier economy could not be concealed from central state supervision as easily as Monika Albers' dealings. The emergence of the border—at the time, hardly visible and sparsely guarded—made its mark on the options for legal border-crossing economic transactions. Frontier residents could cross the border almost at will in those early years, as shown by the Albers case. But the economic activity many of them routinely engaged in was subject to regulation by state agencies and was very difficult, if not outright impossible to conceal. Fields cannot be hidden, nor can dairy farms, orchards, or forests. Production facilities, machinery, warehouses, and harvested produce are also unlikely to escape regular monitoring by state agents. Administrations in each occupation zone prioritized efforts to feed and house residents within their territorially defined jurisdictions. This preference dramatically transformed formal economic practice along the inter-German border in the Eichsfeld, which was predicated on extensive cross-border dependency. Topography and historical development created many ties across administrative and state borders. When the occupying powers tried to make these borders into the limits of economic transaction, official frontier economy suffered a blow, as demonstrated by the example of the Werra Valley communities.

In 1945, the Werra Valley was the site of one of the most extensive territorial exchanges between the Allies. The communities of Neuseesen and Werleshausen were traded to the Americans (transferred from Thuringia to Hesse) because the railway connecting the bulk of the US zone with the port of Bremerhaven passed through them. In return, the Soviets received a territory that included five communities: Asbach, Sickenberg, Weidenbach, dietzenrode, and Vaterode.[35] All the valley communities, exchanged or not, were part of the same economic space around the river valley towns and the railway that connected them. They had

[35] The treaty was signed on 17 September 1945 in the town of Wanfried and is known as the 'Wanfried Treaty' (*Wanfrieder Abkommen*). This territorial exchange is discussed in more detail in Chapter III.

Fig. 1.3. View of the Werra Valley from the ridge of the Eichsfeld to the East.
Photo by the author, July 2008.

their main market, as well as most economic and administrative interactions, in the nearby towns of Bad Sooden-Allendorf, Witzenhausen, and Eschwege in Hesse. Furthermore, the new border separated Asbach and Sickenberg, traded from the US to the Soviet zone, from respectively 40 and 20 per cent of the land tilled by their inhabitants. The territory ceded to the Soviets also included most of the forest of the town Bad Sooden-Allendorf. It was not immediately clear in 1945 that this demarcation line would limit economic transactions, but it did so quite soon thereafter.

The longstanding district, province, and state borders were set according to many historical political developments. They showed little regard for the topography of the Eichsfeld and the economic interdependencies that resulted from it. These networks were affected to a great degree by the steepness of slopes and their implications for transportation and other costs. In its southwestern margins, the Eichsfeld dramatically slopes from the 1,300–1,650 feet high peaks of the Höheberg ridge towards the valley of the Werra river (see Figure 1.3).

The villages of the plain along the northeastern bank of the Werra—Wahlhausen, Lindewerra, Neuseesen, and Werleshausen—were consequently integrated economically into Hesse to the southwest of the river and not into the mountainous Thuringian lands to the northeast (see Figure 1.4). The railway constructed south of the river, with a station just a mile from Lindewerra, and the proximity of the

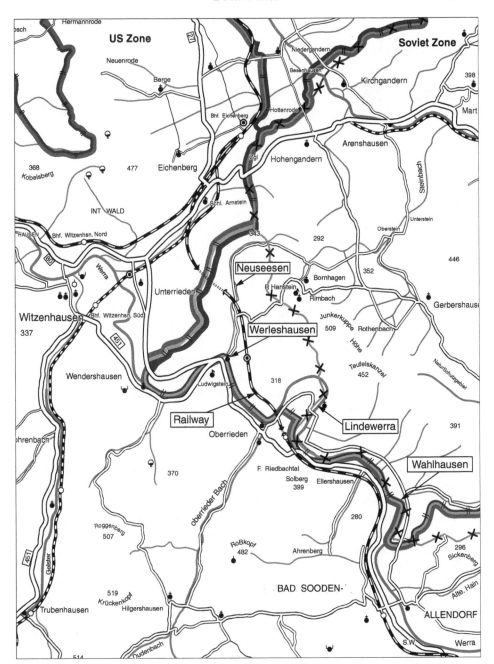

Fig. 1.4. Map showing the locations of the Werra Valley communities.[36]

[36] Dipl. Ing. W. Störmer, Map of Landkreis Göttingen, Verlag W. Stüwe, Braunschweig (undated) in StADud, KEF.1/0066. I thank Joachim Störmer for allowing me to use his father's map.

Fig. 1.5. The Werra bridge connecting Lindewerra to Hesse. Originally constructed in 1901, the bridge was blown up in 1945 by retreating Wehrmacht soldiers and reconstructed after the unification of Germany. Above the bridge, the photo features the peaks of the Eastern part of the Eichsfeld.

Photo by the author, July 2008.

towns of Witzenhausen (4–6 miles away) and Bad Sooden-Allendorf (2–4 miles away) contributed to the orientation toward Hesse.

Administratively, some of these communities belonged to Hesse and others to Thuringia, but prior to 1945 their economic integration into Hesse was not challenged or interrupted by borders. The occupation and division of Germany changed this situation from its earliest days when, on 8 April 1945, retreating Wehrmacht soldiers blew up the bridge connecting Lindewerra to the West (Figure 1.5). In September, when American and Soviet occupation forces agreed on the territorial exchange in the region, Werleshausen and Neuseesen were politically integrated into the district of Witzenhausen, in line with their long-standing economic integration. For Lindewerra and Wahlhausen, Asbach and Sickenberg, the emergence of the economic border spelled trouble. The demarcation line between the Soviet and American zones quickly became a more restrictive dividing line than the borders that preceded it.

In early 1946, a plea from the village of Lindewerra to the President of the county of Kassel in Hesse to transfer the village from Thuringia (Soviet zone) to

Hesse (US zone) described the changes to the village's economy since the occupation. The letter, endorsed by the mayor of Lindewerra, was written by Bernd Hintze, a native of the village who had moved to Witzenhausen.[37] The letter laid out the historical connections between the Werra Valley villages and the towns of the district of Witzenhausen. Hintze presented a dense, multi-layered social and economic regional unit conjoining the communities of the Werra Valley. The mail for the villages was handled in Bad Sooden-Allendorf. Villagers of the valley went to the Hessian towns when they needed to see a doctor; they sent their children to school in these towns. The products of their dairy farms were transported to Bad Sooden-Allendorf, and this is also where additional supplies of bread and meat came from when local stocks were depleted.

All of these links, Hintze wrote, were disrupted in one way or another since the occupation. Under Soviet occupation, the residents of the Soviet zone were instructed to turn for all services and economic functions to Heiligenstadt or one of the larger villages in the district of Heiligenstadt. Heiligenstadt lies over 13 miles from the Werra Valley villages and is over a thousand feet higher. During the winter, the roads to Heiligenstadt often freeze, requiring strong horses or motor power to get through. Hintze gave several examples of the implications of the new policies to the economy of Lindewerra. For instance, the village had been instructed to supply Heiligenstadt with 2,800 zentner (approx. 154 US tons) of potatoes. To carry this weight as far as Heiligenstadt, the village required, according to the letter, 90 horse-drawn carts; for the steepest four miles of the way, each cart would need four horses to pull it. The total number of horses in Lindewerra was ten, making the whole idea quite impossible.

The tone of the letter was dramatic and ominous, and no doubt it exaggerated both how strictly the border was guarded and how disastrous the economic effects on the village were. Nonetheless, it reflected the anxieties about what the solidification of the border might bring about.

Six months later came the laconic reply from the County President in Kassel: 'After examining the matter, I do not find it advisable to pursue it any further at this time.'[38] The chief administrator of the county clearly did not want to shoulder additional problems. He added that it was not unheard of that communities would have economic difficulties, and in such cases it was up to the authority in charge to deal with them. In this case, he suggested, the problems were not his to solve because the communities were on the other side of the border. Acknowledging the jurisdiction of state organizations across the border, this West German official recognized division and thereby helped construct it.

The ease with which frontier residents crossed the border and their uncontrolled border-crossing economic activities posed a threat to the two state-building projects in occupied Germany. Directing official economic activity towards the needs of these projects required supervision and resources, and state organizations in East

---

[37] Bernd Hintze to Regierungspräsident Kassel, 14 March 1946, HeStAM, 401/11, Nr. 27.
[38] Regierungspräsident Kassel to Landrat Witzenhausen, 3 October 1946, HeStAM, 401/11, Nr. 27.

and West increasingly tightened the screws of these mechanisms. Reining in the unofficial economy was much more complicated and required greater resources. The primary instrument in the administrative efforts to curb unofficial border-crossing transactions was border guarding.

BETWEEN STATE AND SOCIETY: BORDER GUARDS IN FRONTIER ECONOMY

On both sides of the border, border-guarding forces were a major focus of state agencies' efforts to curb the unofficial economy and to impose a growing separation between zonal economies. Border guards are the immediate medium of state–society interaction along many borders. In the early years of the inter-German border, border guards occupied an intermediary position in these relations. In no area was the internal conflict of border-guarding organizations as clear as in border-crossing economic activity. On both sides of the border, the types of organizations guarding the border, the social make-up of these organizations, and the changing roles they assumed in the frontier economy were largely responsible for shaping the frontier economy in general and the cross-border trade in particular.

George Gavrilis has argued that, when left to pursue their task to the best of their judgment, border-guarding forces tend to cooperate across borders to achieve more effective border security. However, such cooperation is rare, because central state agencies, preoccupied with state-building, seldom grant border guards the autonomy to work together.[39] One of the criteria Gavrilis lists as a precondition for cross-border cooperation between border-guarding organizations is the compatibility of state-building strategies on both sides of the border. In the case of the inter-German border, such compatibility was certainly absent. State agencies on both sides of the border were anxious to ensure the strict application of their conflicting state-building strategies. To achieve this, they endeavoured to make border guards obedient enforcers of state policy.

State agencies' movement on two fronts—centralized control and direction of border guarding on the one hand, and the improvement of material conditions of border guarding on the other—determined their success in this effort. As this section shows, border guards were gradually pulled away from society and from the temptations of frontier economy and made to play the role assigned to them by central state agencies. In this process, they turned from active participants in border-crossing trade into obstacles in its path.

The length and terrain of the zonal demarcation lines in occupied Germany made guarding them an immensely difficult task. In a memo from April 1945, British military planners estimated that they would require 12 to 16 infantry battalions to guard British zonal boundaries with the Russian and US zones of

---

[39] George Gavrilis, *The Dynamics of Inter-State Borders* (Cambridge: Cambridge University Press, 2008), 14–17, 27–36.

occupation. The same memo stated: 'The boundary between the British and Russian zones is approximately 400 miles in length... Crossing the British and Russian boundaries are approximately 115 roads and railways, of which there are 74 main roads and 10 main railway lines.'[40] Unwilling or unable to raise the massive manpower required, all Allied occupation forces turned early on to German personnel to guard their zonal borders.[41] These Germans were assigned to sections of the zonal border and given a chain of command to report to, but they were given little in terms of equipment and instructions for dealing with a very complicated reality. Under these conditions, border guards in all three occupation zones often developed their own tactics. They thus acted as semi-independent agents, manoeuvring in the interstice between state and non-state groups and organizations. Allied occupation forces and forming German administrations sought to improve their supervision of border guards. But it took them time to amass the political and economic resources needed to establish this control and turn border guards more clearly into instruments of state building.

The Western Allies and West German state agencies, more adamant about economic reconstruction, commanding greater economic resources, and more dependent on border measures for framing economic policy, moved more decisively than the Soviets. The original reservations of the Western occupiers regarding centralized German armed forces were overcome in the face of more pressing concerns. In the period between 1949 and 1953, Western border guarding along the inter-German border was centralized. Local and *Länder* forces assigned to the border in previous years were replaced with more numerous federal, professionalized ones, and centralized control of their command was ensured.

On the Eastern side, thorough control over organizations and resources was seen as a more immediately crucial task than economic growth. Securing party domination began at the centre, where power was concentrated, and spread gradually. As they set out to gain control of East German society, the periphery was not as important for the Soviets and the German communists as it was for their Western counterparts. Consequently, border guarding was not high on their agenda and border guards were poorly trained and equipped. Organizational structures changed several times during the 1950s, but East German state organizations did not mobilize the resources and organization necessary to achieve effective control over border guarding until the second half of the decade.

In May 1946, in one of his weekly reports, the US military governor of the districts of Witzenhausen and Eschwege included the following story, which he found indicative of the population's attitude towards the border police:

[40] 'Memorandum on the Control of Inter-Zonal Boundaries', 9 April 1945, NARA-Mil, RG 260, 390/40/19/3–4, Box 32.
[41] Torsten Diedrich, 'Die Grenzpolizei der SBZ/DDR (1946–1961)', in *Im Dienste der Partei*, edited by Torsten Diedrich, Hans Ehlert, and Rüdiger Wenzke (Berlin: Links, 1998), 201.

A boy carrying a package was walking along a road near the border when he was stopped by a border policeman who proceeded to search the package. Upon finding twenty eggs, the border policeman demanded ten. The boy offered the lot to the policeman, saying: 'Here, uncle, take them all. We don't need them, my father is a border policeman, too.'[42]

Regardless of its authenticity and accuracy, the fact that this story was spread by frontier residents and recorded by the office of the military governor reveals the economic-historical context of early border guarding. Underproduction, devastation, and difficulties in transportation led to great shortages in staple foods. Germans lived under strict rationing; they could not buy 20 eggs legally. In border areas, a primary channel for circumventing rationing was thus border-crossing trade, which operated outside the reach of the government and therefore escaped the registrations and quotas applied by each side. Western occupation administrations tasked border guards—recruited from among frontier populations—with the task of stemming the black-market tide. Among other measures, they ordered border guards to search border-crossers' belongings. This was a delicate position of power for people who were themselves far from drowning in luxury.

Unsure how much to trust rumours about border policemen's involvement and complicity in illegal trade, the military governor's office ran a small experiment. A disguised soldier was sent to sell a group of border policemen American cigarettes on the black market. The border policemen bought the bait-cigarettes and were promptly arrested. Despite this and other accumulating evidence, the governor was of the opinion that the local office of border police was doing an overall good job. But he added that closer supervision by US officers of the work of border police commissioners and 'prompt payment of salaries sufficiently large to encourage efficiency would help'.[43]

US military administrators realized that under the existing conditions, it would be almost impossible to prevent border policemen from taking advantage of their position and increasing their incomes through participation in illegal economic activity. Border policemen in the Western zones were settled locally with their families and were part of the fabric of frontier society, which made it very difficult to isolate them from the economic interests and practices of frontier residents in general.

The Witzenhausen governor's recommendation for increasing salaries seems to have gone unheeded, at least in the early years of occupation. The Border Police was under the German administration of the re-emerging federated states. The material conditions of border guards therefore depended primarily on the priorities and resources of Hesse, Lower Saxony, Bavaria, and Schleswig-Holstein and not only on the wishes of the American or British military governors. Two and a half years after the above-mentioned story was recorded, and five months into the Berlin Blockade, officers of the US military government of Hesse joined the Hessian

---

[42] Office of Military Government for Landkreise Witzenhausen and Eschwege, 'Weekly Detachment Summary Report', 11 May 1946, NARA-Mil, RG 260, 390/49/16/3–4, box 569.
[43] Office of Military Government for Landkreise Witzenhausen and Eschwege, 'Weekly Detachment Summary Report', 11 May 1946, NARA-Mil, RG 260, 390/49/16/3–4, box 569.

Minister of the Interior for a tour of the border of the Soviet zone. They reported that the policemen had to carry out their jobs under utterly inadequate conditions, in crowded accommodations and without winter clothing and/or winter shoes. They were under the impression that the minister would take action after their visit to improve these conditions.[44] By that time, the border police along the border with the Soviet zone was reinforced with policemen previously stationed on the border to the French zone. But the responsibility for the border police was still in the hands of the border states. This meant that there was no central coordination or funding to equip, feed, and pay border policemen.

On the Eastern side, border guarding was structured and controlled differently, with greater emphasis placed on central supervision. During the early years of occupation, the material conditions of border guarding units were significantly worse than those of their Western counterparts, partly because the guards were not assigned from within a local police force and could not count on a home base in the region. Their involvement in unofficial, border-crossing economic activity was also extensive. In a random inspection of the border police quarters in one unit in Thuringia in September 1947, for example, a police inspector found 1,000 cigarettes hidden within the belongings of one constable. Questioning soon revealed that five other colleagues were involved in illegal trade and accepted bribes.[45]

East of the border, the supplies of the border-guarding units and their material conditions remained very poor for a longer time than in the West. This had implications for the units' position within the regional, cross-border economy. A series of inspections of border police units in the Eastern part of the Eichsfeld from early 1951 gave ample evidence of the policemen's meager equipment and of their involvement in local unofficial trade. One report stated that the policemen 'are forced to carry out their duty in ragged, worn-out uniforms, to the point that they are ashamed to go home on leave, because they are mocked . . . in their home communities.'[46] The same report also mentioned that the policemen's diet was almost unchanging. They suffered from a very poor supply of vegetables and their bed linen was washed only once every eight weeks. In another village, the housing situation was the main problem—the unit stationed there was housed in three different farmer houses, with the guards sharing their roofs with local families and sometimes with their farm animals. Border policemen had run out of batteries for their flashlights, a situation that made night patrols ineffective.[47] Like boots, uniforms, and winter clothes, so with flashlight batteries: almost all units complained about the shortage of items, without which border guarding could not be carried out effectively, especially in a forested mountainous area like the Eastern part of the Eichsfeld.

[44] Office of Military Government for Hesse, 'Monthly Summary Report for the Period 1–30 November 1948', 7 December 1948, NARA-Mil, RG 260, 390/49/24/4–5, box 966.

[45] Chef der Grenzpolizei Thüringen, 'Tätigkeitsbericht der Grenzpolizei für die Zeit von 21.-30.9. 1947', ThHStAW, Land Th, MdI, Nr.1126, 75–7.

[46] 'Bericht über Grenzkommado Neuendorf' (undated), BArch-B, DO1 20.0/638a. See also 'Bericht über Grenzkommado Freienhagen' (undated), BArch-B, DO1 20.0/638a.

[47] 'Bericht über Grenzkommado Bebendorf' (undated), BArch-B, DO1 20.0/638a.

The picture that emerges from these reports is of a very miserable and ragged lot, poorly equipped and generally dispirited and angry at their superiors and their state. Gerhard Sälter writes that, already by the summer of 1948, and more so from 1949, central authorities in Berlin made an effort to improve the conditions of the border guards. Central administrations aimed to supply adequate uniforms and construct barracks, and at the same time increase the political training of border guards to make them more independent of society and more loyal to the state and party. Despite this declared commitment, he shows that material conditions, training, equipment, and morale remained poor in border police units until 1950.[48] The set of reports analysed in this section indicates that actual changes in the conditions of border guards were effected very slowly, even after 1950. No wonder, then, that many of the border guards found approaches by local villagers irresistible and accepted all sorts of goods, especially food, from known smugglers in return for turning a blind eye.

One of the most negative of the reports to come out of the inspections dealt with the unit stationed in Siemerode.[49] This report suggested more clearly than others that border policemen were involved in illegal border-crossing trade. The explanation of this finding is especially interesting. While the American officer from Witzenhausen, quoted earlier, identified adequate salaries as the primary means to stop border policemen from engaging in illegal economic activity, the communist party inspector sent to Siemerode had a different interpretation. Although he too reported guards' miserable material conditions, he did not regard these conditions as the main cause for illegal activity by policemen. For him, the problem lay instead in insufficient leadership and political instruction, which left too much room for the negative influences of the surrounding social environment.

Opinions about Eichsfeld frontier communities in East German party and state circles were generally very negative. These opinions were largely based on two factors—the rich and active ties of locals to the West and their Catholic faith. Religiosity in general, and Catholicism in particular, were perceived by the communist regime as markers of disloyalty to the state. With a population that was 85 per cent Catholic and a culture marked by a strong attachment to tradition, the Eichsfeld was a difficult case for party work and mobilization.[50] The opening paragraph of the report on the unit stationed in Siemerode is typical of this attitude:

> The village of Siemerode is very isolated. The population is entirely Catholic. Approximately 70% of the men work in the West . . . The area is known for intensive smuggling. The majority of the population is hostile to the GDR and shows a negative attitude to the people's police. There are attempts to spread corruption among the

[48] Sälter, *Grenzpolizisten*, 63–5, 68–9.

[49] 'Bericht über Grenzkommando Siemerode' (undated), BArch-B, DO1 20.0/638a.

[50] Behrens, 'Regionale Identität und katholisches Milieu,184–6; Petra Behrens, 'Regional Kultur und Regionalbewustsein im Eichsfeld 1920 bis 1990', in *Regionalismus und Regionalisierung in Diktaturen und Demokratien des 20. Jahrhundert*, edited by Petra Behrens et al. (Leipzig: Leipziger Universitätsverlag, 2003), 41–4; also Heinz Mestrup, *Die SED: Ideologischer Anspruch, Herrschaftspraxis Und Konflikte Im Bezirk Erfurt (1971–1989)* (Rudolstadt: Hain, 2000), 133.

young people's policemen and to draw them to attend the Catholic Church. Young girls initiate relationships with them, and then influence the people's policemen to visit church.[51]

The report stated that a few of the policemen, including one constable, had dealings with two different families of known border-crossing guides (in other words, smugglers of people). Corruption and professional misconduct were, in the political analysis of party inspectors, an inevitable result of close relations with frontier residents.[52] It is telling that the first recommendation of the report was to move the unit, composed of many young Catholic refugees, away from the Eichsfeld to a section of the border populated by Protestants. This would reduce the threat of social association with frontier residents, a major cause for their 'corruption'.[53]

In February 1949, following complaints from civilians, a criminal police investigation revealed that the entire border police unit in Ellrich-Nord in the Harz region, a bit north of the Eichsfeld, was involved in smuggling in return for various bribes. The police sensed that the scope of illegal activity in this unit was far greater than the investigation could prove.[54] Even the limited list of illegal activities the police managed to get some of the men to confess to—using evidence discovered while searching their quarters and their homes and reading their letters—reveals a great range of opportunities and temptations. One constable, for example, admitted to the following:

a. Receiving money from a man guiding people across the border in return for letting the man and his group through. In one instance, the constable received a considerable sum of 100 (Western) Marks. The interrogators could not prove, but assumed, that this was the rate for many other instances as well.

b. Allowing a truck belonging to an East German moving company to cross from East to West illegally in return for an unspecified compensation.

c. Crossing the border himself carrying a sack full of animal skins to a Western factory for unspecified compensation.

d. Receiving sausages, live geese, liquor, and cigarettes from different people in return for helping them cross the border illegally.

e. Smuggling a person from East to West and back in return for 100 Western Marks and a few packets of cigarettes. Both the guard and his wife helped carry the person's bags to his Western destination.

f. Together with some of his colleagues, receiving Western money and in return letting a resident of the British zone with a motorbike through to the Soviet zone.

---

[51] 'Bericht über Grenzkommado Siemerode' (undated), BArch-B, DO1 20.0/638a.
[52] See also 'Bericht über Grenzkommado Volkerode' (undated), BArch-B, DO1 20.0/638a.
[53] 'Bericht über Grenzkommado Siemerode' (undated), BArch-B, DO1 20.0/638a.
[54] 'Vorkommnisse beim Grenzpolizei Kommando Ellrich-Nord', 24 February 1949, ThHStAW, Land Th., MdI, Nr. 1133, 86–9.

    g. Helping a girl with whom he had intimate relations cross illegally to the West.[55]

Illegal border crossing, of goods and people, was clearly a very lively economic activity and border policemen were in a key position to play a profitable role in it. Many more Germans in East and West than were legally permitted wanted to cross the border and/or get merchandise and belongings across. Frontier residents were the most active agents in the effort to keep border-crossing channels open. Many of them had property, work, raw materials, markets, and other economic interests across the border. In addition, they benefited from the illegality of much of the cross-border economy, as many frontier residents became smugglers or guides for smugglers. Avoiding border-guard stations and patrols was in many cases possible for those who knew their way around. But it appears, at least in some cases, that finding an arrangement with individual border guards and whole units was the easier method.

STATE AGENCIES TRY TO REIN GUARDS IN

The benefits of this economic activity were distributed between frontier residents, border guards, and the buyers and sellers involved. A significant volume of trade escaped the reach of state agencies on both sides of the border. Part of state-building efforts in West and East, from as early as 1947, focused on accessing and controlling these resources. State agencies on both sides of the border sought ways to eliminate border guards' participation in the unofficial economy by improving guards' material conditions and increasing central supervision of their work. Available resources—combined with economic priorities, legal frameworks, and organizational structures—shaped the eventual path of action in West and East.

East of the border, the already-centralized border police was further centralized in the years 1948–52, as part of the covert re-militarization of East Germany. The number of policemen recruited increased rapidly, and more party activists were assigned to border police units. The resources invested were not sufficient at this stage to effect a significant change in the equipment or training, although the plans foresaw such changes. As noted above, the material conditions of the guards remained very poor.

The Thuringian police tried to encourage confiscation of illegally traded goods along the border by securing the sole use of everything confiscated to the police as an organization. Border-crossing trade was a potential source of revenue and power not only for individual border guards. Ministers and police chiefs sought to limit the role of individual border guards in border-crossing trade through stricter supervision and hoped to increase in this way the share of the police as an organization in the profits. The idea was to convey to the guards that by imposing

---

[55] See 'Vorkommnisse beim Grenzpolizei Kommando Ellrich-Nord', 24 February 1949, ThHStAW, Land Th., MdI, Nr. 1133, 87 for the items this constable admitted to.

more effectively state regulations on border-crossing trade, they would collectively benefit from traded goods more than if they were tempted to act illegally for personal gain. This way they would also avoid criminal and disciplinary procedures.

In late May 1948, the Thuringian Minister of Provisioning, Gillessen, suggested to his colleague, the Thuringian Minister of the Interior, Gebhardt, an agreement for the division of confiscated goods. He quoted a note by an undersecretary, detailing the goods confiscated by the border police during a two-week period from mid-March to early April of that year. It was a long list and he only mentioned the few items that caught his attention as a minister assigned to the task of supplying a population of millions in times of wide-spread shortages and hunger:

45 bottles of liquor [Schnaps]
2,100 herrings
Approx. 1,300 kg flour
1,164 cigars.[56]

The undersecretary who wrote the note suggested putting before the cabinet a proposal for the sole use of these goods by the police. The Minister for Provisioning thought that he and the Minister of the Interior, responsible for the police, could reach an agreement about this without involving the entire cabinet. He suggested half of the captured goods should be divided through the Ministry of Provisioning to certain groups of workers, leaving the other half to the police.[57]

Could border policemen be persuaded to do the state's bidding, surrendering their individual room for manoeuvre for this institutional arrangement and reverting from participants to regulators of border-crossing trade? Judging from the bitterness border policemen expressed regarding their superiors demonstrated in the reports about border guards' units in the Eichsfeld, it seems unlikely that this plan would have worked very well. In the late 1940s and early 1950s, there was enough unofficial trade for both arrangements to co-exist. Despite the fact that large parts of the border-crossing trade were in the hands of smugglers and border policemen, the Thuringian border police generated every ten days very long lists of goods confiscated along the border.[58] The Minister for Provisioning did not object to channelling these confiscated goods according to organizational priorities; he just wanted to control at least some of this flow himself. Illegal border-crossing trade generated revenue and power positions, not just for border guards but also for whole police forces and ministries. These organizations had an ambivalent

---

[56] Minister für Versorgung to Minister des Innern, 25 May 1948, ThHStAW, Land Th, MdI, 835, 157. For the supply conditions and the wide-spread problem of hunger see Alice Weinreb, 'Matters of Taste: The Politics of Food and Hunger in Divided Germany' (PhD diss., Ann Arbor, MI: University of Michigan, 2009).

[57] Minister für Versorgung to Minister des Innern, 25 May 1948, ThHStAW, Land Th, MdI, 835, 157.

[58] See the successive reports titled 'Tätigkeitsbericht der Grenzpolizei', ThHStAW, Land Th., MdI, Nr. 1126 for 1947–8. See also the more standardized quarter reports, titled 'Aufstellung über beschlagnahmte Waren und Gegenstände' for the entire GDR border from 1951–2, BArch-B, DO 1, 20.0/639.

attitude toward initiatives that aimed to stem the flow of goods across the border altogether. This was the case not only in East Germany.

Across the border, the issue of illegal border-crossing trade and attempts to control it pitted Allied occupation administrations and the emerging Federal Republic's government against regional and state authorities. The conflict was partly about revenue, but it also involved questions of authority, priorities of local and national economy, and different perspectives on the inter-German border. The significance of this border increased after the currency reform, and even more during the Berlin Blockade. The Bi-zone authorities issued many new regulations, increasingly limiting legal border-crossing movement of goods, which amounted to a de facto counter-blockade along the inter-German border.[59] The Western Allies—and the German federal authorities emerging under their authority— tried to make this border into a more efficient instrument of economic isolation. It was supposed to protect the stability of the West German market and polity from cheap competition and orchestrated sabotage, as well as allow effective central planning and policy. For example, the local press in Hesse reported in February 1949 that as part of the border-control effort, Hessian border police forces oversaw the digging of trenches that severed all border-crossing roads in order to prevent the passage of unauthorized vehicles.[60]

Starting in early 1949, Western state organizations initiated the assignment of a new, centrally controlled customs service to the inter-zonal border. This force was to take over all border checkpoints, removing them from the hands of police forces that were controlled by each of the border states. The Customs Border Guard (*Zollgrenzschutz*, henceforth ZGS) was established by the British to supervise the movement of goods across the international borders of their occupation zone. It brought to the inter-German border a very different perspective from that of locally anchored police forces, representing more faithfully the interests of state building. The four states bordering on the Soviet zone opposed this initiative, which was presented as an attempt to relieve them of a heavy burden that they had not handled successfully. The governments of these states and their border-guarding organizations raised many objections.

By taking over the border checkpoints, the ZGS removed not just the labour from the hands of border states and districts but also control over the volume and flow of goods across the border. In previous years, border police, under border-state and district supervision, treated smuggling with an eye to the needs of local economy. In the district of Braunschweig, for example, the police noted that many small-time smugglers sold textile products cheaply in local markets. Police-men therefore began to routinely search incoming train passengers' belongings for smuggled textile products. If caught, smugglers were forced to sell their products to

[59] See, for example, Senat der Hansestadt Hamburg, Organizationsamt, Hamburg, 8 November 1948, BArch-K, Z33/100 bd. 1, 2–4. See also Runderlass, Nr. 45/49, 30 March 1949, NLA-HStAH, Nds. 100, Acc. 57/89, Nr. 91, 6.

[60] See the newspaper report about this operation as saved in the Hessian police files: unknown author, 'Gräben entlang der Zonengrenze', *Hessischen Nachrichten*, 4 February 1949, HeStAM, 401/13, Nr. 84.

the police for fixed-item prices.[61] The police would then sell these items to local textile producers on a not-for-profit basis. Interestingly, the police did not confiscate but rather bought the items and did not press charges against the smugglers. This practice had little to do with curbing illegal border-crossing trade and much with harnessing it for the benefit of local Western industry. It prevented competition, while still allowing the illegal flow of goods from the East. Small-scale illegal border-crossing trade by frontier residents was in many cases quietly tolerated by local police forces. Police in border districts were well aware that many border crossers, even without permits, could be just visiting friends and family, maintaining professional or other support networks. Even though these crossers often carried modest amounts of different goods with them, border policemen routinely let them through if caught. Policemen, who were in many cases part of frontier communities themselves and could identify the crossers, did not insist on complete paperwork if they knew crossers were working in the border area or had relatives there.[62]

Goods that Western border guards confiscated along the border were, by and large, integrated into the border-states and districts economies, even if not all of them so smoothly as in the above-noted example from Braunschweig. The sums involved were not of huge consequence to the overall revenues of state organizations, but they were significant direct additions to state budgets. At the time that the occupying Allies were pushing to replace the border police with the ZGS, the Hessian Minister of the Interior forwarded to his colleagues in the cabinet a long, detailed report—compiled by the director of the state's police office—on the achievements since 1946 of the border police in Hesse. In the six months since September 1948, the border police had confiscated goods worth approximately 1,700,000 DM, the director wrote.[63] The minister who forwarded the report added that even if state police did not manage to completely seal the border to illegal trade, the solution should be to add manpower to the (state's own) police rather than replace it with a federal force.[64]

In arguing for the need to add men to the border police, the report mentioned, alongside successes in combating large-scale smuggling, the methods and practices employed by smugglers and the difficulties of tracking them down and preventing such deals. Many West German companies were, according to the report, eager to sell their products in East Germany, circumventing their own government's regulations. A common practice was to find accomplices in frontier communities, companies that would agree to serve as official buyers for the goods in question,

---

[61] President d. Verwaltungsbezirk Braunschweig to Nds. Minister für Wirtschaft u. Verkehr, 18 June 1949, NLA-StAW, 12 Neu 18, Nr. 1188.

[62] Chef d. Polizei, pol.-Bez. Hildesheim to Lower Saxon MdI, 17 March 1951, NLA-HStAH, Nds. 100, Acc. 57/89, Nr. 45, 128.

[63] Hessisches MdI to many recipients, 2 February 1949, HeHStAW, Abt. 531, Nr. 143. The sums are mentioned in the bottom of p. 14 and top of 15 of this report. The planned state income for Hesse in 1949 was just over 1.5 billion DM, making this sum (if doubled for a full year) just over 0.2%. The laws instating the state budget for each year since 1947 are available online at the information portal of the state's parliament (http://starweb.hessen.de/starweb/LIS/haushalt.htm).

[64] Hessisches MdI to many recipients, 2 February 1949, HeHStAW, Abt. 531, Nr. 143. This argument is in the very last page of the report.

giving a legal cover to the shipment up to the border. From warehouses near the border, even large shipments could then be smuggled across quite easily, going unnoticed with the help of professional smugglers from the border area and some railway employees or border policemen willing to turn a blind eye in return for bribes.[65]

The most staggering failure described in the report could actually serve as a strong argument against letting *Länder* police guard the border. The chief of police described the successful smuggling of 12 tractors to the Soviet zone, planned and orchestrated by the head of the council of the state of Brandenburg in the Soviet zone, Fritz Köppler. This large-scale operation 'went smoothly, because Köppler managed, *through contacts among Hessian authorities*, to illegally move the six tractors in 1948 and six more in the last days of January 1949 . . . across the border into Thuringia' (emphasis added).[66]

This was not an isolated incident. West German companies and bureaucrats, along with frontier residents and administrators, were involved in illegal border-crossing trade of various scales, which eluded legal supervision and taxation, and all seemed to be making a profit. The Allies therefore agreed that more men were required on the border but insisted that these men should not be under border-state supervision but rather under Bi-zonal, later federal, control. Despite stiff resistance, especially from Bavaria and Hesse, the ZGS Act went into effect in April 1949.[67] The four states bordering on the Soviet zone were required to bear at least some of the financial burden of hiring and paying 5,000 additional men. Bavaria insisted on keeping its own border police intact alongside the ZGS, whereas the other three border states transferred some personnel to the new federal force.[68]

The new customs officers quickly transformed the economic function of the inter-German border. They brought with them a set of considerations different from those applied to guarding the inter-German border prior to that point. Their mindset and their manuals were shaped by work along international borders, and they drew their priorities from the perspective of the entire West German economy. They examined border-crossing traffic much more thoroughly than their predecessors, and they confiscated all goods disallowed by the regulations, which were elaborate and restrictive.

Unlike locally rooted state police officers, they had little regard for the social or economic context of border crossers, were not interested in determining causes and

---

[65] This was the procedure in several of the cases reviewed in the report of Hessisches MdI to many recipients, 2 February 1949, HeHStAW, Abt. 531, Nr. 143. See especially p. 9.

[66] Hessisches MdI to many recipients, 2 February 1949, HeHStAW, Abt. 531 Nr. 143, 15.

[67] Jürgen Ritter and Peter Joachim Lapp, *Die Grenze: Ein deutsches Bauwerk* (Berlin: Links, 2006), 159. See also 'Verordnung über die Überwachung des Verkehrs mit Vermögenswerten zwischen dem Gebiet der Bundesrepublik Deutschland und der sowjetisch besetzten Zone Deutschlands sowie dem Ostsektor von Berlin', *Bundesgesetzblatt* Teil I, 1951, 439–42. The ZGS was renamed Customs Border Service (*Zollgrenzdienst*).

[68] During the first half of 1949, financial ministries in the border states exchanged views about how best to counter this initiative and eventually how to protect as much as they could of their independence when legislation was pushed through. See HeHStAW, Abt. 531, Nr. 143 beginning on 12 January 1949.

motivations, and were not concerned about the possible positive uses of confiscated goods in the frontier economy. The result was a dramatic rise in the quantities of confiscated goods, which rapidly filled overflowing warehouses, awaiting evaluation and use, sometimes long enough to rot or become unusable. The list of goods that ZGS officers in the county of Brauschweig (one of three counties in Lower Saxony that bordered the GDR) confiscated during 1950 is indicative of this change: among other things they listed 22 tons of meat products, 28 tons of flour, and 160 tons of steel and iron products intended for export to the GDR, and 80 tons of coffee, almost 6 million cigarettes, 80 tons of chemicals, 81 vehicles, 24 tons of textiles, and much more imported from the GDR.[69] The ZGS was not responsible for the next stage; its officers were tasked only with the job of protecting the West German economy, as demarcated by the inter-German border, from unauthorized mixing with the economy of the Soviet zone. Officials in Lower Saxony tried to convince ZGS officers to dampen the zeal with which they pursued their task and recognize the unreasonable implications of such a high volume of confiscation. But they found that ZGS officers did not share their reasoning.

During the second half of 1949, Lower Saxon district and county offices' frustration and anger at the new situation continued to grow. The customs service produced large amounts of confiscated goods every day, issuing standardized price estimates for different items and transferring them to border districts. The districts did not have the manpower to sift, pack, and market such quantities. They had serious doubts as to whether many of the items could be marketed at the prices given by the ZGS, and as to whether some of them could be marketed at all. Some of the confiscated items were very old or of very low quality. Selling East German low- quality goods cheaper than the market prices for parallel Western goods might make economic sense, but it would threaten local producers. Pricing these products according to average Western market prices, on the other hand, would render the products impossible to sell.[70]

These problems were most acute in the district of Helmstedt, which was home to the main checkpoint between Lower Saxony and the Soviet zone/GDR. The district was not prepared for the volume of goods that began to pile up quickly in its warehouses. With its limited manpower, the district administration found it very difficult to sell or distribute these goods in an orderly fashion and generate income from them while still protecting local producers. District administrators' indignation erupted when they learned in late 1950 that the state's financial offices regarded these goods—valued at the price assigned by customs—as part of the district's taxable income. According to official numbers, the district had accepted

---

[69] 'Umfang des Schmuggels im Bezirk des HZA Braunschweig im Kalenderjahr 1950', March 1951, BArch-K, Z33, Nr. 58, 36. This was not unique to this area or to 1950. See the bi-monthly reports with lists of confiscated goods and a discussion of the successes and targets of the work in BArch-K, Z33, Nr. 89.

[70] A series of emergency meetings, reports, and memos on this topic can be found in NLA-StAW, 12 Neu 18, Nr. 1188. See especially Der Präsident des niedersächsischen Verwaltungsbezirks Braunschweig, 'Vermerk', 17 June 1949 and 'Bericht über die Besprechung beim Wirtschaftsamt Helmstedt', 23 November 1949.

from the customs goods estimated as worth 11 million DM in 1949–50 and paid sales tax on only 691,768 DM. When the Lower Saxon Tax Office requested permission to inspect the books of the district, the district refused to open its books. In the correspondence that ensued between state, county, and district offices, all parties eventually agreed that the customs' estimates were too high but that the district was nevertheless forced to open its books for inspection.[71] West German federal offices regarded establishing an economic barrier from East Germany an essential step on the road to economic reconstruction and growth. The practices of the forces they assigned to the job effectively brought the demarcation line with the Soviet zone closer to the function of a state border. The negative consequences to frontier economy were negligible in the overall planning in Bonn, but not for border districts. For frontier residents and administrations, the inter-German border thus assumed new economic significance.

The problems of local and state agencies with the ZGS did not begin or end with the ZGS's zealous confiscation of goods at the checkpoints. In 1949, the chief of police in a Lower Saxon border county wrote that customs officers might be well trained in supervising the movement of goods, but they were missing the more critical aspect of border guarding—security.[72] He and his colleagues saw hundreds of policemen transfer to the federal force and saw the police being forced to pull away from the border. They believed that the ZGS was not equipped to tackle border guarding. Its men were not trained to control the movement of people and were not aware of the many problems of keeping order, protecting the local economy and preventing crime—all affected by the vicinity of the border and the quality of border control. Customs officers concentrated their work at the checkpoints and roadblocks, by and large neglecting the long stretches of border between them. While most goods crossed the border through main roads and railways, many goods and many people (especially those who wanted to avoid being spotted) did not. During 1949 and 1950, police chiefs repeatedly clamoured for mobilizing more policemen and assigning them to the border areas, advocating for more active patrolling along the border. Local policemen knew the area well, they wrote to the Lower Saxon Minister of the Interior. In contrast to the new force, they could quickly tell the difference between harmless locals on their way to visiting family or back from working their fields and smugglers or enemy agents who needed to be taken in.[73]

---

[71] NLA-StAW, 4 Nds, Zg.1-1981, Nr.117. Most documents bare the title 'Einsichtnahme in die Bücher und Belege des Wirtschaftsamtes Helmstedt'. See especially Landkreis Helmstedt, Oberkreisdirektor, 23 January 1951, Der Präsident des niedersächsischen Verwaltungsbezirks Braunschweig, 6 February 1951, and Der Niedersächsische Minister für Wirtschaft und Verkehr, 2 October 1951.

[72] Chef der Polizei Lüneburg to Lower Saxon MdI, 5 July 1949, in NLA-HStAH, nds. 100 Acc. 57/89, Nr. 52, 2–6.

[73] NLA-HStAH, Nds. 100 Acc. 57/89, Nr. 45. See especially Chef der Polizei Hildesheim, 9 September 1950 (40), Chef der Polizei Hildesheim, 1 October 1950 (60–1), Chef der Polizei Braunschweig-Land, 18 October 1950 (59–60), and Chef der Polizei Lüneburg, 12 December 1950 (85–7).

Police chiefs had a personal and institutional stake in increasing the manpower under their command and the responsibilities assigned to them, but they were not alone in raising these concerns. With the cementing of the fronts in the Cold War and the outbreak of the war in Korea, West German civilians and authorities gradually grew more concerned about possible security threats along the border. The federal government worried that Eastern forces were intentionally trying to destabilize the situation along the border in order to present the Western state as incapable and weak.

Since the early years of occupation, West German state agencies had lobbied the Western Allies to approve the establishment of a second federal border guarding organization, one dedicated to security. In 1951, they finally received permission. As soon as possible thereafter, the federal government sent reinforcements to the border and encouraged border states to do the same.[74] In 1950–51, the West German federal government was under the impression that civilians in West Germany did not feel secure enough and considered their state ill-prepared for threats from Soviet-backed East German forces. This led to many reactions, not all of which can be treated in this chapter, but for present purposes it is relevant that federal responses were very much in line with the above-discussed recommendations of the Lower Saxon police chiefs.[75] The new Federal Border Guard was tasked with patrolling the length of the border and trained to undermine attempts of subversion and possible invasion from East Germany.[76]

THE REDEFINITION OF BORDER-CROSSING ECONOMY

The new Federal Border Guards introduced much more powerfully than their predecessors the priority of national and international security to the inter-German border. They conducted manoeuvres based on the assumption that 'internal enemies' of the Federal Republic were supported and assisted by the GDR, a reasoning that transformed smuggling from a purely economic issue into something

---

[74] For the West German campaign to win Western support for a federal border guard and its culmination in 1951 in the federal legislation establishing the force, see Dierske, *Bundesgrenzschutz*, 30–9. For preparations in Lower Saxony to work with the new force and reactions of police county chiefs, see Lower Saxon Minister of the Interior, 27 February 1951, NLA-HStAH, Nds. 100, Acc. 57/89, Nr. 45, 138; and Chef der Polizei im Polizeibezirk Hildesheim, 'Gedanken zum Aufbau einer bundes-Grenz-Polizei', 27 February, 1951, NLA-HStAH, Nds. 100, Acc. 57/89, Nr. 55, 20–5.

[75] See, for example, Bundesminister des Innern, 31 January 1952, NLA-HStAH, nds. 100, acc. 57/89, Nr. 55, 52.

[76] There is very little research about the federal border guard and it is quite outdated. David Livingstone's dissertation, 'The Federal Border Police: Reshaping Order and Security in West Germany's Democratization, 1948–1978', which he is working on at the University of California in San Diego, promises to fill this gap in scholarship.

perceived as a grave security threat.[77] When BGS units were actually deployed along the rural border though, their routine work did not uncover such activities, and their primary task remained that of combating smuggling. Border-crossing activity was not as sinister, it appears, as the BGS command assumed, but officers of the Göttingen unit still sought ways to curb it. After their night patrols found no criminals along the border, they concluded that smugglers used hidden trails that they could not find. They then decided to move their patrols further inland and try to surprise smugglers in places where they might already be off their guard.[78]

BGS units were added to, and in principle coordinated their work with, local police forces and ZGS officers. The presence of uniformed personnel along the border increased significantly with their arrival in late 1951 and even more so when their number was doubled a year later. Regular patrols between checkpoints by day and night were added, and BGS troops were given special legal authority along the border to stop and search people. They also took over the task of checking passports at the checkpoints.[79] Even if they could not locate smuggling trails, the stationing of the BGS troops stretched the border into a broader zone in which all movement could be monitored as potentially illegal. This extended border guarding, by a federal military organization (disguised as police) cast a shadow of criminality and security threat over all border-crossing transactions.

For frontier residents, the stationing of more troops on the border was a mixed blessing. Frontier residents knew the reality along the inter-German border first-hand and recognized that additional border guards would not engage invading Soviet tanks but would more likely contribute to a growing solidification of Germany's division. Some West German manufacturers benefited immensely from the Western embargo on products from the Soviet zone during the Berlin Blockade, which lasted almost a year. Producers especially, who in this way got rid of their stiffest competitors, were quite dismayed when the blockade was lifted in the spring of 1949. The Chamber of Commerce and Industry in Coburg, for example, lamented the damages that the thoughtless lifting of the blockade wrought on the budding West German glass industry. The letter from the Chamber of Commerce stated that unfair competition of cheap East German products would ruin Western producers unless greater limitations were imposed on the importation of glass and ceramic products from the Soviet zone.[80] This was not an isolated letter but part of a broader phenomenon. As Edith Sheffer has shown, Western producers and traders were quick to find ways to manipulate border controls so as to eliminate competition from across the border.[81]

---

[77] See Grenzschutzabteilung Nord III S, 'Lage Blau', 21 February 1952, NLA-HStAH, Nds. 100, Acc. 57/89, Nr. 55, 32–51.

[78] Grenzschutzabteilung Nord II to Grenzschutzkommando Nord, 5 April 1952, NLA-HStAH, Nds. 1150, Acc. 108/92, Nr. 143.

[79] For the legislation founding the BGS and detailing its authorities and numbers of men see Dierske, *Bundesgrenzschutz*, 37–49.

[80] Industrie- und Handelskammer zu Coburg to the Industrie- und Handelskammer Braunschweig, Coburg, 10 August 1949, NLA-StAW, 12 Neu 18, Nr. 1545.

[81] Sheffer, *Burned Bridge*, 61–6. See also Kreisrat Helmstedt, 7 January 1950.

Such reactions, however, were common only in industrial areas. In rural communities they were quite rare. In the small agricultural communities typical of the Eichsfeld and many other border districts, economic interests were tied to cross-border connections. Frontier residents in these communities therefore were not at all eager to see additional forces and greater limitations on border crossing.

Two documents written by the mayor of the small community of Nesselröden in the span of four years demonstrate the dramatic increase in the presence of uniformed state agents along the border in that period and local reactions to it. In 1946, the responsibility for guarding the border was assigned to the community itself. Nesselröden was ordered by the British occupation forces to appoint guards to man the roadblock erected on the road leading to the neighbouring village in the Soviet zone and make sure it was manned around the clock. The mayor was unsure how to finance the guarding and asked the district authority for money to pay the guards.[82] In July 1950, the mayor of Nesselröden wrote to his district administrator a letter of complaint on the stationing of additional policemen in his village. Villagers complained, the mayor wrote, that their hard-earned taxes were being spent on new police barracks. He did not understand why a village, which had until recently been policed by a single man, and had only recently seen the settling of a federal customs unit, should also become the seat of several additional state policemen.[83] The county police chief in Hildesheim replied a few weeks later, saying that the vicinity to the border was the reason that more than four policemen were needed for the village. He added that, while the mayor might not know it, customs officers were not engaged in routine police work; they had other responsibilities. Besides, the police chief added caustically, the mayor and some of his neighbours in Nesselröden were more likely worried that the police would enforce the law more strictly in their village.[84]

Indeed, when federal reasoning gradually turned border crossing of almost all kinds into a suspicious activity, there was apprehension in frontier communities about strict policing. The distance from Nesselröden to Böseckendorf (Figure 1.6) in the GDR was a mile and a half and the two villages had many kinship ties, as well as lively social and economic relations. Villagers from Böseckendorf owned—and at that point still worked—fields in Nesselröden. Many from both sides crossed the line between the two villages daily, as they had always done. Subjecting their border passages and the contents of their rucksacks to even potential police inspection was not a happy thought for these villagers.[85]

---

[82] Bürgermeister Nesselröden to Kreisverwaltung Duderstadt, 24 June 1946, KrAGö, LK DUD, Nr. 22.

[83] Gemeinde Nesselröden, Gemeindedirektor, to Kreisdirektor Duderstadt, 26 July 1950, KrAGö, LK DUD, Nr. 22.

[84] Chef der Polizei Hildesheim to Oberkreisdirektor Duderstadt, 21 August 1950, KrAGö, LK DUD, Nr. 22.

[85] When the GDR closed the border and abolished the 'little border traffic' in May 1952, villagers from Nesselröden worked the fields of their relatives from across the border and made sure they received at least part of the income. In conversation, a native of Böseckendorf told how, when her baby brothers were very sick, relatives from Nesselröden smuggled medicine from the West for them. When, in October 1961, over 50 people left Böseckendorf for the West during one night, they went to

Fig. 1.6. Memorial of the border between Nesselröden and Böseckendorf.

'Mahnmal deutsche Teilung.' Photo by Dehio, downloaded from Wikimedia commons: http://commons.wikimedia. org/wiki/File:Mahnmal_deutsche_Teilung.jpg. The memorial, called 'Movement' (*Bewegung*), was constructed in 1991 by Roger Bischoff.[86]

The police chief's response to the mayor shows that, in state agencies' view, frontier areas were dangerous and lawless, not just because of threats from the outside but also because of the frontier residents themselves and their behaviour. The Lower Saxon government adopted the view that more police were needed around the border. The federal government and border states invested resources to install police and customs units in border communities with sufficient salaries and working conditions so as to limit their temptation to engage in illegal border-crossing trade. In the span of one year the village residents saw a jump from four to over 60 uniformed personnel; in a village of roughly 2,000 residents, this meant that the ratio of uniformed personnel to residents jumped from 1:500 to 1:32. Two separate housing facilities were constructed for the two forces, and they brought with them vehicles, equipment, and orders from central authorities.

As mentioned previously, the ZGS focused initially on controlling the traffic through the official checkpoints, and its officers did not seriously try to control the movement of goods along the stretches of border between their posts. In a series of reports in March 1951, regional customs offices estimated that they were able to prevent 70 per cent of all smuggling attempts in the checkpoints but only 20–25 per cent of smuggling attempts along the border between checkpoints. In the views of the reporting officers, this was not worrisome: smuggling along what they termed

Nesselröden, where they knew they would be received and taken care of. Some of them lived in Nesselröden for the rest of their lives.

[86] For additional details about this memorial see Ulrich, *Geteilte Ansichten*, 251–2.

'the green border' was small in scale and not very consequential, they reasoned.[87] But in federal and state financial offices, concern mounted over the volume of illegal trade carried out by the thousands of people who crossed this border daily, either legally—with work, study, or other permits—or illegally.

In December 1951, at about the time the first BGS troops arrived in the border areas, a subcommittee of the zonal border-states' commission (*Arbeitsausschuss der Zonengrenzländer*) met to discuss the problem of border-crossing trade through the 'little border traffic' (*kleine Grenzverkehr*).[88] Representatives of different federal ministries and of the four border states discussed proposals to increase supervision of this unofficial trade, which the assembled parties believed to be quite extensive in volume. They did not work with concrete numbers or even estimates of the volume of illegal trade, but they had heard rumours and were generally displeased with unsupervised border crossing. The only evidence for the existence and scale of the problem was the income in West DM of a certain East German trade organization store near the border.

The original Allied directive instituting the 'little border traffic' had not allowed for a restriction of crossing points and times, but the civil servants who met in 1951 thought that the new regulations introduced in November 1948 as part of the counter-blockade on the Soviet zone allowed them to oblige all those who held daily crossing permits to report any goods they carried with them across the border two years after the blockade ended. They believed, for example, that it made sense to order anyone bringing goods with him, even goods intended for personal use (including seeds for sowing fields, food for lunch, etc.) to cross the border at specified main roads, where checkpoints would be established to control these goods. The committee also suggested a yearly rationing card, which would be issued to permit holders, listing the products and quantities they were allowed to take with them.[89] All of this was not idle talk. The institutions of the fledgling West German state were making a considerable effort to assert sovereignty and attain control along the inter-German border. A few months later, customs offices in the border counties of Lower Saxony were asked for their opinion on a list of suggestions for increased supervision of the daily crossings in the framework of the 'little border traffic' and the goods that crossers carried with them. The suggestions included

[87] BArch-K, Z33 Nr. 58, 35–40.

[88] 'Tagung der Arbeitsausschuss der Zonengrenzländer', 12 December 1951, NLA-HStAH, nds. 220, Acc. 144/95, Nr. 9. 'Little border traffic' was a set of arrangements allowing the issuing of permits for daily crossing of the inter-German border for purposes such as work or study. These arrangements were made possible from the fall of 1946, after the Allied Control Committee issued directive number 42, creating the legal framework for these arrangements. See Dirketive Nr. 42, 31 October 1946, NLA-StAW, 4 Nds. Zugangsnr. 48/1993, Nr. 833 for the text of the directive. For the arrangements thus created in different regions and how they worked see the report from the Lower Saxon Minister of Interior to the Federal Minister for all-German Questions, Hanover 24 February 1950, BArch-K, B 137/1530, 22. Reports from the Lower Saxon Minister's colleagues from Bavaria (15 March 1950, 30–1) and Hesse (27 March 1950, 33–6) follow in the same file.

[89] 'Tagung der Arbeitsausschuss der Zonengrenzländer', 12 December 1951, NLA-HStAH, nds. 220, Acc. 144/95, Nr. 9. The policy change in November 1948, during the Berlin Blockade, was discussed above in this chapter. See Senat der Hansestadt Hamburg, Organizationsamt, Hamburg, 8 November 1948, BArch-K, Z33/100 bd. 1, 2–4.

designating a limited number of roads the crossers could use, specifying the hours during which they could cross and instituting a rationing system.[90] Judging from the custom offices' responses, the idea was to assign greater portions of the existing police forces to the border in order to supervise border-crossing trade.

The assumption of almost all parties to this correspondence (with exception of the customs office at Northeim) was that almost without exception, farmers, workers, and businessmen with crossing permits were involved in illegal trade. The regional offices tried to come up with ways to impose supervision on these people without completely undermining their work, but did not dispute the basic tenet. Most of the permits were given to farmers who worked fields in remote areas. The requirement that these farmers pass through main roads meant a loss of work time and thus a considerable inconvenience. Limiting the hours of crossing further limited work time by extension and was quite impractical for farmers, who were dependent on the weather and seasons. But, at least among the customs officials who were polled, it was agreed that increased supervision and restrictions were required.

CONCLUSION

State organizations and border guards on both sides of the border were concerned about border-crossing economic (and other) activity and sought to supervise and regulate it. State agents saw border-crossing activity as a potential threat to state power and criminalized most unsupervised border crossings. The driving concern of East German state organizations' border policy was not efficient extraction as in the West, but coercion. East German state organizations were more preoccupied with the exertion of power through party hierarchies than with the implications of these practices for the actual function of the border. More importantly, East German state agencies did not possess the same resources as their Western counterparts and could not transform border guarding in a similar fashion, although they were just as anxious to turn the border into a statement of power and statehood. As the next chapter will show, they found a way to do so with more modest resources, through a much less subtle exertion of power in 1952.

Just two months after the correspondence between Western customs offices regarding supervision of goods carried across the border by permanent permit holders, and before Western border states instituted any changes in the crossing procedures, the GDR unilaterally announced the abolition of the 'little border traffic'. For many Eastern and Western workers, students and traders, and especially for the thousands of farmers who owned fields across the border from their

---

[90] The request came from the Lower Saxon main customs office in Hanover in early February 1952 and the responses came a few weeks later. They all bear the title 'Kontrolle des Verkehrs zwischen grenzdurchschnittenen Güttern' and follow each other in NLA-HStAH, nds. 220, Acc. 144/95, Nr. 9.

residences, this was a serious economic blow.[91] But the development of Western policy regarding border-crossing trade in the years 1948–52 suggests that for financial planners, customs officials, and border police in West Germany, this East German initiative came as a relief. They could profess powerlessness in the face of 'Eastern aggression', and they no longer had to take the blame for the difficulties of unhappy border crossers—the GDR took care of this for them.

Before it became a frontline of a potential Third World War, the inter-German border emerged as the fault line between two parallel efforts to design and control economic activity from the centre. In the span of a few short years, the initial resolve of the Allies to manage occupied Germany as a single economic unit was forsaken for conflicting strategies of separate economic reconstructions. The demarcation line between the Western and Soviet zones of occupation assumed growing importance in this process, especially through its function in the Western state-building project.

Occupation forces and German state organizations on both sides of the inter-German border assigned a growing number of men to guard the border between them, transforming this border in the process. The efforts of Western and Eastern state organizations to eliminate unofficial border-crossing economic activity were not very effective in the years 1948–52, but they did achieve important changes in the function and perception of this border. State agents assigned to the border area defined as suspicious or illegal increasingly greater proportions of routine border-crossing movement of people and goods. They consequently subjected more people and goods to different measures of supervision in increasingly larger areas along the border. Economic motivations, plans, and goals played the most important role in shaping policies and practices of state organizations in these early stages of Germany's division. West German organizations took most of the initiative in constructing the inter-German border as an economic divide in those years.

As the next chapter shows, the GDR seized the initiative in the spring of 1952. The construction of physical barriers, the clearing of forests and fields, and the deportation of frontier residents were visible and violent actions. They changed the reality and perception of the border almost overnight. These dramatic steps should not conceal, however, the more subtle division processes affected by the transformation of the economic function of the border prior to 1952.

[91] The transformation in GDR border policy in the summer of 1952 and its effects of frontier agriculture are the focus of Chapter II.

II

Bounding the Land
Border Formation and Land Ownership, 1952–3

The farmer Stamm from the village of Zwinge rented his fields twice in the years 1952–4, to two different farmers.[1] First he rented to the farmer Falck from Fuhrbach and a year later to the farmer Lapp from Brochthausen because Falck did not pay the rent as agreed. Lapp plowed his newly rented fields and prepared to grow potatoes, but Falck sowed wheat in the fields, thus indicating that he still regarded them as his own. At this point Stamm decided to involve the authorities. While this story is reminiscent of the myriad stories about agricultural feuds that every chronicle in any rural area has recorded, this tale is different. This is a story about the Cold War and the division of society along the Iron Curtain. Before 1952 these three farmers, from villages not more than three miles apart, had not been rivals.[2]

The conflict between these three farmers was caused by the inter-German border which passed between them, and by the policies of East and West German state agencies. The borderline left Zwinge in the GDR and the other two villages in the FRG. Until 1952, farmers from all three villages crossed the border daily to work fields they owned on the other side of it. Following a dramatic overhaul of the GDR's border regime in May 1952 that was no longer possible. This is when Stamm had to rent out his fields. Falck would have liked to do the same with his fields east of the border, but under communist rule in the GDR he was not allowed to do so. Having lost the ability to work his land, he managed to at least secure a rent contract for alternative land. But since he was not compensated for his loss, he decided not to pay the rent.

Falck's vigilantism was an act of defiance against the GDR's wanton confiscation of his land and against the FRG's unwillingness to compensate him accordingly. But it pitted him against two other neighbouring farmers who were also exposed to the new realities created along the border in the summer of 1952. All three (and many thousands of frontier farmers who found themselves in similar situations) reacted to the changing conditions and attempted to protect their land ownership

[1] Parts of an earlier version of this chapter appeared as an article. See Sagi Schaefer, 'Border-Land: Property Rights, Kinship, and the Emergence of the Inter-German Border in the Eichsfeld', in *Praktiken der Differenz: Diasporakulturen in der Zeitgeschichte*, edited by Miriam Rürup (Göttingen: Wallstein, 2009), 197–214.

[2] Landkreis Osterode to Fuhrbach, 'Bewirtschaftung von Ländereien an der Zonengrenze', 22 November 1954, StADud, Rep 51, Fuhrbach 7330, Fuhr 327.

and incomes. All of them had to contend with state agencies' positions and practices and in this process made each other into rivals. The current chapter tells the story of this process as it unfolded during the dramatic year of 1952–3 along the rural border between East and West Germany. It begins with the policy change which undergirded the process.

On the evening of 26 May 1952, East German state organizations took the initiative in constructing the inter-German border, announcing decisive policy measures. This step entailed grave implications for frontier farmers. Thousands of farmers along this border lost access to their fields on the other side. In one stroke, ownership of plots passed on through generations was threatened as East German state organizations tried to assert their authority along the border. This chapter traces the reactions of frontier farmers and state agencies to this new reality, and the interactions between them. Examining these interactions, the chapter uncovers early connections between border construction and the changes in perceptions and orientations of frontier farmers along both sides.

Like most of the land traversed by the inter-German border, the Eichsfeld (Figure 2.1) was a predominantly agrarian region. When the GDR announced the sealing of the border, frontier agriculture along the 1,000-mile frontier was immediately thrown into chaos. In the Eichsfeld, family plots had been traditionally apportioned among siblings according to southwest-German tradition (*Realerbteilung*). Centuries of plot division had created a society of mostly smallholding farmers, producing at or below subsistence levels. A survey of land ownership in the GDR part of the Eichsfeld in 1950 showed that 29 per cent of the land in the district belonged to farmers owning five ha (a bit over 12 acres) or less of land and only 7.6 per cent of the land was owned by farmers with more than 20 ha (a bit under 50 acres).[3] When the proto-industry lost out to the growing industry in the towns during the first half of the nineteenth century, labour migration became widespread in the region, and the economy of many households came to depend on labour performed all over Germany and across the ocean.[4] But reliance on migrant labour did not reduce the attachment to land ownership as an important economic resource and as an anchor of self-esteem. In the postwar period, the size of a family's farm still determined its status and political power in the village.[5]

The GDR's attempt to close the border threatened the property rights of many frontier farmers; for others it created opportunities to gain additional land. To protect

[3] 'Landwirtschaftliche Betriebsgrößenklassen im Eichsfeld', 29 May 1951, BArch-B, DE 1, 5296, 193. For the historical origins of this situation and its consequences see Matthias O. Gleitze, 'Die Verteilung und Bedeutung der Betriebsgrössen in der Landwirtschaft des Kreises Duderstadt' (PhD diss., Rostock University, 1926). See especially part II of the dissertation, beginning on p. 45.

[4] For the development of proto-industry see Peter Kriedte et al., *Industrialization before Industrialization: Rural Industry in the Genesis of Capitalism* (Cambridge: Cambridge University Press, 1981). For this transition in the Eichsfeld see Behrens, 'Regionale Identität, 177–8. For the specifics of work-migration in the Eichsfeld see Detlef Schnier and Sabine Schulz-Greve, *Wanderarbeiter aus dem Eichsfeld: Zur Wirtschafts- und Sozialgeschichte des Ober- und Untereichsfeldes seit Mitte des 19. Jahrhunderts* (Duderstadt: Mecke, 1990).

[5] See the first four chapters in Daniela Münkel (ed.), *Der lange Abschied vom Agrarland* (Göttingen: Wallstein, 2000).

Fig. 2.1. Map of Germany showing the location of the Eichsfeld region.[6]

their inherited property and to acquire more land, Eichsfeld frontier farmers learned to use language and logic to which the authorities were amenable. In 1952, and for a number of years thereafter, the border did not significantly hinder their movement or sever their contacts across it. However, it generated land-related incentives and opportunities which made frontier farmers develop divergent orientations and emphasize different qualities and values. Depending on how the border's emergence affected their land ownership, and on the social make-up of specific areas, frontier farmers developed different approaches to their regional community and state.

[6] Copied and edited from Bundesministerium fur Gesamtdeutsche Fragen (ed.), *Im Schatten der Zonengrenze* (Bonn, 1956), 5.

Because of the limited communication between Eastern and Western state agencies, border formation on both sides was unusually dependent on the cooperation of frontier residents. As this chapter shows, the result was a process that entailed intensive interactions between state agencies and frontier residents. The latter acted in their own interests, attempting to harness policies designed in Bonn and East Berlin to locally relevant ends. In this process, frontier farmers adopted assumptions and agendas required in order to present their case to separate Eastern and Western state agencies and oriented themselves to the rules these organizations established.

From the early nineteenth century, the borders between German principalities gradually diminished in function and became less significant. The German customs union (*Zollverein*), established in 1833, eliminated the economic purpose of many of the borders between German principalities. Throughout the following three decades, it expanded to encompass most of the territory that in 1870–1 became the Second German Empire. Borders between the federal states of the German *Kaiserreich* opened to free movement of people and goods following unification. Under the Saxon and Prussian states, as well as under Imperial Germany, the Weimar Republic, and the Third Reich, Eichsfeld residents inherited, bought, leased, and rented landed property irrespective of these borders. Following the collapse of the Third Reich, restrictions on movement were tight all through occupied Germany. Crossing zonal borders was prohibited for Germans, and the Allies only granted permits for special causes. Within a year, restarting and increasing production, especially agricultural production, became a priority for the occupiers in the face of developing hunger in their occupation zones. They realized that in many factories, mines, and fields, production depended on crossing zonal borders.

In October 1946, the Allied Control Committee for Germany issued 'directive 42', authorizing and regulating zonal border crossing for Germans who resided in one zone and worked in another.[7] Following this directive, zonal commanders authorized district administrations to issue permits and regulate passage in their districts. The local arrangements thus created all along the inter-German border were referred to as *Kleine Grenzverkehr* ('little border traffic', henceforth KGV). These arrangements enabled most farmers along the inter-German border to work their fields and harvest them from early 1947 onwards.[8] Farmers who lived in one zone and owned or leased land in another were one of the biggest groups benefiting from this opportunity. In the Eichsfeld they constituted the majority of those receiving crossing permits under the new regulations.[9] For most frontier farmers of the time, zonal borders reassumed the marginal role in their economy that they held before 1945.[10]

---

[7] 'Dirketive Nr. 42', NLA-StAW, 4 Nds. Zugangsnr. 48/1993, Nr. 833.

[8] See the report from the Lower Saxon Minister of Interior to the Federal Minister for All-German Questions, 24 February 1950, BArch-K, B 137/1530, 22. Reports from the Lower Saxon Minister's colleagues from Bavaria (15 March 1950, 30–1) and Hesse (27 March 1950, 33–6) follow in the same file.

[9] 'Grenzpassierscheine in Thüringen', 8 January 1952, ThHStAW, LBdVP, Nr. 176, 4–7.

[10] See Landkreis Dud to RP Hildesheim, 9 June 1951, NLA-HStAH, Nds. 120 Hildesheim, Acc. 82/77, Nr. 21.

During the early occupation years, a more ambitious policy affected land-ownership patterns in large parts of occupied Germany. Land reform aimed to transform the rural social structure and the Soviets pushed it very determinedly in their zone.[11] Initially, the British also favoured some kind of redistribution of land in their zone.[12]

Unlike the northeast German planes, the Eichsfeld had very few large estates and state domains. Most of the farmers in the region owned medium or small plots and did not fall into any of the groups whose land was targeted for confiscation by the Soviet zone's land reform. In the fall of 1945, district authorities in the Eichsfeld found only 55 farms in the district with more than 100 ha (approx. 247 acres, the bar set for land reform in the Soviet zone). These farms held 6.5 per cent of the land in the district.[13] In addition, the district also confiscated and redistributed land belonging to 28 people defined as former Nazis or war criminals.[14] Compared to other regions in the Soviet zone of occupation, these were low numbers, but they were quite typical for Thuringia, where estates were traditionally smaller and fewer than in the northeast.[15] Consequently, the overall effect of the land reform in this region was not dramatic. District authorities took over some of the more successful estates to use as district agricultural schools. Some villages received additional land and distributed it among farmers. As in other areas of the Soviet zone, this land distribution reinforced rather than undermined traditional village hierarchies.[16] By 1947, land reform had come to an end in the Eichsfeld.[17]

THE WATERSHED OF 1952 AND THE CRISIS OF FRONTIER AGRICULTURE

For the next five years there were no more major upheavals in land ownership in the Eichsfeld, but on 27 May 1952 frontier residents faced a new reality. East German state organizations announced drastic changes in the border regime, making the

[11] Arnd Bauerkämper, '*Junkerland in Bauernhand*?: *Durchführung, Auswirkungen und Stellenwert der Bodenreform in der sowjetischen Besatzungszone* (Stuttgart: F. Steiner, 1996).

[12] For the debates and plans for land reform in the British zone see Günter J. Trittel, *Die Bodenreform in der Britischen Zone 1945–1949* (Stuttgart: Deutsche Verlags-Anstalt, 1975). For a broader perspective on the reasons why the reform was never enacted in the British zone see Farquharson, *Politics of Food*.

[13] Astrid Klinge, 'Anmerkungen zur Durchführung der "demokratischen Bodenreform" 1945 im sowjetsich besetzten Eichsfeld', *Eichsfeld-Jahrbuch* 13 (2005): 175–6.

[14] Klinge 'Demokratischen Bodenreform', 180–1.

[15] See Andrew I. Port, *Conflict and Stability in the German Democratic Republic* (Cambridge: Cambridge University Press, 2007), 29.

[16] For the general argument see Bauerkämper, 'Junkerland in Bauernhand?' The central Thuringian archive in Weimar holds many reports on land reform from the Eichsfeld district. See for example: ThHStAW, Land Thür. Landesbodenkommission, Nr. 323, 3–6, 8–10, 12–13, 183–6. For a summary of land reform in the Eichsfeld see Klinge, 'Demokratischen Bodenreform', 167–92.

[17] See 'Bericht über die Dienstreise am 28.1.1949 in den Kreis Heiligenstadt', ThHStAW, Land Th. Landesbodenkommission, Nr. 42, 159–67. These issues are discussed in more detail in Chapter IV.

zonal demarcation lines officially impenetrable. There is disagreement as to how long in advance this policy was planned and discussed, but it is clear that the timing of its implementation was a response to the FRG's joining, on that very day, the European Defense Community.[18] The new policy included the abolition of all local and regional arrangements of the KGV. Community councils received a detailed copy of the new order stating explicitly that 'the regulations governing the little border traffic are abolished as of May 26, 1952'.[19]

The border was to be fortified by erecting a fence, clearing a ten-meter strip along the eastern side of this fence and declaring a 500-meter strip and a five-kilometer-strip as restricted areas with ascending levels of security. The state promised certain benefits, including economic ones, to residents of these areas.[20] On the other hand, the new border regime imposed many restrictions on movement and other free-doms for frontier residents. During the following weeks, East German forces deported thousands of 'untrustworthy people' from the declared restricted areas into the GDR hinterland and mobilized or coerced thousands of others to build fences and clear forests.[21] District and community councils were instructed to notify the population that crossing the control strip along the border was prohib-ited. The text of the order further stated that 'the border police received instructions [that] in cases of non-observance of orders weapons should be used.'[22]

Despite these strong words, crossing the border did not become significantly more difficult for frontier residents after 27 May 1952. Knowing the terrain better than the border policemen, they could and did cross it more or less at will. As described in Chapter I, frontier residents bribed border policemen in many cases, threatened, or simply ignored them in others, but more often they just tried to avoid them. Smugglers, refugees, and people going to work or to visit family had to be more careful, but if they really wanted to go to the neighbouring zone they still did so. On 26 June 1952, a month after the new border regime was announced, the

---

[18] For the preparations to the announcement of the new border regime in the GDR, beginning in early May 1952, see BArch-M, DVH 27, Pt7493. For the purposes of the argument in this chapter see especially 'Entwurf für Befehl Nr. /52', 20 May 1952, 50, and documents on pp. 63–7. See also 'Besondere Massnahmen an der D-Linie auf Veranlassung der SKK', 3 May 1952, BArch-B, DO 1, 20.0/642 for measures to tighten and even seal parts of the border as early as 3 May 1952. For the broader context of this policy change in East Germany see Corey Ross, *Constructing Socialism at the Grass-Roots: The Transformations of East Germany, 1945–1965* (New York: St. Martin's Press, 2000). See especially part two, beginning on p. 51.

[19] See for example Kreisrat d. Kreises Worbis to Bürgermeister Kirchgandern, 26 May 1952, KrAEich, Kirchgandern, B14. For an earlier version see 'Entwurf für Befehl Nr. /52', 20 May 1952, BArch-M, DVH 27, Pt 7493, 50.

[20] Edith Sheffer, 'The Foundations of the Wall: Building a "Special Regime" in the Borderland (unpublished paper given at the GSA annual conference 2006). See also Rainer Potratz, 'Zwangsaussiedlungen aus dem Grenzgebiet der DDR zur Bundesrepublik Deutschland im Mai/ Juni 1952', in *Grenzland: Beiträge zur Geschichte der deutsch-deutschen Grenze*, edited by Bernd Weisbrod (Hanover: Hahnsche Buchhandlung, 1993).

[21] 'Arbeitskräftebeschaffung für die umgesideleten Betriebe', 27 June 1952, KrAEich, EA HIG, 192; 'Protokoll über die Beschrecung am 24.6.52 im Dienstzimmer der Genossen Ministerpräsidienten', ThHStAW, Land Thür. MdI Nr. 3039, 7–9; BArch-B, DE 1, 6084, 178–9, 185–6.

[22] Kreisrat d. Kreises Worbis to Bürgermeister Kirchgandern, 26 May 1952, KrAEich, Kirchgandern B14.

chief of the People's Police (*Volkspolizei*) in Thuringia wrote to the Minister of the Interior that the police had reinforced its units along the border but was powerless to stem the tide of 'flight to the West'.[23]

However, the new border regime immediately prevented farmers along the border from working their fields across it. They could still cross illegally and get to their fields, but working an open field near the border meant that patrols could see them, arrest them, or prevent them from actually performing the work they came to do. Even if they could somehow maintain their fields this way, they could not expect to be able to transport their harvest across the border unobserved.[24] The most immediate consequence of the new East German border policy was therefore to plunge frontier agriculture into uncertainty and chaos. My estimate is that around 1,200 households were affected in the Eichsfeld alone.[25] The new policy was announced in the midst of the fieldwork high season, when every day mattered. By then, farmers had already invested work and capital in their fields and depended on the expected returns. Many of the plots involved were small and many of the households were worker-peasant households not relying exclusively on agriculture for their living. Most of the affected farmers lost access to plots which were too small to support a family.[26] That said, even families which only had a kitchen garden were not only attached to it emotionally but depended on it in many ways. This is much before the *Wirtschaftswunder* reached the Eichsfeld. Saving on food expenses was crucial for some families, especially for pensioners and widows.

On both sides of the border, state agencies and frontier farmers followed different political and economic interests and agendas in an attempt to maximize benefits and reduce damages in the new situation. The official border policy did not determine the actual arrangements of land ownership and field work along the border. Nor were these arrangements determined exclusively by the reactions of state agencies and frontier farmers. Such arrangements were rather the consequence of the interactions between four broad groups of agents: state agencies and frontier residents in the FRG and the same two groups in the GDR (see Figure 2.2). The

[23] LBdVP Thüringen to Innenministerium d. Landes Thüringen, 26 May 1952, ThHStAW, Land Th., MdI, Nr. 3039, 96. See also Buckler, *Grenzgänger* and Röhlke, *Erzählungen von der deutsch-deutschen Grenze*.

[24] Stadt Duderstadt, *Die Grenze im Eichsfeld: Leid, Hoffnung, Freude* (Göttignen: Verlag Göttinger Tageblatt, 1991), 12–13; See also Landrat Witzenhausen to Regierungspräsident Kassel, 'Ernte an der Zonengrenze', 8 August 1952, HeStAM, 401/13, Nr. 5 for an example of a farmer attempting to bring part of his harvest across the border from West to East. See BArch-K, B 137, Nr. 58 for reports that in some areas Western border guards allowed it.

[25] See Kreisrat d. Landkreises Worbis to Thüringischer MdI, 28 March 1951, ThHStAW, Land Th., MdF, Nr. 1397 for an estimate of over a thousand farmers in the Worbis and Heiligenstadt districts who owned land in the FRG. In June 1951, a report from the district of Duderstadt (the Western part of the Eichsfeld) counted 169 farms in the district with fields across the border. See Landkreis Duderstadt to Regierugnspräsident Hildesheim, 9 June 1951, NLA-HStAH, Nds. 120 Hildesheim, Acc. 82/77, Nr. 21.

[26] Entschliessung des Rates der Gemeinde Fuhrbach, 13 June 1952, NLA-HStAH, Nds. 120 Hildesheim, Acc. 55/78, Nr. 393. For example, in the village of Fuhrbach, only 12 of the total 117 affected households were 'strictly peasant' (*rein bäuerliche*). See Landkreis Duderstadt to Regierungspräsident Hildesheim, 17 June 1952, NLA-HStAH, Nds. 120 Hildesheim, Acc. 60/78, Nr. 2.

Interactions around and across the Inter-German Border

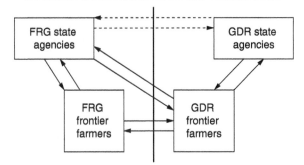

Fig. 2.2. Frameworks of interaction around the border

touchstone of these interactions was the lack of official relations between Western and Eastern state agencies.[27] Eastern state agencies did not interact with Western frontier farmers. Thus we can speak of four different interaction spheres, all affected significantly by the absence of a fifth.

In the summer of 1952, the centrality of land ownership for frontier farmers and the political and symbolic significance of the border for state organizations on both sides added an edge to these interactions. Under these strained conditions, the different groups of agents used the resources available to them in order to attain the best possible outcome. Frontier farmers turned to their social networks across the border for support and used their superior knowledge of agricultural conditions and of the terrain to secure their property rights or acquire more land. State agencies used legal and economic measures and applied instruments of coercion in the attempt to enforce certain practices of land ownership along the border. State agencies were in most cases able to enforce the rules of legitimate land use in their territory, but they were often powerless to determine de facto ownership as farmers learned to play these rules in their favour. Conflicts over property rights thus affected the relations of frontier residents on both sides of the border with their state agencies and with each other.

The chapter analyses these processes during the year following the announcement of the new border regime, comparing three areas in which different conditions produced different reactions of both state agencies and frontier farmers. The first is the Lower Saxon part of the border in the Eichsfeld (see Figure 2.3 for a map of the Eichsfeld borderlands). In this area, a conflict over the arrangements of field work along the border evolved between two groups of frontier residents, those who lost and those who gained land, and different state agencies intervened in this conflict. In the parts of the inter-German border in the Eichsfeld which fell to Hesse in 1945, the border separated Protestant communities from each other.

---

[27] This was largely due to the decision of the Western Allies and the West German state not to recognize the GDR, and to the campaign they launched to isolate it internationally. The impact of this decision and its determined application are discussed in Chapter III.

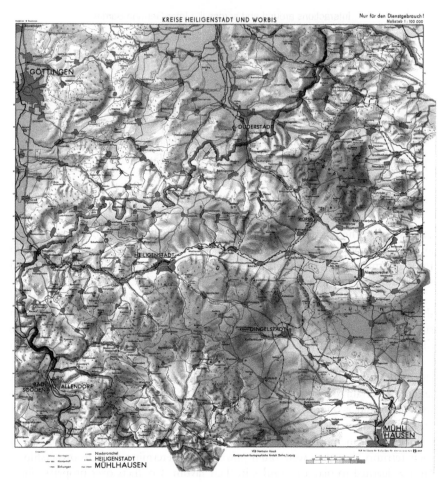

Fig. 2.3. Map of the Eichsfeld borderlands, produced in the GDR in 1960s.[28]

Protestants constituted a small minority in the Eichsfeld and were connected differently to the surrounding regions. This fact, combined with administrative problems created by the Allies' territory swaps from 1945, introduced opportunities for taking over land which were not available elsewhere. State agencies in the Eastern part of the Eichsfeld had an abundance of available land following emigration and deportations from the border areas. Frontier farmers could get land, and in return state agencies demanded that they relinquish claims for property in the West.

---

[28] I thank the staff of the Eichsfeld district archive in Heiligenstadt, and especially Regina Huschenbeth, for allowing me to take a copy of this map with me.

MY BROTHER'S (LAND) KEEPER: ACQUIRING
LAND IN LOWER SAXONY

The new border policy was not a complete surprise for West German authorities. Rumours and early indications circulated at least several days in advance of 26 May.[29] And yet, the scope of the change, and especially the immediate effect it had on agriculture along the border, caught Western state agencies completely unprepared. While state agencies studied the situation and debated solutions, frontier farmers reacted to the new reality, attempting to protect or further their economic interests.

A struggle ensued between groups of Western frontier farmers over fields in their district, previously owned by Eastern frontier farmers. On one side were frontier farmers who had lost access to their land in the East. They demanded these fields as a compensation for their loss. On the other side stood frontier farmers from communities in the territory of which were fields owned by frontier farmers from the East. These frontier farmers used their cross-border networks to secure private agreements with the owners for working these fields. They presented themselves therefore as the guarantors of private property in the name of the owners.

Ascending levels of state agencies entered the fray in three distinguishable stages starting in early June 1952. The district, the lowest level of administration above individual villages, was the first to intervene. Looking to alleviate the plight of those worst hit by the situation, the district administration, seated in Duderstadt (West), sought to ensure quick and effective compensation for these farmers. Lacking financial resources to compensate them, and lacking the legal authority to confiscate land, the district tried to assign farmers who had lost access to land in the East as trustees for fields of farmers from the East. Several weeks later, the Lower Saxon federal state, from its capital in Hanover, actively engaged this issue. Lower Saxon state agencies emphasized the challenge of maximizing agricultural production. In practice, that meant giving the untended land of East German farmers to those best equipped to work it immediately.

The West German federal government took the better part of the summer and fall before addressing the problems of border agriculture. When federal agencies intervened, they pushed a policy driven not by economic but rather by symbolic-political considerations. The main concern of the federal government was to avoid recognizing or in any way admitting the division of Germany. This was more important for West German federal agencies than the economic problem of frontier regions. Changing as little as possible in the legal status of property around the border was the main thrust of the policy favoured in Bonn. Therefore, although commanding sufficient resources, the federal government was very careful not to offer frontier farmers financial compensation for land they owned in the East.[30]

---

[29] 'Schließen Sowjets die Zonengrenze?', *Göttinger Tageblatt*, 24 May 1952, 2.
[30] For an analysis of the West German strategy of denying the existence of a second German state and its (much broader) implications for border policy, see Chapter III.

Table 2.1. Stages of land ownership conflict in the Lower Saxon Eichsfeld

		Drama in Three Acts	
	Beginning on	State agency determining policy	Primary objectives of the state agency in charge
Act One	early June 1952	Rural district (*Landkreis*) of Duderstadt, (Western Eichsfeld)	Solving the economic plight of frontier farmers in the district and preventing the collapse of farming households
Act Two	late June 1952	State (*Land*) of Lower Saxony, Hanover	Ensuring agricultural production was maximized
Act Three	October 1952	Federal Government of West Germany (*Bund*), Bonn	Preventing recognition of legality or legitimacy of the division, the border and the GDR.

Such compensation might be perceived, they reasoned, as legitimizing the confiscation of these lands by the GDR.

Each of these stages (see Table 2.1 for a summary), with the specific policies introduced and the agents involved in it, changed the rules and the power balance in the local struggles along the border. One group of Western frontier farmers depended more on interactions with state agencies, the other on interactions with frontier farmers from the East. Their scramble for economic assets gradually turned into a conflict about the meaning of the border. This heated struggle forced frontier farmers into different ideological and political positions and made them adopt certain views of their relations with their state and with their kin and neighbours across the border.

The East German border policy reform in May 1952 created different sets of problems in different areas along it. The rural district of Duderstadt, covering the Lower Saxon part of the Eichsfeld, gained 277.21 ha (approx. 685 acres) and lost 204.52 ha (approx. 505 acres) of agricultural land. Had the gains and losses been spread evenly along the border, this problem might have been quietly solved. But nine-tenths of the land lost beyond the border belonged to farmers in the two northernmost frontier villages in the district, Brochthausen (36.54 ha) and Fuhrbach (144.74 ha). Brochthausen also gained ten ha, Fuhrbach did not gain any land. The two southernmost frontier villages, Nesselröden and Immingerode, gained 105 ha and lost no land. The district town, Duderstadt, gained more agricultural land than any other community in the district (see Figure 2.4).[31] Consequently, the closing of the border pitted two groups of Western frontier farmers in the district, losers and gainers of land, against each other in a competition for Eastern farmers' land. State agencies found themselves in the position of arbiter between these two groups.

---

[31] Landkreis Duderstadt to Regierungspräsident Hildesheim, 17 June 1952, NLA-HStAH, nds. 120 Hildesheim, Acc. 60/78, Nr. 2.

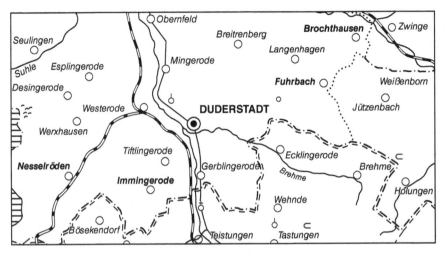

Fig. 2.4. Map of the border region in the Lower Saxon Eichsfeld from 1947. The names of communities which gained and lost most land in the district are highlighted in bold.[32]

The district administration in Duderstadt began its inquiry into the problems of agriculture along the border on 7 June 1952. A memo was sent to all the border communities requesting detailed data regarding the effects of the border closing, listing especially land lost in the East and the owners of this land.[33] After receiving replies, the district sent an official report on the situation ten days later to the County of Hildesheim. The district administrator in Duderstadt, Matthias Gleitze, was primarily concerned with the fate of the farmers who had lost land. They were the worst hit by this new policy, he wrote, and in some cases were facing real subsistence problems. They lacked the resources to even keep working the land they still had on the Western side of the border. The district suggested making as many of them as possible the trustees for fields belonging to farmers from the East. They should be prioritized as trustees over other farmers who had not lost land of their own, reasoned the district administrator in this report. He also stated that these farmers must first be compensated in cash for the losses they would suffer in expected harvest income and in the supply of fodder for their livestock. Lacking such immediate compensation, he wrote, they would not be able to take up trusteeships and the entire compensation scheme might collapse.[34] But this scheme encountered other problems on the ground. In the three communities which together held 95 per cent of the land gained in the district, Immingerode, Nessel-röden, and Duderstadt, almost none of these fields were subject to the district's policy. By the time of the first report from the district, private agreements regulated

[32] Adapted from BArch-B, DE 1, 5295, 8.

[33] Landkreis Duderstadt to Gemeindedirektor Fuhrbach, 7 June 1952, StADud, Fuhr 256.

[34] Landkreis Duderstadt to Regierungspräsident Hildesheim, 17 June 1952, NLA-HStAH, nds. 120 Hildesheim, Acc. 60/78, Nr. 2.

the work in nearly all these fields. Frontier farmers from the East had made agreements with their relatives in the West to take care of the fields for them. The district thus could not assign them as trusteeships to the farmers from Fuhrbach and Brochthausen. Immingerode and Nesselröden were too far for that purpose anyway; fields in Duderstadt's jurisdiction were more relevant. But, as the district reported, most of the fields in Duderstadt owned by farmers from the East (mostly for the community of Ecklingerode, in which almost every household had relatives in Duderstadt) had been rented through private contracts to relatives. The only fields not privately rented had poor soil and were therefore unwanted by trustees.[35]

Some of the most pressing problems in Brochthausen were solved through the land gained in the community and in the neighbouring district of Osterode. But the Duderstadt district did not find solutions for Fuhrbach farmers, the worst hit in the district. One hundred and seventeen households in Fuhrbach owned land on the eastern side of the border. The vast majority of them (102) were worker-peasant households with less than five ha.[36] As mentioned above, this did not mean that the land was less important to them, economically or otherwise.

Fuhrbach did not wait for the district to act. The community council realized that the authority and resources to offer real help and compensation lay not in the district but with the state of Lower Saxony and the federal government. Two weeks after the announcement of the new policy, the council sent a plea to Hanover, the Lower Saxon capital. Private farmers in Fuhrbach and the community itself (which lost income from the communal forest and orchard) required urgent help, they wrote. Only an immediate tax deferment and substantial cash grants to farmers and to the community could, in their opinion, prevent collapse. They wrote that:

> [the new conditions along the border] ... impede the financial situation of the community of Fuhrbach and all its residents to such an extent, that they face complete economic collapse ... Most of the potato fields are in the Russian Zone ... cattle would have to be sold out of hardship unless emergency steps will be taken soon.[37]

The district administration was the first to raise the idea of compensating Fuhrbach farmers with alternative land. The district was unable to offer financial resources but could use its authority to supervise land-ownership arrangements. It was actually a neighbouring district, the rural district of Göttingen, which first suggested appointing trustees to work fields whose owners resided in the GDR.[38] The district, according to the proposed scheme, would open special accounts under the names of the owners in a regional bank and the appointed trustees would deposit a

---

[35] Landkreis Duderstadt to Regierungspräsident Hildesheim, 17 June 1952, NLA-HStAH, nds. 120 Hildesheim, Acc. 60/78, Nr. 2.

[36] Landkreis Duderstadt to Regierungspräsident Hildesheim, 17 June 1952, NLA-HStAH, nds. 120 Hildesheim, Acc. 60/78, Nr. 2.

[37] 'Entschliessung des Rates der Gemeinde Fuhrbach zu den Schäden, die ihr und ihren Einwohnern durch die Ziehung des Eisernen Vorhanges enstanden sind', 13 June 1952, NLA-HStAH, nds. 120 Hildesheim, Acc. 55/78, Nr. 393.

[38] Landkreis Göttingen prepared a form for such trusteeship agreements. See Landkreis Göttingen, 'Beschluß', 1 June 1952, NLA-HStAH, nds. 120 Hildesheim, Acc. 60/78, Nr. 2.

yearly rent and a certain percentage of their profits from these fields into the accounts. The rural district of Göttingen conceived this as the way to ensure tilling of fields owned by Eastern frontier farmers.

The district of Duderstadt perceived this proposed trusteeship system as a potential scheme to compensate frontier farmers who owned land in the East. The district administration informed frontier farmers hurt by the new border policy that they could expect compensation in alternative land. District officials recognized them as victims of the new border policy and acknowledged the state's responsibility to compensate them. In the following months, the district administration tried to promote compensation within the framework defined by Lower Saxon policy, stretching to the limit this framework and the patience of superior state agencies.

The Lower Saxon government convened an inter-ministerial forum with representatives from the border counties on 23 June 1952, to discuss the new situation along the border. The convened officials agreed that the most pressing problem was that of frontier farmers who owned land in the East. Lower Saxony's reserves were not large enough to compensate them, and the federal government promised very modest support for this purpose. A decision was made to gather more accurate information about the land that was lost—not just the size but also the quality of the soil, previously paid taxes, and more.[39] The following day, the Lower Saxon Minister for Agriculture sent a memo to the border counties. It was not clear, he wrote, when the 'little border traffic' would be renewed, and until that time temporary measures to ensure agricultural production along the border would be necessary. He pointed out that the law could be of use in this case: the Land Cultivation Order, enacted by the British military government in 1947, gave state agencies extreme powers in order to ensure agricultural production. Using this order, state agents could force trusteeships on untended fields even if the owners objected. He asked that frontier districts be advised to make use of this legal instrument should the need arise, adding that where the owners already made private arrangements to work their land districts should not interfere with such arrangements. He accepted the position of the district of Duderstadt that farmers who had lost access to their land in the East should be the first to be given trusteeship. Beyond these general guidelines, the minister left specific decisions to the border districts which should 'consider to a large extent the local conditions'.[40]

The legal measures suggested by the Lower Saxon Minister came at a very opportune time for the district of Duderstadt. He essentially placed the responsibility for agricultural production in designated fields with the district, which applied this power quite differently than the minister foresaw, ignoring the comment regarding private contracts. On 2 August the district announced that all private contracts for the working of fields owned by residents of Thuringia (GDR)

[39] Regierungspräsident Hildesheim, 'Vermerk', 24 June 1952, NLA-HStAH, nds. 120 Hildesheim, Acc. 55/78, Nr. 393.
[40] Niedersächsische Minister für Ernährung Landwirtschaft u. Forsten, to Regierungspräsident Hildesheim, 24 June 1952, NLA-HStAH, nds. 120 Hildesheim, Acc. 55/78, Nr. 393.

should be submitted for inspection. All residents of the district who had made such agreements were called to present within two weeks written and signed contracts. The announcement also required them to submit proof that they had the resources and skills to work these fields to optimal productivity. Knowing that many of these agreements were unwritten, and that relatives who signed them were not always farmers themselves, district authorities hoped in this way to replace them with trustees from Fuhrbach.[41] This was clearly not what the Lower Saxon government had in mind when it advised the border districts to use the Land Cultivation Order. While ostensibly following instructions to ensure or increase production, the district aimed to determine who the producers would be. Forced changes of trustees and renters in mid-season could not be seen as conducive of production. The district manipulated the language and framework of the legislation in order to promote a different agenda.

The district of Duderstadt failed decisively in this attempt. A few weeks after announcing the inspection of private contracts, the district reported to the county of Hildesheim that the programme was not working. The report mentioned three obstacles: the ease with which frontier farmers crossed the border; the thick cross-border kinship networks they had; and their mistrust of the state and the mechanism of trusteeships it offered.[42] Frontier farmers from the East preferred private arrangements with relatives in the West to district-sponsored trusteeships. They feared that accepting trusteeships would be used down the road to restrict their ownership rights. More than trust in relatives and friends, the preference of private contracts may be taken, as the report specifically stated, as evidence of mistrust of the state's long-term commitment.[43] Trusted relatives and friends in the West promised them easier and quicker control over their land and the income from it. These renters cooperated with the owners to produce all the necessary documentation, subverting the district's plans. Consequently, very limited territory was left for the district to assign for trusteeships, which could not suffice as compensation for those farmers who owned land in the East. From the roughly 1,000 plots belonging to Eastern farmers, the district succeeded in creating only 63 trusteeships in two months and predicted that these too would be challenged in the courts.[44]

All along the border, West German authorities respected private contracts. In fact, the county of Hildesheim reported to Hanover that the number of private contracts kept growing. Fields marked for trusteeship were taken over through

---

[41] Oberkreisdirektor Duderstadt to Regierungspräsident Hildesheim, 14 August 1952 and 'Bekanntmachung', 2 August 1952, NLA-HStAH, Nds. 120 Hildesheim, Acc. 60/78, Nr. 1.

[42] Regierungspräsident Hildesheim to Niedersächsische Minister für Ernährung, Landwirtschaft u. Forsten, 1 September 1952, NLA-HStAH, Nds. 120 Hildesheim, Acc. 60/78, Nr. 1.

[43] Regierungspräsident Hildesheim to Niedersächsische Minister für Ernährung, Landwirtschaft u. Forsten, 1 September 1952, NLA-HStAH, Nds. 120 Hildesheim, Acc. 60/78, Nr. 1. Farmers' mistrust for the state as guarantor of their rights had a long history. See Robert G. Moeller, *German Peasants and Agrarian Politics, 1914–1924: The Rhineland and Westphalia* (Chapel Hill, NC: University of North Carolina Press, 1986); John E. Farquharson, *The Plough and the Swastika: The NSDAP and Agriculture in Germany, 1928–45* (London: Sage Publications, 1976).

[44] Regierungspräsident Hildesheim to Niedersächsische Minister für Ernährung, Landwirtschaft u. Forsten, 1 September 1952, NLA-HStAH, Nds. 120 Hildesheim, Acc. 60/78, Nr. 1.

private agreements.[45] It brought a welcome decrease in the workload of district administrations, but also left them powerless to help the farmers in their districts injured by the closing of the border. No compensation could be as effective as alternative land, wrote the County President in this report. The ideal solution would be to give them fields of equivalent value and size in their own or in neighbouring communities. The combination of the Lower Saxon resolve to respect private agreements with the mistrust for the state among farmers and the resilience of their cross-border networks stood in the way of this solution.[46]

Western frontier farmers who owned land in the East relied on state agencies to compensate them. And they had reason to do so. Initially, their district administration assured them that they would be appointed as trustees for fields owned by farmers from the East. At the same time, other frontier farmers managed to ensure control over these fields for themselves, effectively blocking their fellows from accessing this form of compensation. These frontier farmers capitalized on contradictions in policymaking and subverted what state agencies initially viewed as the ideal solution. They won additional land, usually not far from their own fields. Rents and other payments to the owners notwithstanding, they improved their own situation.

As this turn of events demonstrated, cross-border kinship networks in the Eichsfeld were strong and effective in 1952. During the 1950s, West Germans could apply to visit family in East Germany and usually received a crossing permit and a residence permit for two to three weeks. In the early fifties, frontier residents in the Eichsfeld frequently crossed the border for a day or two to visit their family but would still go to the village council of their family and apply for food stamps for the entire period stamped in their passports. They would thus leave their families with food stamps for an additional person for a couple of weeks, a very substantial assistance involving minimal effort.[47] Some Western frontier residents came to see the payments for fields as part of this assistance to relatives rather than a simple rent contract. However, we should not overstate the degree of altruism involved. At least in some cases, owners from the East complained later that relatives and other renters cheated them—they packed up cheap items which were rare in the East and sent them to the owners, saying that they cost as much as the rent for the field. This way they kept to themselves most of the income from these fields.[48]

By late August 1952, a clear pattern emerged regarding the handling of fields owned by farmers from the East in the Lower Saxon Eichsfeld: private contracts governed the work in a vast majority of these fields. There remained the problem of frontier farmers who owned land in the East. Most pressing was the problem of the

---

[45] Regierungspräsident Hildesheim to Niedersächsische Minister für Ernährung, Landwirtschaft u. Forsten, 1 September 1952, NLA-HStAH, Nds. 120 Hildesheim, Acc. 60/78, Nr. 1.

[46] Regierungspräsident Hildesheim to Niedersächsische Minister für Ernährung, Landwirtschaft u. Forsten, 1 September 1952, NLA-HStAH, Nds. 120 Hildesheim, Acc. 60/78, Nr. 1.

[47] Land Thuringen, Ministerium d. Innern to Landrat Heiligenstadt, 20 September 1951, ThHStAW, LBdVP, Nr. 409, 3.

[48] W. L. to Fritz Bönning, 28 January 1954, StADud, Fuhr 326.

farmers from Fuhrbach. When it became clear that the state failed to give them alternative land, financial compensation became the only option. This placed the federal government at the epicentre of action, and all involved set their eyes on Bonn.

It was not very long before federal agencies realized that they needed to address the problems that the Western borderlands had experienced since late May 1952. In late June, opposition parties in the Bundestag petitioned the government to present and respond to updated information. At that stage, the federal government felt greatest urgency in the managing of the resultant wave of refugees, and the threat to the energy supply sustained by some border areas. In early July, the cabinet allocated 36 million Marks to deal with these problems.[49] The federal Ministries of Economy and Finance assigned all other problems and demands to the committee for 'emergency areas' (*Notstandsgebiete*). Economics Minister Erhard wrote to chancellor Adenauer that the republic had many such regions and there was no reason to prioritize the border regions.[50]

The issues on the table pertained to infrastructure, the economy, and agriculture, but for the federal government, border policy was first and foremost a symbolic issue. From Bonn's perspective, the most crucial aspect of this new border situation was that it originated in the GDR. Any reaction to it had first to consider existing policy regarding relations to East German statehood. The West German government did not recognize the existence of a second German state. Consequently, federal agencies developed great sensitivity to texts and subtexts, to gestures, allusions, and hidden meanings.[51]

The Federal Ministry for All-German Affairs (*Bundesministerium für gesamtdeutsche Fragen*, henceforth MfgF) convened on 12 July at the first forum to discuss the problems created along the border. The only significant decision arrived at in this meeting was to form an inter-ministerial committee.[52] When this committee met two weeks later, ministry representatives reviewed demands that their ministries had received for assistance to border areas and summarized the costs of accepting them. The demands received by the Ministry for Agriculture came to 2 million Marks, and were the only ones presented as urgent. The ministry's representatives requested that the committee reach a decision within two weeks.

The participating federal civil servants emphasized that in this case the federal government had no legal, but only a moral responsibility to help. The federal government should take some of the financial burden upon itself only because it

[49] Bundesministerium für gesamtdeutsche Fragen, 'Niederschrift über die Ressortbesprechung betr. die Koordinierung der Massnahmen', 12 July 1952, BArch-K, B 137, Nr. 58.

[50] BArch-K, B 136, Nr. 695. Erhard reacted in this letter to the demands of the four border states (Bavaria, Schleswig-Holstein, Hesse, and Lower Saxony), which pressed Adenauer to direct his minister to allocate emergency funds to the border regions.

[51] This Western strategy and its implications to border formation are the subject of Chapter III.

[52] Bundesministerium für gesamtdeutsche Fragen, 'Niederschrift', 12 July 1952 BArch-K, B 137, Nr. 58. The convened officials, representing many offices, discussed mostly the different motions presented in the Bundestag and the situation of refugees.

was too heavy for the border states to manage on their own.[53] Thus the committee chose to interpret the problem as a local one. Any other understanding of the problems and their causes might have entailed considering the causal connection between West German positions and policies and the closing of the border. The economic development of West Germany, the escalation of the Cold War, and the insistent refusal of the FRG to recognize the GDR, all contributed to the attempt by the GDR to seal the border. As discussed in Chapter I, the guarding of the Western side of the border was, by that time, almost entirely controlled by federal organizations. Thus, it would have been very problematic to assign border-formation-related problems to the jurisdiction of border states.

Over the next few months, the committee mostly registered claims for assistance and debated questions of responsibility of the border states and different federal ministries.[54] By October, pressure from the border states and the Bundestag on the federal government to take additional action grew. The press reported extensive damages and frontier residents' disappointment with the federal government. Finally, in early October, the Federal Minister of Finance decided to allocate 6 million Marks for assistance to the border areas. Twenty per cent of this sum was immediately transferred to the Ministry of Agriculture for the claims presented three months earlier as most pressing. The cost of the border states' total claims to federal agencies had by that time reached 65 million DM. The inter-ministerial committee decided that 'in light of the large volume of claims, dividing the five million according to economic urgency would not be possible.' Rather, the committee reasoned that 'out of political considerations, the available sum of five million should be divided as soon as possible in such a way as to support as many small measures broadly spread along the entire border as possible.'[55] The Ministry of Agriculture informed the committee that the 1.2 million it received was far from enough for even the emergency help needed. The committee replied that the ministry provided assistance to private people whereas federal funds should be invested more directly in alleviating damages to public interests.[56]

When federal money was directed to help frontier farmers, it did not resolve the conflict between these farmers and state agencies. On the contrary, it added friction. Beginning in mid-October, the 1.2 million Marks were directed from the Ministry of Agriculture primarily to the frontier farmers who owned land in the East and had lost access to it. For months, frontier farmers in the Lower Saxon Eichsfeld pleaded with state agencies for compensation for the land they had 'lost' across the border. Just then, in early October, a few of them got some alternative

[53] Bundesministerium für gesamtdeutsche Fragen, 'Niederschrift über die Sitzung der interministeriellen Ausschusses für sofort- und Sondermaßnahmen', 24 July 1952, BArch-K, B 136, Nr. 695, 17–23.

[54] Interministerieller Ausschuß, 12 September 1952, BArch-K, B 136, Nr. 695, 70–4.

[55] The committee met on 23 October. The Minister of Finance originally allocated 5 million. He added another million after Hesse announced 1 million Marks to be allocated of its own means for that purpose. Interministerieller Ausschuß, 24 October 1952, BArch-K, B 136, Nr. 695, 96–103. The political pressures and reports in the press are mentioned in the opening comments of the report on the meeting. The quote is from p. 97.

[56] Interministerieller Ausschuß, 24 October 1952, BArch-K, B 136, Nr. 695, 96–103, here 98–9.

land as trustees. State agencies expected them to pay rents for these fields, and a percentage of profits as well. The same state agencies did not, until then, give them any compensation for their own land. Finally, the bureaucratic process appeared to be over, and it seemed that money was about to be apportioned. It soon became clear that the compensation did not meet the farmers' expectations.

Federal funds were meant to compensate frontier farmers for their lost income from the expected harvest of that season alone. Not for farmhouses, machinery or animals, and most importantly, not for the land itself. This compensation was conceived rather like compensation for a drought harvest, a one-time unexpected natural disaster. As such, it was defined not by needs but according to budget limitations. The federal government insisted that it had no legal obligation to compensate for damages, thus trying to de-politicize the problem and remove it from the context of the Cold War and the division of Germany. For frontier farmers who had lost access to their fields, this insistence bore concrete financial consequences.[57] Bonn and Hanover sent strict instructions that the money should be allocated only for expected harvest income. No connection should be made between these sums and the obligations of frontier farmers as trustees and taxpayers. The district of Duderstadt soon found that these criteria did not evoke much sympathy with frontier farmers. The farmers held very different perceptions regarding state agencies' responsibility for their plight.[58]

Through the winter of 1952, frontier farmers received compensation of up to 50 per cent of lost harvest profits calculated for their fields east of the border. By the time they got the last payment for these 50 per cent, it was almost spring, and many farmers were already concerned with next year's harvest.[59] More crucially, frontier farmers viewed these payments as part of the overall attempt to compensate them for damages they suffered. They therefore immediately compared them to rents the state demanded for trusteeships, which some of them got. Trusteeship conditions required them to pay 50 per cent of their profits for grain crops, and lower percentages for other crops in addition to the rent.[60] Altogether, these farmers argued, state agencies asked them to pay for trusteeships as if they had not lost anything themselves, while compensating them for only half of their expected harvest.[61] The federal government, they concluded, took better care of frontier farmers from the East, than it did its own citizens. They repeated their threats to

[57] See NLA-HStAH, Nds. 220, Acc. 144/95, Nr. 9; Nds. 120 Hildesheim, Acc. 60/78, Nr. 1 and Nr. 2 for the many exchanges between the state offices in Hanover, the county in Hildesheim and the border districts on the uses and allocation of these funds.

[58] See the exchanges between Bonn, Hanover, Hildesheim, and Duderstadt on these issues at NLA-HStAH, Nds. 120 Hildesheim, Acc. 60/78, Nr. 1. Frontier farmers did not really care if the money came from this or that budget. Both Lower Saxony and the federal government were responsible for compensating them and the district authority represented both on ground level, hence the indiscriminate use of 'state' when conveying their concerns.

[59] Landkreis Duderstadt to Regierungspräsident Hildesheim, 7 February 1953, NLA-HStAH, Nds. 120 Hildesheim, Acc. 60/78, Nr. 1.

[60] Niedersächsiche Minister für Ernährung Landwirtschaft u. Forsten to Regierungspräsident Hildesheim, 22 November 1952, NLA-HStAH, nds. 220, Acc. 144/95, Nr. 9.

[61] See their complaints as published in the local newspaper in March 1953. 'In Fuhrbach herrscht einmütige Empörung', *Göttinger Tageblatt*, 3 March 1953.

withhold payment for trusteeships until they received full compensation for their own losses.[62] The district supported this demand of frontier farmers who had lost access to their land in the East, whereas the federal government and Lower Saxony maintained that trusteeships and compensations were separate issues. This difference of attitude is partially attributable to the fact that it was the same district official who told the same frontier farmers that they must pay full rents and percentages, and that they would receive full compensation. This district official recognized that for the farmers these issues were one and the same. By November, some frontier farmers in the Duderstadt district who owned land in the East had already received trusteeships. When it had become clear that their threats were serious and they did not intend to pay for the land, the Lower Saxon Minister for Agriculture ordered the county to withhold payments of compensations to these farmers. Thus, the previous insistence on keeping compensation distinct from payments for trusteeships notwithstanding, state agents readily made this connection when it served their goals.[63]

The district was forced to give up at least its active support of the demands of frontier farmers. In the same memo from 22 November the Lower Saxon Minister of Agriculture specifically instructed that private contracts made by farmers from the East with Western farmers should be respected and encouraged. Throughout the winter of 1952–3, the federal government, commanding overwhelmingly superior resources, made the border states and districts fall in line with its perspective. For Western frontier farmers who owned land in the East, this meant a denial of their losses and the fullness of their plight. Through the winter, these farmers sought ways to improve their economic conditions by circumventing the regulations instated by state agencies. Some of them managed to get alternative land through private contracts with farmers from the East. State agencies did not regulate these contracts, enabling renters, like the aforementioned farmer Falck, to renege on rents without risking their compensation payments.[64]

For frontier farmers, the issue was foremost an economic one. The federal government, on the other hand, justified its position in political terms anchored in the international conditions of the Cold War. As victims of 'Soviet aggression', frontier farmers found that they had a public political voice. They still made primarily economic demands, but realized that they must use political instruments in order to further them. In early March 1953, one local newspaper published a story about Fuhrbach farmers' deep disappointment with the support they got from both Lower Saxony and the federal government. The paper wrote about the grave economic conditions along the border, the great losses caused by the sealing of the border, and the meagre 50 per cent compensations. It also detailed the trusteeship payments and showed that they were higher than the compensations. Lower

---

[62] Landkreis Duderstadt to Regierungspräsident Hildesheim, 14 August 1952, NLA-HStAH, Nds. 120 Hildesheim, Acc. 60/78, Nr. 1.

[63] Niedersächsiche Minister für Ernährung Landwirtschaft u. Forsten to Regierungspräsident Hildesheim, 22 November 1952, NLA-HStAH, nds. 220, Acc. 144/95, Nr. 9.

[64] I know only of two such cases, which reached legal claims in 1954. See Landkreis Osterode to Gemeinde Fuhrbach, 19 February 1954, 21 September 1954, and 22 November 1954, StADud, Fuhr 327. The attention to this issue by state authorities suggests that these two cases represent a broader phenomenon.

Saxony and the federal government did not do enough to protect their frontier population, concluded the article. The district administrator attached the article in a letter to the county as a problem which required addressing.[65] This was only the first round in a protracted conflict about the issue which lasted more than a decade, analysed in Chapter IV.

Two groups of Western frontier farmers developed different interests in reaction to the change in GDR border policy in the summer of 1952. Farmers in one group lost access to the land they owned east of the border. The farmers in the other group gained additional land through private contracts. At first, low-level state agencies tried to take land from the gainers and give it to the losers as compensation for their losses. In the second stage, intermediate-level state agencies severed the link between land gained and land lost, demanded production and extraction from land gained, and promised financial compensation. In the third stage, federal agencies prevented compensation with alternative land and provided partial compensations for lost income. The gainers of land learned how to utilize contradictions and weaknesses in state policy. Taking advantage of their ability to cross the border and engage their strong kinship and social networks, they were able to maintain possession of the land they gained. They learned that championing private property could produce economic benefits. The losers learned that state agencies were too weak to protect their interests across the border. They knew how easy it was to cross this border, but recognized that for state power it was impenetrable. State agencies were too feeble to enforce their own decisions on the Western side of the border and give them alternative land. As Chapters III and IV show, farmers who had lost access to land resented the state's insistence on ignoring the reality of the border for which, they felt, they paid the price. Eventually, both groups of farmers learned that to protect their interests they should identify the state agency with most resources in a given territory and work with the policy it dictated.

Western frontier farmers found their cross-border connections to be a valuable asset. To get hold of additional land they had to present themselves as the protectors of their relatives' property and interests. Western frontier farmers who owned land in the East failed to use the same networks in order to retain ownership and income from their land. At least one resident of Fuhrbach tried to mobilize his relatives east of the border for this purpose. Fritz Bönning wrote to his cousin in Weissenborn-Lüderode (GDR) to ask if something could be done regarding his plots. The response he received amounted to what many Western frontier residents were told at that time: his cousin explained that there was no way around the regulations in East Germany, that the GDR government compensated its citizens for lost land but does not consider itself responsible for West Germans.[66] In the face of the East German regime's resolute policy reform, not only

---

[65] Göttinger Tageblatt, 'In Fuhrbach herrscht einmütige Empörung', 3 March 1953 KrAGö, LK DUD, Nr. 1117.

[66] W. L. to Fritz Bönning, 28 January 1954, in StADud, Fuhr 326.

West German state agencies, but East German frontier farmers too professed weakness—they could not look after the property of Western frontier farmers.

LAND GRAB UNDER THE BORDER'S COVER IN HESSE

In September 1945, a small part of the Eichsfeld was traded from the Soviet to the American zone and consequently became part of Hesse and the FRG. This small area contained two villages, Werleshausen and Neuseesen, and was appended to the rural district of Witzenhausen. This exchange was made official on 17 September 1945, in a treaty signed in the town of Wanfried between the regional commanding officers on both sides. The Americans wanted this territory because the railway between their northern port of Bremerhaven and the bulk of their occupation zone passed through these two villages. They gave the Soviets in return a comparable territory with four villages in it a few miles south along the Werra river. This treaty drove the inter-German border into the Eichsfeld in this region, as shown in Figure 2.5.

In this area, Western frontier farmers did not own land on the Eastern side, but there were fields in it owned by Eastern frontier farmers. Knowing how things

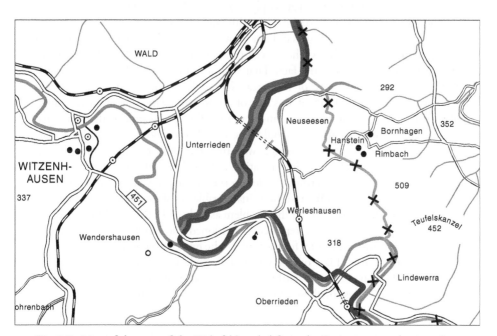

Fig. 2.5. Map of the part of the Eichsfeld traded from the Soviet zone to the American zone in 1945. The old provincial border (also the western border of the Eichsfeld) is the thick double line to the left and the new border, from September 1945, is the thinner line with black Exes to the right.[67]

---

[67] The map in Figure 2.4 is partly adapted from StADud, KEF.1/0041.

developed in the Duderstadt district, one would expect similar regulation of work on these fields. Frontier farmers from the East could cross the border with the same ease in this area; therefore it would be reasonable to assume that they made private contracts for working their fields. Should that not happen, the district could appoint trustees to work them.

In fact, developments took an almost opposite direction. In the Duderstadt district, frontier residents relied on strong active cross-border kin and social networks. They knew the owners from the East well and interacted with them to agree on arrangements to work their land. Frontier farmers in the Witzenhausen district claimed not to know the owners of these fields. Further, they claimed that they were not able to find out who the owners were or contact them. In October 1954, the district administrator from Witzenhausen reported property-rights problems in the two Eichsfeld communities of Werleshausen and Neuseesen. He wrote to his superior in Kassel that these village councils were not able to determine the ownership of over 200 Morgen (approx. 149 acres) of land near the border. He stated that the owners of these fields resided in neighbouring villages in the East, and had not been able to access their fields since the summer of 1952. All attempts by the two communities to locate them had failed. Consequently, the villagers could not even determine the plot borders and the communities had simply taken over the land and leased it.[68]

The explanation the memo offered for this land grab was almost certainly bogus. It is highly unlikely that villagers did not know who owned which plot next to their village. This was nevertheless the official position transmitted from the district to the county two years after the fact. That such a claim was at all possible was the result of the recent history of this area. When the Soviets and the Americans swapped territories in 1945, it was out of ad-hoc necessity. They did not think about the long- term implications and certainly did not imagine at that time that two independent German states would be established on both sides of the demarcation line. The territory exchange was therefore not complemented by an exchange of all the relevant administrative and legal records. The land registries and court records for the territory added to the district of Witzenhausen in 1945 were still kept in the GDR and were inaccessible to West German authorities. Authorities in Hesse pointed out this problem as early as 1946,[69] and from then on the district of Witzenhausen repeatedly petitioned the neighbouring district of Heiligenstadt across the border for these files. The first correspondence began in the winter of 1947–8.[70] Like others which followed, it failed to lead to record exchange. Only in 1974 did authorities in Hesse give up hope of getting the original land registries for these plots and decided to create new land registries.[71]

---

[68] Landrat des Landkreises Witzenhausen to Regierungspräsident Kassel, 8 November 1954, HeStAM, 401/13, Nr. 6. The memo does not give many details about the use of the land in those two years. Just that the fields were leased.

[69] Präsident des Großhessischen Oberlandgerichts to Regierungspräsident Kassel, 8 April 1946, HeStAM, 401/11, Nr. 27.

[70] See KrAEich, EA HIG, Nr. 402/I for the correspondence saved on the Thuringian side, including internal memos.

[71] Hessische Minister der Justiz to Hessische Ministerpräsident, 9 October 1975, BArch-K, B 369, Nr. 77.

Consequently, Western authorities had no official means of identifying the owners of these fields and so could not disprove frontier farmers' claims.

Furthermore, Hessian state agencies were not very keen on disproving them. In the summer of 1952, Hesse responded to the new border regime with a policy starkly different to that of Lower Saxony. On 30 July, the Hessian Minister of the Interior announced a new border policy. Hesse decided to seal the border for crossing by Eastern frontier farmers. The minister sent reinforcement of riot police and border guards' units to border areas and instructed border counties to use them in order to prevent Eastern farmers from accessing their fields. The border districts were told they should supervise the collection of the harvest from these fields to be used for the needs of the district.[72] Protecting the property rights of Eastern frontier farmers was clearly not a priority in Hesse. It was more important to ensure the allocation of these fields' produce for feeding Hesse's own population. The district of Witzenhausen did not have to worry about the fields of Eastern frontier farmers in Werleshausen and Neuseesen; they had already been taken by Western frontier farmers.

The state organizations' approach does not fully explain this land grab by the two Eichsfeld communities. As described above, it was not state policy which prevented similar acts in the district of Duderstadt. Frontier farmers from the East made private contracts for working their fields in the West before any Western state agency intervened. Kinship networks were the determining factor in making this pattern the rule in the Lower Saxon part of the Eichsfeld. Such networks were less effective in the Hessian part. This difference was most likely a result of the different confessional make-up of both areas. The Eichsfeld is a Catholic enclave surrounded by Protestant populations. Centuries of widespread endogamy among Eichsfeld Catholics produced thick kinship networks binding together families and communities. Werleshausen and Neuseesen were part of a Protestant minority which counted for 10–15 per cent of the Eichsfeld population. As Protestants in communities bordering on large Protestant populations, the residents of these two villages had a broad choice of marriage options. Consequently, the ties which bound them to the (also Protestant) neighbouring communities across the border were weaker than those exhibited in the Duderstadt district between Catholics.

Hesse's border-closing policy was short-lived. Federal funds were crucial for Hesse as well in order to address the many economic and infrastructure problems created by the border.[73] These funds were accompanied by the federal government's policy regarding the handling of property-ownership questions along the

---

[72] 'Sperrung der Zonengrenze', 30 July 1952, HeStAM, 401/13 Nr. 4. This was not an empty declarative statement. Border forces were indeed instructed to keep an eye on these fields. At least in one case, Hessian border guards prevented an East German farmer from harvesting his field. See HeStAM, 401/13, Nr. 5. This policy ran counter to the federal government's interest in not recognizing the border as presented above and that it was introduced and pursued is testimony to the lack of active policy on these issues by the federal government at that time.

[73] See Interministerieller Ausschuß, 26 June 1952, BArch-K, B 136, Nr. 695, 17–23 detailing demands for help from the federal government according to the state. Hesse requested the highest amount of all four border states for the building of new roads along the border.

border. On 6 October 1952, the Hessian Minister of the Interior called off the sealing of the border.[74] Hesse, too, came to support private contracts and to form trusteeships for fields owned by frontier farmers from the East. This change of policy did not, however, change anything in Werleshausen and Neuseesen.[75] The perseverance over time of the land grab highlights the convergence of several exceptional conditions in these communities: the different options of Protestant populations in the Eichsfeld, combined with the territorial exchange between occupation zones.

Frontier residents in Werleshausen and Neuseesen benefited from the new border regime. By solidifying the inter-German border, it cemented their belonging to the Western side, a reality only seven years old at the time. They still remembered the three months of Soviet occupation in 1945 and were not sorry to see fences between them and the Soviet forces.[76] In addition, their communities (and through them some of them privately) won additional land in the summer of 1952. In Hessian state agencies they found active and later passive support for their land grab. Hesse worried about refugees from the East and their reception and about solving the problems of its own frontier farmers. As long as production from all these fields was ensured, the state agencies' actions showed that they were not interested in the property rights of GDR citizens.[77]

CONTROL AND PRODUCTION: UNDERMANNED AGRICULTURE IN THE GDR

On the evening of 26 May 1952, Herr Gassmann from the Thuringian Ministry of the Interior in Efrurt spoke to about a hundred residents of the village of Lindewerra, near the GDR border with West Germany. The meeting was called by the local SED party branch to introduce and explain the new policy announced that evening, which amounted in principle to a complete sealing of the border to the West. The party official gave a speech about the political conditions and why his government was forced to take protective measures against Western aggression. The villagers repeatedly interrupted Gassmann, shouting, cursing, and openly contradicting his words. When the speech ended, the speaker was barraged with angry questions from farmers for which he had no good response: what were farmers

---

[74] Hessisches MdI to Regierungspräsident Kassel, 6 October 1952, HeStAM, 401/13, Nr. 4.

[75] As mentioned above, the owners of the land were still reportedly unknown in October 1954.

[76] See the testimonies on the occupation months in Frieda von Christen, 'Die sowjetische Besatzungszeit in Werleshausen und Neuseesen (Juli bis September 1945)', *Schriften des Werratalvereins Witzenhausen* 4 (1981): 15–27. See also Ansbert Baumann, 'Thüringische Hessen und hessische Thüringer. Das Wanfrieder Abkommen vom 17. September 1945 wirkt bis heute nach', *Deutschland-Archiv. Zeitschrift für das vereinigte Deutschland* 37, nr. 6 (2004): 1000–5 for a short analysis of the attitudes of the residents of Werleshausen and Neuseesen to the decision to move them from Thuringia to Hesse.

[77] The website of Werleshausen has a map and list of the names of the plots in the village's territory. Some of the names retain indications that they once belonged to the community of Bornhagen across the border. See www.werleshausen.de/information/flurname.htm, accessed 20 August 2013.

supposed to do, whose fields lay across the border? Where could they get hay for their cattle, if they could not harvest their hay across the border? Many fields were close to harvest time, would it really make sense to leave the hard-earned crops unharvested? Had the government decided to force frontier farmers to go bankrupt? Lacking satisfactory answers, Gassmann retreated from the stage, as did his colleagues in other villages along the border that evening.[78]

The GDR initiated the new border regime and prepared for it in advance. Even so, the initial consequences for agricultural production were devastating and like Gassmann, party activists and leaders could not come up with effective solutions. Loss of access to fields in the West was just one of the problems. The new measures included deporting 'unreliable persons' from the restricted zones. It also gave rise to a widespread flight to the West from the border areas. In the Eichsfeld, about 330 persons were deported from border areas to the GDR hinterland in early June and about 760 fled to the West.[79] Under these circumstances, state organizations could easily offer alternative land to farmers who had lost access to fields on the Western side, assuming they were still around. Party and state organizations quite quickly shifted from deportation and border-construction projects to calming the population, preventing further emigration to the West and ensuring agricultural production.[80] By the end of July, the Thuringian police registered 99 family farms in the Eichsfeld, whose owners had moved to the West or had been deported to the hinterland. State agencies referred to such plots as 'having become free' (*freigewordene*) and preferred assigning them to agricultural collectives. But there were very few such collectives in the Eichsfeld in 1952 and in only six of the total 99 cases was this solution possible.[81] In 83 cases, the land ended up in the hands of private farmers appointed by the district or the community.[82] Central state offices in East Berlin were not concerned with issues of legal ownership over the plots in question. Actual control over who worked the land and who derived the income from it was of interest to them; legal matters could be settled later.[83] The people who were

---

[78] Kreisvertreter d. Amtes für Information d. Landes Thüringen beim Rat d. Kreises Worbis to Amt für Information Erfurt, 27 May 1952, ThHStAW, Land Thüringen, MP, Amt für Information, Nr. 1161, 35–7.

[79] Many fled because they feared deportation: quite a few were tipped off that their names were on the list. Of the 760 people, 121 indeed were on the deportation list. See ThHStAW, LBdVP Nr. 176, 263–90, 331–46. On the deportations in general, see Inge Bennewitz and Rainer Potratz, *Zwangsaussiedlungen*.

[80] See KrAEich, EA HIG, Nr. 192; ThHStAW, Land Thür, MdI, Nr. 3039, 96; BArch-B, DE 1, 6084, 145–6, 178–9.

[81] The connection between agricultural collectivization and border formation in the GDR is analysed in Chapter IV.

[82] Freigewordene Ländereien und ihre Bestellung in Kreis Worbis, 6 August 1952, ThHStAW, Land Th., MdI, Nr. 3040, 25–6.

[83] Seven years later, when collectivization became obligatory, at least one village in the Eastern Eichsfeld requested a landowner in West Germany to sell (for a set price) a plot in the village that he still legally owned. He was not really given another option, but clearly the legal situation was not changed until then. Private collection of M. from Paderborn.

assigned to work these lands were officially defined as trustees, but in practice worked these fields as their own.[84]

East German state agencies registered little active resistance to the new regime. Some people resisted deportation from border villages. The most common act of resistance was crossing to the West. Mass desertion from the already manpower-starved regional agriculture created a big problem for East German authorities. Many of those who left for the West took their livestock and equipment with them, making it very difficult to resume production on their farms. In some cases, communities appointed persons with no farming experience, leading to a decline in production. In other instances, farmers from other districts or refugees were assigned to farms and discovered that cattle and essential tools were missing or that the farm was in debt and needed additional funds.[85] The deportations deterred frontier villagers from open confrontation with state agencies.[86] There was ample room for *Eigen-Sinn* and non-compliance, however. Many cases were recorded of farmers who undermined border-construction work. The clearest illustration of successful passive resistance by Eichsfeld farmers at this time was their ability to prevent collectivization. In other examples, frontier residents refused to observe curfew rules and removed red flags from public buildings during the night.[87]

Records of redistribution of land belonging to Western frontier farmers were carefully kept by different Eastern state agencies. There is no evidence for passive or other resistance to this process by Eastern farmers, who were its primary beneficiaries. The plots were divided, as described above, mostly to private frontier farmers. First in line were farmers who owned land in the West and had lost access to it. This was in many cases unrealistic because land was gained by communities in which not much land was lost and vice versa. Under shortage of experienced and able farmers, land was often given to anyone who agreed to take it. Contrary to what happened in Lower Saxony, frontier farmers did not produce private contracts with relatives across the border. With widespread fear of further deportation, no one wanted to openly challenge the regime. The lack of more subtle attempts to preserve property rights is nevertheless surprising in light of the very effective efforts in this regard in the Duderstadt area discussed above.

We have seen an excerpt from Fritz Bönning's letter, asking his cousin in the GDR to help maintain ownership and income from his plots. In his response, the cousin emphasized that if the frontier farmers from Fuhrbach would turn to the GDR government and ask for trusteeships for their fields, they would only cause trouble to their fellows in the East. If the farmers from Fuhrbach would expose the private contracts and trusteeships made by Eastern farmers for lands in the West, he

---

[84] For instructions in this spirit from the central government see Richtlinien zur Besetzung von Bauernstellen und gewerblichen Betrieben , 12 June 1952, BArch-B, DE 1, Nr. 6085, 9–13.

[85] See many examples in KrAEich, EA HIG, Nr. 192. These problems are analysed in more detail in Chapter IV.

[86] On the deterrent effects of the deportation in the short and long term see Berdahl, *Where the World Ended*. See also Sheffer, *Foundations of the Wall*.

[87] For examples from the Eichsfeld see: ThHStAW, LBdVP, Nr. 176, 141; BArch-B, DE 1, Nr. 6084, 274–5; BArch-M, DVH 27, Pt 7493, 103–10.

wrote, those farmers would suffer. 'You know very well how quickly they deport people here on the border', he wrote.[88] This description of strict control over land use and inability of frontier farmers to take any initiative was not entirely accurate.

Following the deportations in the summer of 1952, there indeed was a widespread fear of additional deportations. But less than a month after the announcement of the new regime, Eastern state agencies changed their tone. They found it difficult to restore agricultural production along the border and were unable to stem the tide of emigration to the West by force. Fearing depletion of the agricultural workforce and the spread of hunger, Eastern state agencies tried to reassure frontier residents. They were still concerned about loyalty and the cooperation of frontier residents, but the winning over of frontier residents and people from other regions for working the fields along the border and preventing a further decline in production became their primary goal. They were not very successful in this endeavour and consequently became more flexible than the above-quoted letter suggested. Already in late June 1952, the district council in Heiligenstadt was desperate enough in its attempts to procure a workforce for untended fields near the border to suggest employing the inmates of a district youth prison for this purpose. The GDR Minister of the Interior vetoed this idea, declaring that prisoners were not allowed in the restricted border zones at all.[89] All manner of inexperienced and incompetent farmers were given farms and funds to work vacant plots. Experienced local villagers were gladly given fields they wanted to add to their farms.[90] With all these efforts, there were still untended fields. State agencies tried to ensure production on as many vacant plots as they could and were not in a position to supervise specific arrangements. Interesting evidence of this came in February 1953 in a letter from a resident of Zwinge, an Eastern frontier village, to the village council of Brochthausen (West) asking permission to graze his cows on a neglected field belonging to a farmer from Brochthausen. His letter shows that some fields at least were still untended, and that Eastern state agencies did not supervise their use. That he bothered to ask for permission might have been related to a disinclination to alienate farmers from Brochthausen who made up most of the trustees appointed for the fields of farmers from Zwinge (and maybe his own fields as well) in West Germany.[91]

When East German border policy changed in May 1952, a great deal of land became available along it in the GDR. To get some of this land, frontier farmers were not required to profess loyalty to the state. It was enough to avoid openly resisting state agencies. Presenting claims on behalf of Western owners or any other legalistic arguments would have put them at odds with the authorities. Instead of tendering such claims, they accepted, at least outwardly, the new border regime and the de-facto confiscation of land from Western frontier farmers and from deported

[88] W. L. to Fritz Bönning, 28 January 1954, StADud, Fuhr 326.
[89] Arbeitskräftebeschaffung für umgesiedelte Betriebe, 27 June 1952, KrAEich, EA HIG, Nr. 192.
[90] KrAEich, EA HIG, Nr. 192. See also BArch-B, DK 1, Nr. 137, 80–8; BArch-B, DE 1, Nr. 6084, 108, 135–7; ThHStAW, Land Th., MfWuA, Nr. 87, 40–5; ThHStAW, Land Th., MdI, Nr. 3039, 7–13.
[91] K. K. to Bürgermeister Brochthausen, 9 February 1953, StADud, Bro 19.

or emigrated neighbours. This acceptance enabled them to enlarge their farms and improve their financial situation. The solidification of the border brought many limitations and changes in their lives; it evoked fear and concern about the future. But it was not a purely negative development for Eastern frontier residents.

Eastern frontier farmers did not need to renounce their commitments to their kinship and other social networks in the West. They just maintained that under the conditions of imminent state violence there was nothing they could do for their Western kin. This position, even if not entirely accurate, allowed them to keep these networks intact. Through these networks, as discussed in the first section of this chapter, they retained the legal ownership and at least some income from their fields in the West.

CONCLUSION

The leaders of the German Democratic Republic aimed to make a strong statement with the announcement of the new border regime in May 1952. The FRG integrated further into the Western Bloc and the Cold War had already turned hot in Korea. The Western strategy was to ignore the existence of an East German state and treat the territory between the Elbe and the Oder–Neisse lines as nothing more than occupied Soviet territory. West Germany, with massive financial support from the United States, was making its first visible steps out of the postwar depression and into what would become 'the economic miracle'. The GDR, meanwhile, was ignored and rejected outside the Eastern Bloc and rendered illegitimate by its bigger and stronger West German neighbour. In 1952–3, it made a conscious effort to consolidate its hold over both territory and population with a series of both negative and positive policies. The new border regime was the centrepiece in this project.[92]

At least in this regard, policymakers of the Federal Republic in Bonn were in complete agreement with those of the German Democratic Republic in East Berlin. For them too, reactions to the new border regime were primarily considered through the prism of recognition of the East German state and the legitimacy of its actions. Both the months-long period of federal government inaction and the eventual policy pushed from Bonn beginning in October should be understood in this light. The federal government recognized the existence of this border and, as demonstrated in Chapter I, contributed importantly to its construction even before 1952. But West German state agencies refused to publicly acknowledge the inter-German border as an international border with another state. In the summer of 1952, federal offices first tried to downplay the effects of the new border regime. When the magnitude of the change forced them to intervene, the federal

---

[92] The context of these developments is discussed in more detail in the Introduction and in Chapter I. See also Ross, *Constructing Socialism*. Ross's part three deals specifically with the years 1952–3, which he terms 'the Rush to Construct Socialism'. See especially his introduction for this part on p. 51.

government framed its policies as ad-hoc aid programmes for refugees (just another of many such waves) and other persons who were affected.

Frontier residents did not initially conceive of the new border regime in national-political terms. For them, it was first and foremost a hindrance in their daily lives and a forced change in habits and practices. In the East, deportation and emigration left many vacancies and evoked widespread apprehension. Those who owned land across the border from their homes were suddenly unable to tend to their fields. Others saw new opportunities open with fields next to their farms left untended. All of them could see from up close that the GDR's presumption to seal the border for illegal crossing was good only on paper. This notwithstanding, frontier farmers on both sides of the border had to come to terms with the reality of the border. For all frontier farmers, ignoring the existence of the GDR and the division of Germany was not a realistic option. East German state agencies asserted their power violently in the lives of frontier residents. If they worked a field across the border from where they lived, they were forced to give the work up immediately. Western frontier farmers learned that Western state agencies were powerless to protect them from the policies of a state they denied the existence of. On both sides of the border, border formation entailed a de-facto confiscation of land from some farmers. This made the new border regime and the state agencies which initiated and enforced it very real for frontier farmers.

West German state agencies seemed weak and disorganized in the fall and winter of 1952–3. They did not supply alternative land or sufficient compensation to frontier farmers who lost land. Furthermore, they could not enforce policy on frontier farmers who gained land and had no influence on what happened on the eastern side of the border. There were clear disagreements between federal and state offices regarding priorities and perspectives. These disagreements and contradictions further weakened the Western position along the border. After May 1952, Western policy became a hindrance for the economy of many Western frontier farmers.

The many economic, legal, and other problems created by the new border regime forced all frontier residents to interact intensively with state agencies. Frontier residents used their proximity to the border, their ability to cross it, and their connections on the other side to leverage state agencies and obtain benefits or avoid damages. Through these interactions, and even when they worked against state agencies' intentions, frontier farmers had to orient themselves according to rules and regulations. Western and Eastern state organizations thus acquired growing consequence in the lives of frontier residents.

The new border regime made frontier farmers recognize the different conditions under which their relatives and friends across the border operated. They witnessed the different reactions to the new reality across the border. This chapter examined the reactions of four different groups of frontier farmers in the Eichsfeld, showing that their initial reaction was similar. All of them were motivated primarily by the wish to add land to their farms and prevent others from taking over their own land. Each group chose a different path towards this goal according to the conditions in the area, the assets it held, and the rules set by the governing state agency. In the

Hessian part of the Eichsfeld, frontier farmers capitalized on the lack of legal documentation regarding land ownership and loose ties to neighbouring villages and took over land owned by farmers from the East. With a strong backing from Hesse, they perceived their actions as a further step in disengaging from their 'Eastern' past and anchoring themselves in the West.

In the Lower Saxon part of the Eichsfeld, two groups of frontier residents competed for land owned by farmers from the East. 'The losers', that is, those who owned land in the East, tried to convince state agencies to give them the land as a form of compensation. They withheld tax and rent payments in an effort to make state agencies more fully address their plight. 'The gainers' of land could not take over land as their Protestant fellows in Hesse did. Their behaviour was circumscribed by their strong kinship networks and by the accessibility of relevant land registries. Instead, they argued in the name of private property and the rights of their relatives across the border. 'The gainers' won the land because of their relatives' suspicion of state agencies and because the combination of respect for private property and minimal change in the legal situation along the border sat well with the federal government's logic.

East of the border, frontier farmers, those who lost land and those who did not, could quite easily acquire additional land because it was available, following extensive deportations and emigration. To gain access to this land, they had to avoid being marked as troublemakers. They consequently avoided open resistance, did not complain to state agencies about the loss of land in the West, and did not champion their relatives' property rights. To maintain some income from their fields in the West, they circumvented state agencies' policy and supervision, crossed the border illegally, and secured private contracts. If asked about it by Eastern state agencies, they denied having any contact to these fields in the West. In all three areas covered in this chapter, frontier farmers had to make some claim regarding their relations with frontier farmers across the border in order to gain additional land. In Hesse, they claimed to have no connections there at all. In Lower Saxony, they had to claim commitment to help Eastern farmers. In the GDR, they claimed not to care about what happened across the border. All of them, then, were called, through their struggles for land, to think of their relations with fellow frontier residents in other parts of the Eichsfeld.

All these groups perceived that different conditions affected the behaviour of other groups. But such different conduct inevitably contributed to developing a perception of difference between groups. Championing conflicting causes and values, frontier farmers of these different groups expressed divergent perceptions of themselves and of the other groups. Chapter IV analyses these dynamics as they evolved over the following two decades to better examine their significance. Chapter III analyses the effects of the Western strategy of non-recognition of the GDR on the formation of the border and the emergence of Germany's division during the 1950s.

III

The Boundaries of Exclusive Representation
The Inter-German Cold War and the Division
of German Society

In January 1958, Hansjochen Kubitz, the district administrator from Eschwege, a frontier town in Hesse (West Germany), sent an exceptionally candid letter to his superior, airing years of frustration with the West German approach to cross-border coordination.[1] Federal policies undermined economy and daily life in his district, and he had decided to take a radical step of defiance (within the bureaucratic code). The issue at hand was the operation of several bus lines crossing the inter-German border. East German authorities had withdrawn the permits previously issued to drivers employed by the West German company operating these lines. Kubitz knew the administrators of the Eastern districts adjacent to his, with whom he regularly coordinated local issues. They told him in confidence that the problem was currency. East German passengers' payments for riding these buses embarrassed Eastern state agencies. If they paid with Eastern Marks, those were then taken out of the country into the pockets of Western operators in defiance of East German law. If they paid with Western Marks, they were paying with an illegal currency.

His Eastern interlocutors reassured Kubitz that their side wanted to allow the buses to run. All they needed was some arrangement to be found for a formal transfer of the currency under legally sanctioned exchange rates. Agreements on transfer of currency were beyond Kubitz's authority and he realized that the Eastern tactic had transferred the embarrassment to his side. He knew from experience that Western state agencies above him opposed cross-border coordination and would not enter into negotiations on this issue.

But before notifying the bus company owners that they would have to give up these lines, he made a desperate move. He asked his colleagues from the East to arrange a meeting about the currency issue and promised that he would bring to the meeting a high West German official empowered to negotiate. Then he wrote to his superior, the president of the county of Kassel and told him that he had arranged a meeting for him to discuss this problem as a representative of the FRG. As Kubitz probably knew in advance, this initiative would not achieve much. The county

---

[1] Der Landrat d. Landkreises Eschwege to Regierugnspräsident Kassel, 28 January 1958, HeHStAW, Abt. 502, Nr. 1114. The following information is based on this five-page letter. An older version of parts of this chapter appeared in Sagi Schaefer, 'Hidden behind the Wall: West German State-Building and the Division of Germany', *Central European History* 44 (2011): 506–35.

president did not take it upon himself to negotiate with the GDR, nor did anyone empower him to do so. The bus lines ran a shorter route; the company lost the income and the residents of the area lost the border-crossing travel opportunity. Another link had been broken in the cross-border networks of this area.

Like Kubitz, many frontier administrators along the inter-German border found themselves between a rock and a hard place during the 1950s. The process of division regularly created such problems all along the border, and many frontier administrators turned to cross-border coordination to solve them. Their efforts were repeatedly undermined by state agencies enforcing a different set of priorities related to their conflicting state-building strategies.

Nevertheless, there were many attempts to keep cross-border communities and networks viable during the 1950s. At the height of the Cold War, just a few months before the outbreak of the Hungarian crisis, thousands of Eichsfelder from East and West joined together in an Eastern frontier village, with the approval of both German governments. As this chapter will show, local politicians saw this event, and the cultural ties binding together both parts of the Eichsfeld, as an opportunity to circumvent state agencies' limitations on cross-border contacts. Their attempts and their failures highlight the conflicts between local and state perspectives on both sides of the border. The analysis below demonstrates the delicate position frontier administrations held in working for the interests of frontier populations and, at the same time, upholding and justifying state agencies' policies. Local interests required cross-border coordination and cooperation; state-building dogmas undermined such cooperation.

This chapter documents the impact of a policy initiated by the FRG and the Western Allies on the history of the Cold War and on the division of Germany. It analyses the implications of the Western 'claim to exclusive representation of the German people' (*Die Alleinvertretungsanspruch*) for the formation of boundaries between East and West Germany. The Western insistence on diplomatically isolating the GDR, with the declared aim of preserving German unity, actually contributed to the emergence of physical and political demarcations as well as long-lasting social divisions. These changes emerged gradually, not as a direct product of a conscious effort by any one actor. The chapter shows how policies connected with the claim to exclusive representation, and Eastern reactions to this claim, worked to further the physical build-up of the border and to undermine regional and cross-border identification.

The predominance of the Berlin Wall in interpretations of the inter-German border has led to the pervasive notion that the border was a project intended primarily to jail East Germans in the GDR. It is widely accepted that the Berlin Wall was constructed in August 1961 by the Soviet-backed government of the GDR, primarily in order to stop East Germans from moving to the West.[2] Viewing the history of the entire inter-German border as having been constructed for similar

---

[2] Thomas Lindenberger, 'Diktatur der Grenze(n). Die eingemauerte Gesellschaft und ihre Feinde', in *Mauerbau und Mauerfall: Ursachen, Verlauf, Auswirkungen*, edited by Hans-Herman Hertle et al. (Berlin: Links, 2002), 203.

causes suited Cold War ideological battles. It was easy to uphold this view because the visible, physical construction of the border was mostly initiated by East German state organizations.[3] This idea was reinforced at the end of the Cold War. Cracks in the Iron Curtain brought a renewed depletion of East German society, as growing numbers of East Germans took to the West in 1989–90. For 28 years the Wall had prevented them from doing so, hence, many reasoned, this was what the border had been constructed for.

Such reasoning, however, confuses result with intention, ignores change over time, and overstates Berlin's impact. For 16 years after the end of the Second World War, the social division of Germany and the physical construction of the border between West and East progressed under different conditions and served different goals. Even after the building of the wall in August 1961, the rural border and the dynamics of state society relations around it changed very slowly, and the forces shaping this border's development continued to operate according to preexisting interests and goals. This chapter exposes some of the dynamics which developed along the inter-German border during the 1950s, and fleshes out the role of Western interests and practices of control in bringing about German division.

Western and Eastern state agencies obsessively pursued goals dictated by the battle over recognition and legitimacy of the GDR. The best-known front of this war was international diplomacy. Along the inter-German border, daily battles were waged on a less glamorous frontline of the same war, which bore important implications for the lives of frontier residents. Western and Eastern state agencies engaged in protracted conflicts over seemingly minor issues along the border—several acres of land, a few permits, a story in a newspaper, some lost cows. They would not compromise on even such small-fry matters because of the Cold War they waged on each other, which endowed even local quibbles with enormous symbolic significance.

The first part of the chapter explores in more detail the development of the Western strategy of non-recognition of the GDR and its implications for border policies and practices, as well as for other aspects of life along the border and for cross-border relations. The second part analyses two attempts to promote regional and local interests and needs through cross-border coordination during the 1950s. The first case demonstrates a common pattern of cross-border contacts and negotiations during that period. The analysis of this case shows that this pattern prevailed even when strong cross-border networks and traditions supplied a viable framework for cooperation efforts. Despite good intentions of frontier administrators, their efforts were frustrated by the interventions of their superiors.

The second case is a rare one in which state organizations on both sides of the border were anxious to resolve a source of tension between them, and resorted to sub-contracting sensitive cross-border negotiations to local administrators. Even under these exceptional circumstances, Western authorization for the negotiation

---

[3] See an example of assigning all the initiative in the division of Germany to the East based on looking at the most visible steps and interpreting them as having exclusively internal Eastern causes in Lindenberger, 'Deutschland als Grenzregion', 102–4.

was informal, both state administrations significantly limited the scope of the negotiations, and the agreements reached were never formally adopted by either state. Nevertheless, this case demonstrates the potential for cross-border negotiation by local and regional representatives to reach quick understandings and promote interests of frontier populations on both sides.

Together, these two cases enable the exploration of the crucial role that the Western claim to exclusive representation played in undermining cross-border communication and cooperation. Paradoxically, West German insistence on ignoring and denying the division of Germany contributed to buttressing and enhancing the process of division. Frontier administrations and residents who were robbed of the option to coordinate across the border were forced to adopt solutions and practices which relied solely on resources available in and rules pertaining to 'their own', that is, their separate states. To do that they adopted patterns of behaviour, expectations and orientations that with time grew more and more divergent. Thus, the Western policy of exclusive representation, aimed at protecting the unity of the nation, in practice contributed to its division.

EXCLUSIVE REPRESENTATION
AND NON-RECOGNITION

Since 1945, Allied policies had pushed apart the Eastern and Western parts of Germany, yet the Allies never officially abandoned their commitment to the future reunification of Germany as written into the Potsdam agreement. However, the Western Allies' rejection of the Stalin Note of 10 March 1952 indicated that unification did not lie around the corner.[4] Under Konrad Adenauer's leadership, the new West German state made securing greater independence and Western integration its central goals, while also professing a commitment to achieving German reunification. The early 1950s demonstrated how difficult it was to form a coherent policy promoting all these goals simultaneously that would be publicly acceptable, diplomatically viable, and politically realistic.[5]

Within the first half of the decade, the FRG reestablished an army and an armament industry, became a founding member of the (West) European Coal and Steel Union, and joined NATO. Partly in return, it gained growing formal independence from the Western Allies, which allowed the West German government to establish a foreign ministry and diplomatic relations. The Western Allies' occupation of West Germany formally ended with a treaty they signed with the

---

[4] See Steininger, *Eine Vertane Chance*, 9 for a summary of the document's content. For many years scholars and politicians in Germany and elsewhere debated the sincerity of this suggestion and the reaction of the Allies and of the German government. See Wettig, 'Stalin and German Reunification', 411–19. See also Loth, *Die Sovjetunion und die deutsche Frage*, 12–26.

[5] Werner Kilian, *Die Hallstein-Doktrin: Der Diplomatische Krieg Zwischen Der BRD Und Der DDR 1955–1973* (Berlin: Duncker and Humblot, 2001), 14–15; Ludwig Auerbach, 'Das ganze Deutschland soll es sein', in *Adenauer und die Folgen*, edited by H. J. Netzer (München: Beck, 1965), 92–105.

FRG in May 1955. Throughout this period, officials of the federal government repeatedly reiterated its commitment to German reunification. Adenauer and other government officials time and again stated the claim to exclusive representation of the German people, enshrined in the republic's Basic Law (*Grundgesetz*). According to this principle, 'until Germany was restored as a unified state, the government of the Federal Republic—which alone had been elected in a free democratic manner—would act as the sole legitimate representative of the German people.'[6] In practical terms, this meant that the FRG refused to deal with East German state agencies or acknowledge that the territory beyond its eastern border was anything other than Soviet-occupied territory.

The Western Allies supported West Germany's claim to exclusive representation of the German nation. After the establishment of the GDR in the fall of 1949, they devised a strategy aimed at deterring any country from recognizing the new socialist state. Bonn followed suit and made the international isolation of the East German regime a cornerstone of its foreign policy. The federal government announced that it would sever relations with any state that would recognize 'the so-called GDR'.[7]

The Soviet Union put this strategy to the test in the summer and autumn of 1955, when Khrushchev invited Adenauer to Moscow. The prospect of diplomatic relations between the FRG and the Soviet Union raised questions regarding the West German policy on relations with the GDR. Preparing for the visit during the summer of 1955, West German policymakers agreed that if the Soviet Union's leader wished to discuss diplomatic relations with the FRG, the Germans would agree to establish committees to discuss the issue, but no more. They decided to stall by demanding progress on German unification first. During the visit in September, the Soviets refused to discuss reunification, insisting that Adenauer should broach this question with the GDR leadership if he wished. As the West German delegation was preparing to depart in protest, the Soviets made an offer: they would release the remaining 10,000 German prisoners of war (PoW) held in the USSR in return for the establishment of diplomatic relations with the FRG. The offer was politically too valuable for Adenauer to pass up: returning the prisoners to their homes and families would be a tremendous achievement. To the amazement of his senior advisers, Adenauer ignored previous decisions and accepted the offer. Before returning to Germany, Adenauer submitted a letter to the Soviets reiterating the FRG's claim to exclusive representation of the German people, and his government's refusal to accept the postwar borders. This was a face-saving gesture, not a negotiating move—Adenauer did not expect the Soviets to accept this position.[8]

---

[6] William G. Gray, *Germany's Cold War: The Global Campaign to Isolate East Germany, 1949–1969* (Chapel Hill, NC: University of North Carolina Press, 2003), 11–12. See also Kilian, *Die Hallstein-Doktrin*, 18–19.

[7] To avoid using the title 'German Democratic Republic' West German speakers usually referred to it as 'the Soviet zone' (*Sovietische Besatzungszone* or SBZ) or 'the so-called GDR' (*die sogenannte DDR*).

[8] Gray, *Germany's Cold War*, 30–7; Kilian, *Die Hallstein-Doktrin*, 13–18; Rüdiger Marco Booz, *'Hallsteinzeit': Deutsche Aussenpolitik 1955–1972* (Bonn: Bouvier Verlag, 1995), 17–20.

By opening an embassy in a city which already hosted a GDR embassy, Adenauer put at risk the practice, if not the whole theory, of exclusive representation. How would the FRG be able to dissuade other countries from establishing relations with the GDR? On the plane back, the top Foreign Office officials began to assess their options given the new situation. Their decision was to claim that nothing had changed. Moscow presented a unique problem, and the FRG had found a unique solution to it. The Soviet Union held the PoWs and was one of the wartime Allies, all of whom had committed to German unity, so Bonn made an exception. In no other state in the world would West Germany accept the existence of two German embassies. It took a few more months before the details were rounded into an official policy, which was presented in a conference to foreign ambassadors in Bonn. The official letter was signed by the Foreign Office State Secretary, Walter Hallstein. All the elements in the diplomatic formula had been used before, but this was the first repackaging of all these elements into an official West German policy, which was thereafter known as the 'Hallstein Doctrine'.[9] Despite internal and external criticism, this policy held firm until the establishment of the CDU/CSU and SPD 'big coalition' government in December 1966.[10]

The Hallstein Doctrine, which denied the existence of a neighbouring state holding much power over the lives of millions of Germans, gave rise to many contradictions. As Chapter II demonstrated, East German state agencies were present and their practices visible. Western state agencies' insistence on ignoring them forced both sides into corners. In no area were these problems more obvious or more relevant to the lives of German citizens than in the West German border policy and its implementation. Exclusive representation-related policies and the ensuing battles over recognition of the GDR hampered frontier residents' ability to overcome some of the negative effects of German division. Convinced that they were paying the price for Bonn's unrealistic position, Western frontier residents criticized and occasionally subverted their state's policies.

Even before the Hallstein Doctrine was formulated, the West German claim to exclusive representation of the German people had turned the recognition of the GDR into the crux of the diplomatic battle between the two German states. The Western Allies and the West Germans were dependent on cooperation with the Soviets for many things (such as ground travel from West Germany to West Berlin). From May 1952, the East Germans and the Soviets used this dependence to force the West to recognize, on at least a de-facto basis, the GDR. As detailed in the previous chapter, the GDR announced a dramatic change in border policy in May 1952, declaring its border with West Germany officially impenetrable.

At the same time, the Soviets notified the Western Allies of a change in procedures for border crossing. West German citizens wishing to travel into or pass through the

[9] Gray, *Germany's Cold War*, 37–40; Kilian, *Die Hallstein-Doktrin*, 18–23; Booz, *'Hallsteinzeit'*, 17–19.

[10] Gray, *Germany's Cold War*, 193–8; Kilian, *Die Hallstein-Doktrin*, 339–40; Booz, *'Hallsteinzeit'*, 97–104; Martin H. Geyer, 'Der Kampf um nationale Representation. Deutsch-deutsche Sportbeziehungen und die "Hallstein Doktrin"', *Vierteljahrshefte für Zeitgeschichte* 44 (1996): 55–86.

GDR were required from then on to have special permits issued by the East German People's Police. The Soviets proceeded to remove passengers who did not possess such permits from trains crossing the border.[11] Their unwillingness to coordinate anything with a police force of a state they did not recognize put the Western Allies and the FRG in the difficult position of being unable to ensure travel to West Berlin for West German citizens. The new GDR border regime worked in similar ways in many other cases as well. Practices which were previously regulated between the Allies or on local level only, such as the operation of border-crossing bus and train lines, had to be renegotiated with East German state agencies. The GDR thus gained leverage for recognition. On a daily basis, it produced thousands of routine demonstrations for West Germans that it existed and had power over their lives, each of them an incentive for these citizens of the FRG to support cross-border cooperation. The timing was no coincidence. As Corey Ross has shown, 1952 marked a turning point in the East German state-building project. Proclaiming its authority more boldly, the GDR also attempted to force the West to accept its existence.[12] This strategic move raised the border-policy stakes on both sides, making the borderlands into a major battlefield in the German Cold War over the recognition of the GDR. Cross-border contacts thus acquired explosive potential and state agencies on both sides began to supervise more closely frontier officials' contacts with colleagues across the border.

Throughout the 1950s, frontier residents and local politicians (e.g., mayors and district administrators) tried to make arrangements and develop mechanisms to meet the routine needs of frontier society in an environment greatly troubled by the emerging political division. Administrators and politicians in frontier communities and districts were forced to engage the contradiction between their superiors' priorities, framed by diplomatic 'all-German' strategies, and the demands of their communities and regions. Many local administrators tried to make cross-border coordination work, knowing from experience that this was an effective way to manage their resources and promote local interests. Frontier administrators were very interesting players in this history, on the boundary between state and non-state parts of society, often embodying the difficulty to differentiate between the two. Some frontier administrators were defiant of authority; others carefully toed the line. But regardless of the approach, all their initiatives for cross-border cooperation failed. The battle over recognition pulled apart at the seams many cross-border networks and communities by diminishing their relevance to daily life.

REGIONAL IDENTIFICATION AS A WEAPON IN—AND AS A VICTIM OF—THE COLD WAR

In the Eichsfeld region prior to 1945, cross-border cooperation had been the most common way to address challenges of local and regional administration and

---

[11] McCloy to State Secretary, 28 May 1952 and 2 July 1952, NARA-CIV, RG 59, 1311/250/59/ 17/7/11/1.
[12] Ross, *Constructing Socialism*, 51.

economy. State and province borders had divided the Eichsfeld since the early nineteenth century. These borders did not stand in the way of cooperation on a local or regional basis. There was no physical obstacle in place and farmers routinely cooperated to return stray cows, to combat fires, or to coordinate hunting. For these purposes, there was no difference between cooperation among neighbours across the border and those on the same side. The management and regulation of water resources presented the best example of large-scale regional cooperation. Due to the topography of the Eichsfeld, mountainous in the east and flat in the west, water in many smaller and a few larger streams generally flowed across the border from East to West. Regulating and clearing riverbeds was routinely carried out in coordination with neighbouring communities along streams, regardless of borders. When the town of Duderstadt (in the Prussian province of Hanover) needed to increase its water supply in the interwar years, it turned to the neighbouring community of Brehme (Prussian province of Saxony). An agreement was struck whereby Duderstadt purchased a patch of land in Brehme where a deep well and necessary canals were dug to lead the water to the town. At the time, no one thought much of the provincial border between the two communities. The project was completed in 1933 and the water flowed undisturbed from Brehme to Duderstadt until the early fifties.[13]

Cross-border cooperation continued to play an important role in the postwar years in the Eichsfeld, even as old administrative borders traversing the region turned into demarcation lines between occupation zones and state-building projects. The ease of cooperation in the Eichsfeld helped frontier residents overcome some of the problems created by the emerging processes of division. The arrangement reached between the Western town of Duderstadt, the farmers of the Eastern village of Ecklingerode and the Eastern district of Worbis provides a good example. To avoid difficulties arising from conflicting regulations regarding currency conversion in East and West Germany, Duderstadt agreed not to collect land taxes from farmers from Ecklingerode whose fields were in its domain. In return, the farmers agreed to pay the sums they owed Duderstadt to the district of Worbis, which would use them to pay foresters for keeping Duderstadt's town forest (east of the border) in order and supplying Duderstadt with wood.[14] The economy of these borderlands depended on many cross-border interactions and arrangements of this kind to stay afloat in the years prior to 1952. But even in the Eichsfeld, after 1952 cross-border cooperation became increasingly difficult, with state agencies on both sides gradually restricting contact options, especially between officials.

The attempts to reopen the border checkpoint in the Eichsfeld demonstrate how state agencies' priorities prevented the development of solutions to problems along

[13] 'Verbindungen nach Westdeutschland, die die Staatsgrenze berühren', 11 June 1963, KrAEich, EA WBS, Nr. 7241.
[14] Correspondence on this issue, beginning in March 1951, is in ThHStAW, Land Th., Ministerium d. Finanzen, Nr. 1397. See especially documents from 28 March 1951 (Kreisrat Worbis to Th. MdI), 30 April 1951 (internal memo Th. Landesfinanzdirektion), and see also many other examples detailed in the document from 5 May 1951 (inspection report of Th. MdF detailing the different local and regional solutions).

the border. The most important issue on the agenda for frontier administrators in the Eichsfeld from 1952 was the quest to reopen the border checkpoint between Gerblingerode and Teistungen. This checkpoint on the road from Hanover to Erfurt, connecting Duderstadt with the Eastern Eichsfeld, was the only one in the region. It was closed as part of the GDR's reform of border regulations in May 1952, turning the roads to Duderstadt and Worbis (both from the West and from the East) into dead-ends, and severely damaging the economy of the region. Appeals by the Western Allies to the Soviets to reopen the checkpoint were met with Soviet refusals to discuss matters falling under the jurisdiction of the GDR. The president of the county of Hildesheim (West) then notified the district administrator in Duderstadt that the government authorized 'local German administrations to discuss technical issues for the reopening of border checkpoints' with their East German counterparts' (emphases in the original).[15] With this limited authorization, the district administrator in Duderstadt tried to engage his colleague in Worbis in a discussion about the reopening of the checkpoint. The chief administrator in Worbis agreed in principle to discuss it but repeatedly stated that border controls were state, not district, matters. He explained that there were issues of currency exchange, permits, and more involved in opening a checkpoint, issues which local administrators could not regulate. Throughout 1954, the two exchanged letters on the subject, but the Eastern administrator showed no inclination to revise his stand.[16]

The cementing of the battle after 1952 over exclusive representation, led West German state agencies to restrict all cross-border contacts between officials, fearing they might be taken as proof of recognition. With increasing problems in the frontier economy and society caused by the political division, and the proven ability of cross-border cooperation for solving such problems, frontier administrators saw these restrictions as undermining their work. The district administrator of the Western Eichsfeld in Duderstadt, Matthias Gleitze, understood his superiors' reservations about such meetings, but saw cooperation with colleagues from the East as the only way to promote some key interests of his district's population. Gleitze was a native of the Eichsfeld and an expert in Eichsfeld agriculture. Between the wars, he was active in the Catholic Centre Party and spoke publicly against the Nazi Party, an act which in 1933 cost him the position he held in the civil service, but allowed him to regain one in 1947. He was elected as head of the district administration (*Landkreisdirektor*) in 1948, a position he held until his retirement in 1967.[17]

---

[15] Oberkreisdirektor Dud to Regierungspräsident Hildesheim, 4 December 1953, and Regierungspräsident Hildesheim to Oberkreisdirektor Dud, 23 January 1954, KrAGö, LK DUD, Nr. 61. The quote is from the second letter.

[16] Further correspondence throughout 1954 is in the same file, including a report from a surprise visit of one council member from Duderstadt in Worbis. Some examples: Oberkreisdirektor Dud to Vorsitz. d. Kreistags WBS, 23 February 1954; Vorsitz. d. Kreistags WBS to Oberkreisdirektor Dud, 4 March 1954; 'Aktenvermerk', 18 August 1954. All in KrAGö, LK DUD, Nr. 61.

[17] Gleitze was born in 1902 in Seeburg, about five miles northwest of Duderstadt as the crow flies. After retiring he served in the district council and in the council of the city of Duderstadt. He died in 1989 just three weeks before the border opened. For details about Gleitze's life and career see http://de.

In the summer of 1953, Gleitze was personally invited to meet with his counterpart in Worbis. He requested permission from his superior in the county of Hildesheim to accept the invitation. He explained that he knew the GDR side was going to try and score propaganda points if he led an official delegation across the border. He then emphasized that despite the political risk, such a meeting would be worthwhile because there were many burning local issues that could be resolved through cross-border coordination in an area like the Eichsfeld, which had enjoyed 600 years of close relations. Among the issues he mentioned were the reopening of the above-discussed border checkpoint, but also permits to cultivate the Duderstadt town forest which lay across the border, the prompt return of straying livestock, and permissions for conversations between relatives across the border fence.[18] His passionate and calculated attempt, and his promises to avoid any overtures from Eastern officials to discuss political matters, did not help. His superiors gave this initiative a bureaucratic burial by stalling. At the council meeting in Duderstadt, Gleitze explained his rejection of the invitation to a disgruntled council in these words:

> To be on the safe side I asked the [county] government whether it would be possible [to go to Worbis]. They needed to consult the [Lower Saxon] Minister of the Interior. It is quite clear that if I or a committee would travel to Worbis, the Leipzig radio would say that today there is a delegation in Worbis. That might be taken the wrong way here. Then we would have a case of lower authorities going against higher authorities.[19]

Gleitze thought he needed explicit permission and he read administrative language well enough to understand that the county officials' stalling beyond the date of the expected visit was their way of rejecting his request. This incident represents a consistent Western policy prohibiting border-crossing meetings between officials. During this period, Bavarian officials also forced city councillors to cancel meetings in which they had agreed to participate.[20]

The breakthrough in the impasse about border-crossing meetings in the Eichsfeld began in the village of Holungen about 3.5 miles southeast of the inter-German border. Holungen was the birth and burial place of Hermann Iseke (1856–1907), regarded as the Eichsfeld's 'homeland poet' (*Heimatdichter*). Iseke was a jurist and a priest who, as a young man, served in both capacities in many communities of the region. He became a military chaplain and travelled with the German army to China in 1900 and to Africa in 1906, where he died a year later. He was, and still is, best known to Eichsfeld residents through his 'Eichsfeld Song',

academic.ru/dic.nsf/dewiki/930693, accessed 27 June 2010. Gleitze earned a PhD in national economy at the University of Rostock in 1927, having written a dissertation about the development of plot sizes in the district of Duderstadt and its consequences. On the front cover of his dissertation, below his name and title, Gleitze added 'from Seeburg in the Eichsfeld'. See Gleitze, 'Die Verteilung und Bedeutung der Betriebsgrössen'.

[18] Oberkreisdirektor Duderstadt to Regierungspräsident Hildesheim, 1 June 1953, KrAGö, LK DUD, Nr. 61.

[19] Undated Kreistag protocol, KrArGö, LK DUD, nr. 61.

[20] Sheffer, *Burned Bridge*, 137.

praising the scenery and people of his native region and expressing a romantic longing for it. The 'Eichsfeld Song' has become the unofficial anthem of the region.[21] In December 1954, a local committee was formed in the village to organize an Eichsfeld celebration for the upcoming centenary of the poet's birth. The village council wrote to the district of Worbis requesting approval and support for the project.[22] The district approved the idea and instructed the organizing committee to join the SED-affiliated 'League of Culture' (*Kulturbund*).[23]

After receiving the green light, the village cultural committee began preparing a regional event celebrating Eichsfeld traditions. SED activists in the region tried to add political overtones, events, and symbols to the celebration in order to highlight the GDR's success and strength. They also sought to tone down the religious emphasis of the planned event. One of the major conflicts between the local committee and the district party chiefs was the giant cross that the committee planned to erect on top of the hill facing west, to be seen across the border, symbolizing the unity of the Eichsfeld. Eventually, the event, as publicized in invitations sent to Western Eichsfeld communities and the district authority, seemed benign enough to win the approval of West German state agencies. It was not a political event but a celebration of shared heritage, and Gleitze was able to win his superiors over for the participation of Western Eichsfeld residents, himself included.[24]

The regional festival that eventually took place in Holungen on 7–8 July 1956, was a true *Heimatfest*. Highlights of the first evening included the unveiling of the Iseke memorial, a torchlight procession, and the lighting of the cross atop the westward-looking hilltop of the Sonnenstein. A bonfire was lit near the cross and was 'answered' by a bonfire from the Western Eichsfeld. The second day began with a public mass, and its climax was a pageant with Eichsfelder from across the region in traditional costumes. The major events attracted around 10,000 participants from the region, including hundreds from the Western Eichsfeld. Western participants were requested to apply for permits in advance and expected to travel for hours through a remote border checkpoint,[25] but many Western Eichsfelder apparently crossed illegally and joined the event unregistered. It is hard to determine exactly how many participants came from the Western Eichsfeld. Jan Palmowski relies on GDR newspaper reports and on locals' memories to say that there were as many as 800 participants from the West.[26] Permits were issued only for

[21] See www.youtube.com/watch?v=YqYsxGH6X1s and www.youtube.com/watch?v=XVhYUYLfz Mc&NR=1 (accessed 21 August 2010) for performances of this song accompanied by romantic Eichsfeld views.

[22] Rat d. Gemeinde Holungen to Vorsitz. d. Rates d. Kreises Worbis, 20 December 1954 in KrAEich, Holungen B58.

[23] For the letter with the reassuring details about Iseke's background see Rat d. Gemeinde Holungen to Vorsitz. d. Rates d. Kreises Worbis, 21 February 1955, KrAEich, Holungen B58. See also Jan Palmowski, *Inventing a Socialist Nation: Heimat and the Politics of Everyday Life in the GDR, 1945–1990* (Cambridge: Cambridge University Press, 2009), 229–31.

[24] See the official invitation, titled 'Eichsfeld homeland gathering, a contribution to peace and unity' (*Eichsfelder Heimattreffen, ein Beitrag für Frieden und Einheit*), KrAGö, LK DUD, Nr. 61.

[25] Oberkreisdirektor kreis Duderstadt to Vorsitz. d. Rates d. Kreises Worbis, 11 June 1956, KrAGö, LK DUD, Nr. 61. See also Behrens, *Regionale Identität*, 227–8.

[26] Palmowski, *Inventing a Socialist Nation*, 230.

250, who boarded buses and travelled the long way through Wartha.[27] The additional participants must have arrived via shorter, illegal routes. The final character of the event was determined primarily by the massive participation of Eichsfelder, and emphasized the shared Catholic traditions of the region.[28] Regional identification and the will to uphold the cross-border community were still strong among Eichsfelder in 1956. Voting with their legs and with the contents chosen for their *Heimatfest*, residents clearly expressed their devotion to the idea of a unified Eichsfeld.[29]

Gleitze, the highest-ranking Western official present, reported no political transgressions upon returning home from Holungen. For the council members from the host district of Worbis, inter-German politics were nevertheless part of the event. Around that time, party circles in the GDR identified regional culture in the Eichsfeld as a potential tool in their quest to win Western recognition. The secretary of the district council sent four of his deputies to engage visitors, especially the politicians coming from the West. Gleitze was not averse to their courting. Having finally acquired official approval for a formal visit in the Eastern Eichsfeld, he was quite happy to re-establish working relations with his colleagues there. In his reports he emphasized the harmless nature of these conversations, which touched only on topics such as the returning of stray animals, regulation of waterways, and warnings in cases of fire along the border.[30]

The attempts of party organs to turn the Eichsfeld *Heimattreffen* into a political display failed. But the SED in the Eichsfeld used this event to plant the seeds for a concerted effort to turn Eichsfeld's cultural unity and tradition into an instrument of 'all-German work' (*gesamtdeutsche Arbeit*). Under this title, state and party officials, organizations, and citizens of the GDR were encouraged to contact West Germans and win them over to the Eastern positions in the Cold War.[31] Party activists in the Eichsfeld had begun to move in this direction even before the Holungen event. During the fall of 1955, plans were made for a concert of the Heiligenstadt (Eastern Eichsfeld) choir in Duderstadt (West). At the same time, the district of Worbis encouraged the mayors of the three towns of the Eastern Eichsfeld (Dingelstädt, Worbis, and Heiligenstadt) to initiate a meeting with the mayor of Duderstadt, the only town in the Western Eichsfeld.[32] The practice of initiating conversations with private visitors from the West and inviting them to public events, a cornerstone of all-German work in the GDR, was also restructured to instrumentalize regional culture. In previous years, visitors were

[27] Stadt Duderstadt, *Die Grenze im Eichsfeld*, 16.

[28] Eichsfelder Heimatbote, 21 July 1956, Das ganze Eichsfeld, KrAGö LK DUD Nr. 61. For more details on the contents of the celebration, and the locals' perspectives on its impact see Palmowski, *Inventing a Socialist Nation*, 229–34; Behrens, *Regionale Identität*, 227–8.

[29] According to Edith Sheffer this was the case in Sonneberg and Neustadt at that time as well. Sheffer, *Burned Bridge*, 137.

[30] Oberkreisdirektor Kreis Duderstadt, 'Aktenvermerk', 12 July 1956, KrAGö, LK DUD, Nr. 61. See also Behrens, *Regionale Identität*, 228–9.

[31] For examples of 'all-German work' in other frontier areas see Sheffer, *Burned Bridge*, 133–5.

[32] Rat d. Kreises Worbis to Rat d. Stadt Heiligenstadt, 24 November 1955, StAHIG, Rep II, IA, Nr. 560.

invited to private conversations with the mayor or to tour factories and schools, and lectured about the progress in East Germany. In April 1956, the town of Heiligenstadt invited visitors from the West to a lecture about 'poetry in the Eichsfeld dialect' followed by a slide show titled 'our Eichsfeld'.[33] By the mid-1950s, SED circles came to view regional traditions, networks, and identifications as tools for persuading West German citizens that the GDR was a stable, peace-loving, and friendly neighbour state.

East German district officials intended to use the contacts with their Western colleagues forged at Holungen as openings for broader interactions. Between 1955 and 1958, these connections supplied an arena for repeated condensed enactments of the drama of the German Cold War over recognition. Both sides had many issues they wanted to coordinate with their colleagues across the border. For residents of these areas, which had turned into frontier lands, the inter-German border was not just a diplomatic or geo-political issue. It had changed many aspects of their daily lives and significantly hampered their economy. Perhaps the most insidious was the change in the region's place on the transportation map. Bus lines were cancelled and the national railway company reduced—and in the West cancelled—services, even to the district towns. Transportation costs for private citizens and businesses rose significantly and people had to cycle or walk miles to get to work.[34]

But when district administrators corresponded and met, they were obliged to consider not just the local perspective, but that of state organizations as well. Western officials were on the alert against any attempt to raise 'political' issues or to discuss controversial questions. Above all, attempts to involve higher levels of state authorities were to be disregarded. Eastern state agencies also tried to control these contacts, but they sought to direct them to the negotiation of more than just local, 'technical' issues. They strove to have these interactions lead to recognition—at least implicitly—of the GDR, and for that purpose sought to draw in higher-level state agencies. District officials from both sides of the border, who participated in these meetings and correspondences, were genuinely interested in solving problems which made not only the lives of the frontier population but also the job of frontier authorities more difficult. But they knew that they could achieve nothing if permission to negotiate were to be rescinded, and so they had to play by the rules. In West Germany, bureaucratic delays and diversions alongside

---

[33] See the invitation to the event in StAHig, Rep II, IA, Nr. 560.

[34] Voluminous correspondence on both sides of the border deals with the effects on transportation. See for example: Oberkreisdirektor Dud to Regierungspräsident Hildesheim, 4 December 1953, KrAGö, LK DUD, Nr. 61 (district administrator explaining to his superior that severing the border-crossing road had turned the town into a 'dead corner'); 'Besprechung über Bahnbuslinie 1200', 14 September 1956, StaADud, Fuhr 142 (administrators trying to convince representatives of the national railway company to reactivate a bus line connecting border villages); 'Kalikombinat Werra-Merkers', 3 May 1962, BArch-B, DY 30, IV 2/12/73, 157–9 (changes in restricted zone regulations creating transportation problems for this company); Gemeinde Wahlhausen to Ministerium d. Innern, 26 January 1946, KrAEich, EA HIG, Nr. 402/I (the damages to dairy farmers in frontier villages who were required to transport their milk to a distant town).

administrative reprimanding were the lot of defiant local administrators. East German administrators who failed to toe the line risked their positions.[35]

To justify his intent to maintain working contacts with his colleagues in the Eastern Eichsfeld districts despite the danger of political manoeuvring, Gleitze prepared a list of 23 issues that required cross-border coordination.[36] This list was produced for Western consumption; he did not show it to his Eastern colleagues. Accordingly, it did not include any item that might have been considered problematic in the West. On the contrary, in addition to many items in which both sides were interested, such as coordinating the containment of epidemics or fires, the list included items that concerned the West. The first two items were access to the Duderstadt town forest east of the border and opening the border checkpoint between Gerblingerode and Teistungen. It also included the mutual regulation of rivers and water sources, an important Western interest, since the Eastern part of the Eichsfeld was mountainous and lay upstream from the FRG part, and as a result controlled most of the water sources. Permission was granted under conditions of close supervision.[37] Along with border-crossing visits of choirs and football teams, the year following the celebration in Holungen also saw lively correspondence between the district administrations in the Eastern and Western Eichsfeld and several border-crossing visits by council members and district executives.[38]

Back in Duderstadt (Figure 3.1) after the meeting in Holungen, Gleitze did not waste time. On 12 July 1956, three days after returning, he began writing memos and making inquiries about the issues he discussed with his Eastern colleagues, hoping to prove his intention to solve some of the problems they asked him about. It was not as easy as he hoped it would be. One of the issues that the Worbis council members asked him to address, and that Gleitze was happy to help with, was an exchange of land registry documents for plots around the border. In several areas along the border between the two districts, Soviet and British occupation forces had swapped land in 1945. Consequently, many plots lay in the de-facto jurisdiction of communities and districts which did not own the land registries of these plots. Thus, these communities, and both districts, were unable to tax these plots or perform and supervise legal actions pertaining to them. Gleitze wanted to deal straight away with what appeared to him to be a simple matter. He was surprised, upon receiving the case summary from Worbis in August, that Worbis had been asking for these documents since 1953, and forwarded the letter to his land registry

[35] Sheffer, *Burned Bridge*, 136. According to Jan Palmowski, residents of Holungen are convinced that the secretary of their district council was fired because he allowed the *Heimatfest* to take place. Palmoski, *Inventing a Socialist Nation*, 233–5.

[36] See memos in NLA-HStAH, Nds. 50, Acc. 96/88, Nr. 705 and see Gleitze's 23-point document (undated) in KrArGö, LK DUD Nr. 61.

[37] See Ministerialrat Nullmeyer to Oberkreisdirektor Gleitze, 1 March 1957, KrArGö, LK DUD, Nr. 61.

[38] Behrens, *Regionale Identität*, 229–31; Stadt Duderstadt, *Die Grenze im Eichsfeld*, 16–18.

Fig. 3.1. Duderstadt Town Hall (photo by the author, July 2008)

asking why.[39] Within days he learned that it was not in his power to complete this transaction.

The head of the land registry office in Duderstadt replied that as of the previous year, the Lower Saxon Minister of the Interior had notified all land registry offices that his office would centrally direct all exchanges of documents with the GDR.[40] Gleitze did not know that since the late 1940s, there had been ongoing internal discussions on this issue between federal and state offices in the FRG and negotiations with the GDR. In 1951, Lower Saxony was actually the first state to raise this matter with federal officials. The major problem for Lower Saxony was the town of Bad Sachsa in the Harz Mountains.[41] The town (along with a neighbouring village) was transferred in 1945 from the Soviet to the British zone. Lacking a land registry, any real estate deal in the town could not be legally recorded. Initially, the parties involved in the West—on the county, the state, and the federal levels—raised no objections to exchanging copies of land registry documents (keeping the originals so

---

[39] Rat d. Kreises Worbis to Oberkreisdirektor Duderstadt, 8 August 1956, KrArGö, LK DUD, Nr. 61.

[40] Leiter d. Katasteramtes to Oberkreisdirektor Duderstadt, 22 August 1956, KrArGö, LK DUD Nr. 61.

[41] For more details about the territory exchange including Bad Sachsa see Gerhard Möller, ' "Keine Gebietsänderung verlief aber so dramatisch . . ." Wie Bad Sachsa und Tettenborn "in den Westen" gelangten', *Beiträge zur Geschichte aus Stadt und Kreis Nordhausen* 30 (2005).

that in case of unification they would have the necessary documents). But as the internal correspondence developed, doubts surfaced regarding such an exchange. What if the GDR used the documents so acquired to disown private landowners and/or to force collectivization of land? In addition, would surrendering copies of these documents to East German authorities not imply a formal recognition of the division of Germany and of the GDR? By 1956, federal and Lower Saxon state offices had decided that land registry documents should not be exchanged. Because they needed some legal documentation for routine administrative and economic activities, Lower Saxon authorities initiated the creation of new land registries for Bad Sachsa and assumed that similar processes would follow to solve the problem in the smaller agricultural areas as well.[42] Gleitze was forced to backpedal from his promise to take care of this issue, but he did not give up his quest to promote local interests through negotiations with his colleagues in the East.

This story provides a striking example of the symbolic-declarative nature of the exclusive representation policy. Anxious to avoid any semblance of recognition of the GDR, West German authorities opted for practices which enhanced and deepened division. In an attempt to eliminate their dependence on cross-border coordination, Western state agencies undermined common infrastructure. They worked to create a separate, self-sustaining administration, responsible for a separate part of the country and its population.

Similar news came quite quickly from the Eastern Eichsfeld. Gleitze conveyed to his Eastern interlocutors in Holungen the urgency of discussing the reopening of the border checkpoint Gerblingerode–Teistungen. By the end of July he received an updated response. The chairman of the Worbis district council, Werner Flächsig, wrote that he had raised this issue with his superiors and that they were very positively disposed towards finding a way to reopen the checkpoint. All that was required, he wrote, was for Gleitze to get his government to come to the discussion table and then official representatives of both states would be able to solve the problem. The least he expected of Gleitze was to have the district council publicly call the federal government to take up negotiations with the GDR on this issue. Gleitze replied politely a few weeks later, explaining that he could not discuss any 'political' issues. Contacts between the governments in Bonn and Pankow were 'a matter of highly political nature' (*Angelegenheit hochpolitischer Art*), he wrote, so he must refrain from even discussing this option and obviously could not accommodate Flächsig's request.[43] Though they allowed contacts and negotiations, superior state agencies in both states had not changed their position on the permitted topics of discussion and kept a close eye on frontier administrators, severely limiting the possible goals and achievements in these negotiations.

---

[42] The whole file NLA-HStAH Nds. 50 Acc. 96/88 Nr. 705 is dedicated to this issue, documenting over a hundred pages of correspondence and memos from the years 1949–58. See especially, DDR minister für Aufbau to Regierungspräsident Lüneburg, 2 November 1950; Bundesminister für gesamtdeutsche Fragen to Nds. MP, 21 December 1951, and Nds. Minister d. Justiz to Oberlandgerichtspräsident Celle, 4 January 1957.

[43] Flächsig to Gleitze, 30 July 1956, and Gleitze to Flächsig, 24 August 1956, KrAGö, LK DUD, Nr. 61.

The lively cultural exchanges, correspondences, and meetings following the celebration in Holungen created a good atmosphere, but resulted in only very modest levels of coordination. Tellingly, district administrators had not managed to establish permanent mechanisms to cooperate even on the most basic levels. Coordination continued to depend on good will and personal commitment. And when the more complicated expectations of both sides were not fulfilled, good will dwindled.

The contradictions between the practical goals and the symbolic restrictions were too great to resolve. They came to the fore after an official visit of the Duderstadt district administrator and several council members to the neighbouring districts of Worbis and Heiligenstadt in April 1957. The problems began when the GDR side refused entry at the border to the journalists who accompanied the delegation from the West. Only the six council members were allowed in. The delegation members knew that this would happen because they had to apply in advance for permits, and no permits were issued for journalists.[44] They nevertheless invited the press to the visit. This way, they got good publicity for themselves and for their efforts to promote local understanding. Moreover, they emphasized their strong commitment to a free press (albeit not so strong as to stay behind with the journalists) and presented the GDR as having something to hide. The three-day visit passed without further incident. The visitors had a rich and busy programme, saw much and met many people. They were very pleased with the atmosphere and friendly interaction. They also succeeded in blocking attempts of their East German hosts to discuss controversial issues or initiate higher-level talks.[45]

At the press conference they held upon returning, the Duderstadt politicians spoke very highly of their hosts and of the prospects for cooperation. According to reports in Western newspapers, the delegates also presented a list of issues that both sides had agreed to address in future negotiations. The list, as published in the newspapers, included 23 items. It was identical to the list Gleitze had prepared earlier for internal consumption.[46] No agreement had been reached with the Eastern Eichsfeld representatives on this or any other list. Whatever Gleitze thought when he decided to make his list public—probably that it would appease the press and positively dispose the public and his superiors toward the visit—he must have realized that it would cause problems with his Eastern colleagues. The 23-item list did not include many items that the Eastern negotiators repeatedly put on the table, like exchanging delegations of high-ranking officials. District officials in the Eastern part of the Eichsfeld and their superiors in East Berlin read these reports carefully.[47] Gleitze wrote to Flächsig to say that he should not take the reports too seriously. Flächsig replied that in his state, newspapers were taken very

---

[44] See Vorsitzende d. Rat d. Kreises Worbis to Oberkreisdirektor Duderstadt, 2 April 1957, KrArGö, LK DUD, Nr. 61.

[45] Behrens, *Regionale Identität*, 230.

[46] The newspaper stories were cut and saved at the district archive in the file that also held the correspondence. See KrArGö, LK DUD Nr. 61.

[47] The story from the Südhanoversche Zeitung was typed verbatim and saved in the district archive in the GDR part of the Eichsfeld. See KrArEich, EA HIG, Nr. 402/I.

seriously, and protested that the report was wrong to say that his council agreed with the Western delegation on a list of issues to discuss.[48] Gleitze argued that the journalists had misunderstood him, that they had just counted issues he mentioned as potential things to talk about and had made them into a fictitious plan. He probably lied. The identical wording of all 23 articles to those in his original memo suggests that he not only dictated them to the journalists, but probably handed out printed copies. This move is significant because it testifies to Gleitze's giving up on the chance of real progress. Prioritizing good public relations in the West over good terms with his Eastern colleagues suggests that he sensed that a public relations boost was the best thing he could achieve in these negotiations.[49]

Starting in 1955, Party circles in the GDR set out to instrumentalize Eichsfeld traditions for their battles of recognition against the West. Three years later, they gave up on this idea. During 1958, the two districts maintained only official contact; no delegations crossed from side to side and correspondence included mostly the subscriptions to local newspapers each district had arranged for the other. A clear indication that the GDR had decided to give up on leveraging Eichsfeld culture for recognition came in the following year. In 1959, the district of Worbis (the Eastern part of the Eichsfeld) made repeated attempts to establish working relations with the border district of Eschwege in Hesse (West). Eschwege bordered on the Eichsfeld from the southwest but did not share the religion, traditions, or regional identification of the Eichsfeld. The district administrator in Eschwege, Hans-Jochen Kubitz, mentioned at the top of this chapter, rejected all attempts from Worbis to send an official delegation. Worbis was relentless, and on two occasions sent a delegation anyway. The delegates crossed the border as private individuals with permits and surprised the district administrator in his office.[50] These tricks may have gained the GDR some marginal public relations points for trying to establish cooperation between neighbours. But with no cultural exchange or shared heritage on which to base cooperation, the political cynicism of such manoeuvres was easily discernible. None of those involved had any illusions about the chances of real cross-border cooperation emerging from this affair.

I argue that the dramatic changes of 1961 have concealed the effect of division processes during the 1950s and the less visible factors behind them. All along the inter-German border, frontier residents and administrations came together during the 1950s to seek ways to overcome difficulties caused by the emerging border. Edith Sheffer analysed in her book a similar series of meetings and negotiations between Western and Eastern frontier administrators.[51] The general contours of

---

[48] See both letters in KrArGö, LK DUD, Nr. 61.

[49] Oberkreisdirektor Gleitze to Vorsitz. d. Rat d. Kreises Flächsig, 15 January 1958, KrArGö, LK DUD, Nr. 61. On the border between Thuringia and Bavaria, another attempt at cross-border cooperation also deteriorated into press wars at about the same time. See Sheffer, *Burned Bridge*, 137.

[50] Full reports by the participants of this delegation, including newspaper reports from the West are in KrArEich, EA WBS, Nr. 2248.

[51] Sheffer, *Burned Bridge*, 136–8 (reduced from pp. 560–70 in the dissertation). I thank Edith for first pointing out to me the similarity between the two stories as I was working out an early version of this chapter.

the affair in the region she studied were quite similar to those analysed in this chapter: throughout the period, frontier administrators met and talked but could not overcome the dynamics of division. The analysis of cooperation attempts in the Eichsfeld presented here demonstrates that regional cross-border negotiations had failed before 1961, and their failure was not a result of changes in East German policy.

In Duderstadt, Gleitze heard about the Worbis administrators' attempts to force Eschwege into official meetings and contacted his colleague Flächsig. He wrote that he was sorry to have dropped the correspondence between them for a long time. After what had happened, he thought that both of them needed to negotiate with their governments in order to prevent high politics from interfering with their quest to improve life in both their districts.[52]

The reply, which Flächsig drafted and probably never sent, is fascinating. It includes an analysis of the interactions of the previous years as seen from the Eastern side—the hopes, the chances, and the frustrations. It explains well why Eastern administrators took up these negotiations, and why and how they gave them up. Finally, it states the conditions for resuming negotiations. The draft opens with an admission that Flächsig, too, felt somewhat guilty that the correspondence between the two had lapsed. Then, for more than a page, he refutes Gleitze's version of why they had lost touch. He did not think that they should both negotiate with their governments, and he did not agree that they should prevent high politics from interfering in their negotiations. On the contrary, he thought that they could advance none of the issues that mattered to them without involving high politics. Their governments should speak to each other and then all the issues Gleitze had defined as 'technical' would be easy to solve on the local level. If the Federal Republic encountered such problems along its border with Switzerland, he wrote, it would not look to a district administrator to negotiate their resolution. It would send the Foreign Minister to negotiate with his colleague across the border because inter-state negotiations are the only way to solve problems between states:

> I know that you will answer me [that] the government of the Federal Republic does not recognize the government of the GDR. Forgive me if I say so, but this is becoming ridiculous. After all, the GDR exists . . . You cannot simply ignore a full-blown fact.[53]

Nowhere was the truth of this statement as clear as it was along the inter-German border, where East German state agencies shaped crucial elements of everyday life. Relying on their influence over frontier realities, functionaries in the Eastern Eichsfeld hoped that negotiating border issues would force the West to recognize the GDR, and that Western negotiators would realize they had to interact with the GDR in order to improve conditions along the border. Eastern politicians accepted lower-level meetings assuming that the urgency of dealing with the situation along the border would draw in higher state agencies. They lost interest when they found

---

[52] I did not find a copy of this letter. I deduce its content from the draft of the reply letter. See 'Entwurf: An Oberkreisdirektor Gleitze', KrArEich, EA WBS, nr. 2248.

[53] 'Entwurf: An Oberkreisdirektor Gleitze,' KrArEich, EA WBS, nr. 2248.

that Western insistence on exclusive representation was too rigid to allow such developments.

In the second part of the letter Flächsig hinted that while he personally had not given up on the hope of negotiating with Gleitze, he had been ordered to change course and was not in a position to do anything about it. He apologized for the 'strategic impoliteness' in going to Eschwege and not visiting Duderstadt as well, and wrote that he could offer no explanation for it. He repeated the same expression, 'I can offer no explanation' (*Ich kann keine Erklärung geben*), several times, suggesting that higher authorities were involved.[54] But, he wrote, none of this was intended to break off the existing relations with the district of Duderstadt. To demonstrate this, he invited Gleitze and a delegation from his district to visit Worbis again on the occasion of the tenth anniversary of the establishment of the GDR. Flächsig thus made clear in this draft that the only way for him to get permission to renew the pursuance of relations with the Western Eichsfeld was to base them on formal recognition of the GDR. By then, Flächsig understood Gleitze's position quite well. He knew that Gleitze would never accept this offer.

Even without receiving this letter, Gleitze must have known that the more ambitious part of his efforts had failed. Beyond celebrating regional traditions and dead poets, he had hoped to promote solutions for practical problems along the border. He wanted to improve economic, ecological, and social conditions for frontier residents. He realized that this would entail recognition of some German authority east of the border and of its power to determine realities along the border. For that he needed authorization from his superiors in state and federal offices, but the authorization he received was limited and conditional. He had been instructed to bypass everything that Flächsig had been ordered to address. But as long as Gleitze avoided 'political issues', Flächsig avoided discussion of 'technical issues'. They ended up sidestepping all issues other than cultural exchanges.

Following the construction of the Berlin Wall in August 1961, GDR state agencies built increasingly ominous and sophisticated barriers along the rural border as well. Triple fences, mines, and trip wires turned illegal border crossing into a more difficult activity.[55] However, these barriers did not interrupt regional, cross-border cooperation. By then, state agencies' obsessive pursuance of their priorities in the battles over recognition of the GDR had already eliminated the possibility of achieving improvement in frontier economy and daily life through cooperation. When Eastern authorities realized that they could not use cultural exchange to achieve recognition, they put a stop to all official contact.

Caught in the web of restrictions woven by the war over exclusive representation, the two district heads felt obliged to give up their attempts to alleviate through

---

[54] For example, he wrote that he could not offer any explanation for the fact that Gleitze did not always receive the newspaper that Worbis regularly sent him. He noted that he, too, did not regularly receive the paper sent to him from Duderstadt, especially during the time of the Geneva Conference. For that too he 'could offer no explanation'. Flächsig knew very well that the GDR secret service that monitored border-crossing mail was responsible for the missing mail. He knew, too, that they would read this letter.

[55] These processes and their consequences will be discussed in Chapters IV and V.

cooperation the difficulties created by the inter-German border. Each side had to look away from the border, towards its 'own' state agencies, for solutions to these problems. Frontier residents gradually realized that the hope of turning the wheel back, enabling easy cross-border contacts, and renewing social and economic interaction was not realistic.

The determination of the West German government to ignore the GDR, together with the determination of the East German leadership to uphold its border regime and use it to win recognition, precluded cross-border cooperation for the first two decades of the inter-German border. Even relying on the thick cross-border infrastructure of long-standing relations, shared beliefs, and kinship networks in the Eichsfeld, frontier administrations could not overcome the growing division produced by the battles over recognition. Cross-border connections on local levels never ceased completely, but the scope of what was possible to achieve through them, and consequently the drive to keep such channels open, narrowed significantly from the late 1950s. Eichsfelder realized that all border-related problems should be addressed to the governments of their respective states and would only be solved within the two separate territorial jurisdictions. The well in the Eastern village of Brehme, which had supplied water for Duderstadt since 1933, was neglected and the water flow diminished over years of separation. Unable to coordinate maintenance projects with Eastern authorities, Duderstadt was forced to turn west for help in finding alternative resources. By the late 1960s, the town was ready to replace all the water from Brehme with Western sources.[56] Thus, even for their water, the two parts of the Eichsfeld were no longer mutually dependent.

As frontier residents' daily activities connected them ever more tightly with Eastern and Western state organizations, their gaze gradually turned away from the border and towards their respective capitals; their regional, cross-border communities and networks assumed an increasingly modest place in their experiences and identifications.

CONDITIONS OF EXCEPTION: SETTLING THE BORDER PATH NEAR ASBACH

The viability of cross-border networks was useful for state agencies in some extreme instances. In cases which threatened the stability and legitimacy of state-building, state agencies could and did sub-contract sensitive settlements to frontier administrators. The analysis of one such case shows that cross-border contacts were viable and effective as a channel for negotiations in the early stages of division along the inter-German border. This section also underscores the limitations of such negotiations, which indeed resulted in reduced tension, but could not yield stable, official compromises.

---

[56] Shears, *Ugly Frontier*, 180–1.

Determining the exact path of the inter-German border had not been a primary concern of the Allies in 1945. It gradually became more important as this border turned into a frontline of the Cold War. In May 1952 it suddenly became an urgent matter, as the GDR tried to seal off its border to the West. This change of policy created delicate conditions along certain parts of the border, which forced Eastern and Western state organizations to show more flexibility on issues of cross-border coordination than they otherwise allowed. The short strip of the border near the village of Asbach in the Eichsfeld was one such area. To avoid a protracted open conflict and the risk of armed clashes, both sides retreated from their positions on non-recognition and allowed low-level officials to negotiate and agree on the border between their jurisdictions. Even in this case, though, cross-border coordination was not allowed to develop into more than a temporary solution for a specific problem.

The exact path of the border between the US and Soviet zones of occupation near the village of Asbach has been disputed ever since September 1945 when the two occupation forces exchanged territory in this area. Four villages were traded by the US forces to the Soviet zone in return for two villages through which the railway passed connecting the US controlled port of Bremerhaven and the bulk of the US occupation zone in southern Germany (see Figure 3.2).[57]

From the fall of 1947, district administrators of the two relevant districts— Heiligenstadt (Soviet zone) and Witzenhausen (US zone)—tried to clarify this question. Both had a clear interest in settling the border path and exchanging land registry documents. Their land registries included listings of fields and houses which lay in another occupation zone. On the other hand, fields and houses which lay within their de-facto dominion were not on their books. Consequently, both districts, like many others along the inter-German border, lost tax revenues and had difficulty with issues like school registration, voter lists, and court files. In the early stages, Soviet and US occupation forces frustrated local understandings. In the winter of 1947–8, the Soviets insisted on solving the problem through formal exchanges of relevant documentation between newly established German authorities, committing both sides to recognize the treaty between the Allies.[58] American occupation administrators notified West German authorities that such exchanges would not be authorized because the border in this strip was 'not to be regarded as final in the sense of constitutional law'.[59]

---

[57] See Figure 3.2. For more details Gedenkstätte Grenzmuseum Schifflersgrund (ed.), *Das Wanfrieder Abkommen vom 17. September 1945* (brochure, no date or place given); Arthur Künzel, 'Das Wanfrieder Abkommen vom 17.9.1945', *Schriften des Werratalvereins Witzenhausen* 4 (1981): 28–36. For the history and details of this territory exchange see Baumann, 'Thüringische Hessen und hessische Thüringer', 1000–5.

[58] Kreis Landwirtschaftsamt Worbis to Kreisrat Worbis, 16 December 1948, KrAEich, EA HIG, nr. 402/I cites a conversation with a Soviet officer from the district headquarters.

[59] Hessisches Staatsministerium der Finanzen to Katasteramt Witzenhausen, 31 March 1947, KrAEich, EA HIG nr. 402/I cites the US military government decision on the matter saying 'die Grenze . . . nicht als endgültig im staatsrechtlichen Sinne festgesetzt anzusehen'.

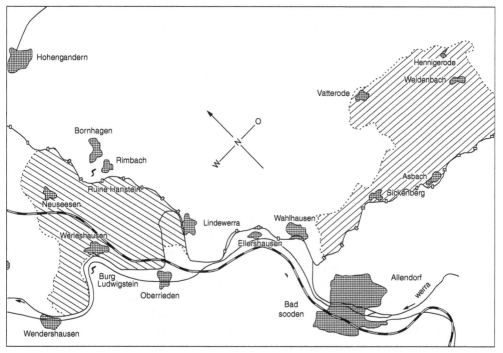

Fig. 3.2. Map of the land swap agreed upon in the Wanfried treaty of 17 September 1945. The diagonal lines mark the exchanged areas. The area to the left was transferred from the Soviet to the US zone in exchange for the area on the right.[60]

Thus, things were left as they were for a number of years, until the summer of 1952, when the GDR tried to seal the border, and turned regulating and finalizing its path into a burning issue. This short strip was one of the areas along the inter-German border that GDR border police could not build a fence or plow the ten-metre-strip along, because the exact path of the border had not been marked. Furthermore, two families inhabited the disputed area, both farming fields within it. The indecision about the border path caused repeated clashes, some almost involving the use of firearms, between East and West German forces. It also brought uncertainty, fear, and much inconvenience to the lives of the two families.[61] Border guards on both sides were acutely disturbed by this situation as well.

---

[60] The map in Figure 3.2 is originally from the border museum Schifflersgrund near Sickenberg, and can be found at www.coldwarhistory.us/Cold_War/The_Whisky-Vodka-Line/the_whisky-vodka-line.html (accessed 29 January 2014). I thank Werner I. Juretzko, who runs the website, and Wolfgang Ruske from the Grenzmuseum for allowing me to use it.

[61] Volkspolizei Berlin, 'Grenzbericht', 5 July 1952, Barch-B, DE1, Nr. 6084, 75; Hessische MdI to Hessische MP, 24 June 1952, HeHStAW, 502, Nr. 7864; Magistrat d. Stadt Bad Sooden-Allendorf to RP Kassel, 23 June 1952, HeStAM, 401/13, Nr. 5.

At the end of June 1952, the Western customs commissioner in charge of the area managed to bring together the mayor of the nearest Eastern frontier community, Asbach, and the chief administrator of the Eastern district to discuss the border path. He could not persuade their Western colleagues to come to the same meeting, so he represented the West by himself. Following this meeting, in which the GDR representatives offered a compromise, and with the background of negative press reports about incidents in this area, the district administrator in Witzenhausen decided—and was probably authorized by his superiors to whom he reported on each meeting—to enter negotiations.[62] The two sides quickly reached an agreement. The Eastern district administrator, though, made it clear that this was a state matter and he was not authorized to sign for his state. Both sides then presented their agreements to their superior authorities.

On 8 August 1952, the district administrator from Witzenhausen wrote to his superior in the county of Kassel to say that so long as the agreement he negotiated was not signed, tension in the area would rise, which played into the hands of the GDR. He asked if negotiations at higher levels were taking place to ratify and finalize the agreement; and if they were not, what should be the next step.[63] There were no negotiations. Lacking final regulation of the border path, Western and Eastern border guards assigned to the area continued to patrol the 'habitual border' (*Gebrauchsgrenze*), and tried to avoid misunderstandings and clashes. The situation remained unchanged for almost a year, with both sides trying to avoid open conflict and at the same time assert their authority in the disputed territory (see Figure 3.3).

Unable to seal this corner of the border, Eastern frontier administrations found it very difficult to address problems to which division gave rise in the community of Asbach. Much of the agricultural land of this community lay in the US zone of occupation, and thus many residents were cut off from their fields.[64] A large number of them decided to move illegally to the West. In the months following May 1952, two families from the village were deported to the GDR hinterland and many others crossed to the West. As long as the border path in the area had not been finalized, regional authorities could not persuade Asbach farmers to take up alternative land. The farmers feared that by doing so they would be giving up legal claims to their fields, which they still hoped to work. The authorities feared that more of them would opt for the West. To prevent this, the GDR had to supply them with fodder for their cattle and cash support just to keep them afloat. Moreover, those who crossed to the West settled mostly in the nearby town of Bad Sooden-Allendorf, and stole across the border at night to retrieve their livestock.[65] During the year following May 1952, 100 residents of Asbach, almost

[62] Landrat Witzenhausen to Hess. MdI, 31 July 1952, HeStAM, 401/13, Nr. 5.

[63] Landrat Witzenhausen to RP Kassel, 8 August 1952, HeStAM, 401/13, Nr. 5.

[64] The reasons for this and similar problems and the conflicts to which they gave rise are the subject of Chapter II.

[65] 'Situationsbericht über die Gemeinde Asbach/Sickenberg', 19 September 1952, KrAEich, EA HIG, 192.

Fig. 3.3. A view of Asbach from the northwest showing the disputed valley.
Photo by the author, July 2008.

a third of the village's population, left for the West, dramatically changing its demography.[66]

The two families residing in the disputed area became exhausted by the uncertainty and repeated run-ins with border forces and sought asylum in the FRG. The story of these two farmhouses and the families that inhabited them is complex and curious. As old mills, the two houses stood on the stream which was accepted (absent accurate maps detailing the agreement) as the habitual border between the occupation zones-turned-states. The residents of these houses received US zone and West German papers, but socially and economically lived in the Soviet zone and the GDR. Following May 1952, they were forced to pick a side. They opted for the West and eventually lost access to their houses and fields.[67]

In May 1953, East German state agencies finally decided to give up on the idea of settling the border path and turn the temporarily patrolled line into a permanent border. Putting many plows to work together, GDR border forces set to plow a ten-metre-strip along one of the last sections of the inter-German border, which

---

[66] 'Bericht über die durchgeführte Komplexuntersuchung in der Gemeinde Asbach', 27 July 1959, KrAEich, EA HIG, 402/II.

[67] Gustav Neuenroth to Bundesministerium für gesamtdeutsche Fragen, 6 June 1953, Barch-K, B137, Nr. 1478.

remained unmarked. The Hessian Minister of the Interior reported to the Federal Minister of the Interior that in doing so they stuck to the path negotiated by the district administrators a year earlier, which neither side formally approved.[68] A few days later he learned that this was only almost accurate. The plowed strip, along which Eastern forces began building a barbed-wire fence, departed from that agreement in one important area in order to include the disputed farmhouses in the GDR. It was not clear if that was a mistake or not, but it very quickly achieved one thing—Western representatives again wanted to negotiate the border path.

Two days later, the district administrator from Witzenhausen met his counterpart from Heiligenstadt, both accompanied by aides and by border police officers. The Western side presented the agreement of the previous summer and asked that it be respected. The Eastern side replied that this agreement had never been ratified and signed. The district administrator from Witzenhausen, the senior representative of the FRG in this negotiation, decided at this point to give up the farmhouses, which had been deserted for almost a year. He traded them for another small patch including an agricultural road used by Western frontier farmers.[69]

The owner of one of the farmhouses was present, working his nearby field, and tried to intervene, but the district administrator excluded him from the discussion. In his complaint letter to the Federal Minister for All-German Affairs, this farmer asked who empowered a district administrator to negotiate away federal territory.[70] The minister had not known about this and asked his colleagues in the Ministry of the Interior and the Foreign Office. He emphasized that local authorities did not have the power to legally change agreements between the Allies. He wrote to the Federal Minister of the Interior that he understood that local-level coordination was required to allow routine border-guarding missions. On the other hand, such coordination robbed the federal government and the Western Allies of the ability to protect their citizens and it had to be made clear that they bore no binding legal power.[71]

Unbeknownst to all parties involved in the local negotiation (except, perhaps, representatives of the federal border guard), the FRG's Ministry of the Interior had had word a year earlier from the US occupation forces that the most accurate map they had of the exchange of territory with the Soviets put the two houses squarely in Soviet territory.[72] After several more months of lively exchanges about this question, somebody in the Ministry of the Interior pulled this information out and it was sent to the Foreign Office. From there it went to the Ministry of All-German Affairs and to the owner of the farmhouse.[73]

[68] Hessische MdI to BMdI, 28 May 1953, HeHStAW, 502 Nr. 7862.

[69] See the detailed report on these negotiations: Landrat Witzenhausen to Hess. MdI, 3 June 1953, HeStAM, 401/13, Nr. 5.

[70] Gustav Neuenroth to Bundesministerium für gesamtdeutsche Fragen, 6 June 1953, BArch-K, B137, Nr. 1478.

[71] Bundesministerium für gesamtdeutsche Fragen to BmdI, 29 August 1953, BArch-K, B137, Nr. 1478.

[72] 'Lage bei Untermühle bei Asbach', 26 August 1952, BArch-K, B137, Nr. 1478.

[73] Auswärtiges Amt to Bundesminister für gesamtdeutsche Fragen, 17 October 1953, BArch-K, B137, Nr. 1478.

It seemed in retrospect that the district administrator negotiated a good deal for the FRG, but this is not the real question. At no point did any of the parties acknowledge that he was empowered to do so, but none of them denied it either. Faced with a challenging question about the authority of a minor official to determine territorial jurisdiction, the federal government remained silent. This silence was telling—West German ministries were clearly aware that the district administrator in Witzenhausen was empowered to negotiate this problem away.

This case demonstrates the sensitivity for both sides of settling the inter-German border. The assertion of state power along the border was crucial for East German state agencies in 1952. It was an attempt to proclaim statehood and force the West to come to terms with it. Effectively sealing the border was also important for Eastern state agencies in order to improve their position vis-à-vis frontier residents, who used easy border crossings to manipulate regulations. Despite these pressing concerns, Eastern forces were cautious, wary that tensions might degenerate into open conflict and threaten the stability of the border, upon which the East German claim to statehood relied. This was the frontline of the Cold War, and even local clashes had ominous potential. Thus, there was a limit to the unilateral assertiveness the GDR could risk.

The volatility of the Cold War border, and the problems that its unclear path caused for border forces and frontier life, forced Western state agencies to deal with the reality of this border. Unwilling officially to diverge from their stance of non-recognition, Western ministries empowered a low-level frontier politician to negotiate what had become an urgent problem. The GDR's closing of the border achieved part of its goal in this case—it forced Western state agencies to deal directly with their Eastern counterparts, implicitly recognizing the existence and authority of the GDR. However, it was not enough to actually achieve official recognition. Having been quite anxious to settle the question as well, Eastern state agencies relented on its demand for agreement on higher levels of state. This was a rare case, in which cross-border coordination seemed the only way for Western and Eastern state offices to avoid the risk of open violence. Immediate interests of stability and state-building trumped Western non-recognition and Eastern insistence on formal recognition.

Asbach remained a troubled spot along the border throughout the GDR's existence. Only in the mid-1970s, through the joint border committee, did both German states officially mark the border near Asbach.[74] The original population of the village lived on both sides of the border and kept up lively contacts across it. Those who remained in Asbach received many added benefits from the GDR in alternative land, increased salaries, and more, and neighbouring communities regarded them as privileged. Despite these benefits, the villagers were reported to have kept up contacts with the West and have held 'negative perspectives' of the GDR. In 1989, when the GDR began to crumble, an initiative from the village

---

[74] The joint border committee and its activity will be discussed in Chapter V.

called for a return of Asbach and the three other villages from Thuringia (former GDR) to Hesse.

CONCLUSION

The Western decision to internationally isolate the GDR had made recognition of the East German state into the most central conflict between the two German states. Both of them were unwilling to risk compromise on recognition in all but the rare, extreme cases during the 1950s and 1960s. In the mid-1950s, party circles in East Germany harnessed regional identification and traditions in the Eichsfeld in an attempt to secure Western recognition. Fearing exactly that, Western state agencies instructed local politicians not to accept discussion of controversial issues and avoid at all cost any formal recognition of the negotiated problems as inter-state matters. Strictly keeping to this line, the Western side exposed the real motivations behind the Eastern initiative. When they understood that even implied recognition was not to be had, GDR party circles ordered the local representatives to withdraw from the negotiations altogether.

As the efforts to settle the border near Asbach demonstrated, when given enough rope, frontier residents and their representatives were able to reach quick understandings and solve even complex problems. But the vast majority of issues frontier residents and administrators hoped to regulate and coordinate could not command the same urgency for state organizations as did avoiding armed clashes along the Cold War border. Frontier residents knew that many of their goals, such as good education, clean water, and preservation of regional traditions, could be partially achieved through stable cross-border coordination. They had been pursuing such cooperation across administrative and state borders for centuries previously. As demonstrated by Duderstadt's relinquishing of land taxes and having its woods tended to in return, cross-border social and economic networks of Eichsfeld residents were thick and effective in the postwar years.

Priorities shaped by the battles over recognition of the GDR led Eastern and Western state agencies to undermine most initiatives for institutional cross-border cooperation. To ensure local interests, frontier administrations had to adapt to the rules and comply with the demands of these new, Western and Eastern, state agencies. Frontier residents adjusted, changing their practices to maximize opportunities and minimize risks. The accumulation of many such changes in orientation and shifts in practice worked to weaken cross-border religious, kinship, and economic networks, thus contributing to the process of German division.

Frontier residents and administrators had a much greater role in this process than scholars have until recently assumed. Edith Sheffer's work most clearly has returned the agency of 'ordinary Germans' to the analysis of the Iron Curtain's evolution. However, this chapter suggests we should interpret their agency cautiously. During the 1950s, there was room for initiative and action on both sides of the inter-German border. In the Eichsfeld and elsewhere, frontier residents initiated cross-border contacts and found ways to persuade state agencies to allow them. But such initiatives ran into the wall of state agencies' obsession with recognition. Local agency was important in shaping life along the border and the meanings attached to the border over time, but only within the limits imposed by state organizations. The infrastructure of long-standing networks in the Eichsfeld remained in place after 1959. But after the short revival in the mid-1950s, official cultural and political exchange dwindled and died out. There remained contacts between district administrations on technical issues, but after 1961 even those deteriorated, and towards the late 1960s they disappeared completely.[75] By 1969, Gleitze's successor had given up on the hope of renewing contact with the East German Eichsfeld districts.[76] As shown in Chapter V, when the border opened frontier administrators in the Eichsfeld were so estranged from their cross-border colleagues that they found it hard to initiate contact.

A key stage in the creation and solidification of the Iron Curtain was the creation of physical, social, and cultural distance between former neighbours, friends, and relatives, and the gradual expansion of these distances. In the 1970s, as Chapter V of this book shows, the inter-German border had become the effective division of a nation and a continent; ominous, controlled, and well-guarded as its image suggested. Under Willy Brandt, the West German federal government had given up exclusive representation and, in 1972, signed an official treaty with the GDR. In the following year, the Eichsfeld checkpoint between Gerblingerode and Teistungen was finally reopened.[77] It had been closed for over two decades. In the meantime, division had become a stable experience. Regional and local problems were solved, festivals were celebrated, riverbeds cleared, land tilled, and produce bought and sold separately. East and West of the border, frontier residents had found ways to pursue their interests within the frameworks created by 'their own' state agencies, and those states had become more 'their own' in this process.

There is no telling how cross-border networks and identifications would have fared had West Germany accepted in 1949 the existence of a second German state. When it decided to drop exclusive representations, these networks were no longer as significant for most frontier residents as they had been two decades earlier. They had become two separate communities. Their energy and time were invested in separate directions. Turning their gaze gradually more towards their eastern and western hinterlands, they also spent more time with their backs towards the border and what lay across it. Chapter IV takes up the processes presented in the first three chapters and discusses their development until the end of the 1960s, including a major shift in GDR policy between 1959 and 1961. Chapter V analyses the dramatic transformation of the inter-German border's function following the Basic Treaty between the two German states in December 1972, and follows the development of division until its demise in 1989.

---

[75] Oberkreisdirektor Dud to RP Hildesheim, 16 June 1964, KrAGö, LK DUD, 1140. Cf. Landkreis Gö to RP Hildesheim, 19 June 1964, KrAGö, LK Gö, A32, Nr. 4.
[76] Oberkreisdirektor Dud to RP Hildesheim, 6 June 1969, KrAGö, LK DUD, Nr. 1140.
[77] These developments are analysed in Chapter V.

IV

For Land or Country?
Frontier Land and the Process of Division, 1952–69

Weeds became a serious problem around the inter-German border in the mid-1960s. The first alarm rang on the western side of the border in 1963:

> The infestation with weeds is progressing quickly within the greatly expanded border-strip. Approximate calculations show that because of the 100–200 meter wide waste-lands along the border, an additional kilometer on either side of the border is suffering from constantly growing infestation with pest plants.[1]

The decline of agriculture on both sides of the border, the expansion of barriers and border installations, and the growing rigidity of East German border regulation had gradually turned a broad strip along the border into a 'no man's land'. The weed infestation was but one consequence of this development, but reactions to it on both sides were typical of state–society relations along the border. East German farmers had no say in the matter. Only collective members still had access to land along the border in some places, and collectives tried to get rid of such fields because working them had become increasingly difficult. East German border-guarding forces resorted to area-spraying with strong herbicides to prevent the overgrowth from turning into a potential hideout. This caused even greater damages to Western farming along the border. West German farmers requested compensation from Western regional and federal authorities. Local authorities pushed complaints up the chain of federal bureaucracy until an agreement regulating compensations was reached between the four border states and the federal government. Cross-border negotiation and coordination was not seriously considered. All negotiations took place within separate territorial state jurisdictions.[2] The unfolding of this problem and its solutions encapsulates the story of the tension between state and society surrounding the process of division during the 1950s and 60s. Border formation gave rise to serious problems in agricultural work. Initially these problems stirred conflicts between frontier farmers and state agencies, but eventually the problems were digested by bureaucratic procedures, alleviated

---

[1] Vereinigung Landwirtschaftlicher Ringe beim Kuratorium für Wirtschaftsberatung e.V. to Landkreis Göttingen, 28 August 1963, KrAGö, LK Gö, A32, Nr. 14.

[2] Vereinigung Landwirtschaftlicher Ringe beim Kuratorium für Wirtschaftsberatung e.V. to Landkreis Göttingen, 28 August 1963, KrAGö, LK Gö, A32 Nr. 14; 'Unkrautbekämpfung im Bereich der Zonengrenze durch das ostzonale Grenzkommando', 30 May 1968, KrAGö, LK Gö, A32, Nr. 2.

through money transfers, or dealt with by military orders; conflict was replaced with compromise and acceptance.

Chapter II covered the first dramatic year of struggle over property rights along the inter-German border. The current chapter investigates the trajectory of this struggle over the following two decades and analyses its influence on the development of German division. Through intensive struggles with state agencies during the 1950s, frontier farmers learned to orient themselves toward the legal and institutional frameworks created by state organizations. In the following decade, state agencies and frontier residents on both sides of the border found ways to reach compromises, protecting the most important interests of all involved. Three factors were crucial in making these compromises possible: economic stabilization and growth on both sides of the border; the diminishing role of agriculture; and an at least de-facto acceptance of the finality of the border.

The fall and winter of 1952–3 were marked by a feverish scramble for land on the part of frontier farmers and for control, authority, and economic viability on the part of Eastern and Western state agencies. The dust began to settle during the spring of 1953; different groups of frontier farmers solidified their positions, and state agencies formed clearer policies. Lines of conflict were drawn between camps. The Cold War stamped heavily the contours of the diplomatic battle between the two German states, and played an important role in border policies on both sides of the border. Frontier farmers were less consumed by this overarching struggle. But, as shown in Chapter III, the conflict between West and East affected them nevertheless.

Interpretive frameworks and opposing interests on issues of agricultural and border policy clashed throughout the 1950s. The inter-German border was thus not just a scene of East–West conflict but also of state–society struggle. The lines of conflict and cooperation shifted according to the issues at hand. At times they paralleled the inter-German border but at others they crossed and challenged border regimes. Many frontier residents interacted continuously with their fellows across the border, using their ability to cross the border to promote their interests. They cooperated with state agencies if and when these agencies offered support for their goals or applied enough pressure on them. They aligned with or against frontier farmers from the other side for similar reasons.

Though the inter-German border did not dictate the lines of alliance and conflict, it did shape the goals and values of everyone involved. Irrespective of their principal stance regarding division frontier residents and state agencies were forced to reckon with it. Their tactics and strategies, even when aimed at undermining the division, oriented themselves towards the reality of the border and its effects.

State agencies and frontier farmers along the border were involved in heated land conflicts during the 1950s. In the GDR, the decade ended with the campaign to impose full collectivization of agriculture in 1959–60. This campaign ended with a compromise, whereby the public showcase of successful collectivization was maintained while the actual practice of farming went almost unchanged in many cases. This kind of compromise exemplifies the way conflicts about land and agriculture played out along the border during the 1960s, in both the West and the East. Changes in policy, economic growth, and shifts in the balance of power between state and non-state organizations and groups framed a calmer dynamic for the 1960s. On both sides of the border, the significance of land ownership diminished markedly during that decade and frontier farmers' positions regarding their land became more flexible. At the same time, state agencies on both sides of the border found ways to allow frontier farmers to protect economic interests without compromising political-symbolic dogmas. On the heels of a decade of conflict, then, came a decade of compromise between frontier farmers and state agencies.

The compromises were made possible by the fact that frontier residents now related differently to the land they inhabited. As demonstrated in Chapter II, the intimate connection between farmers and their land had been a major obstacle to the construction and solidification of the inter-German border. Farmers' insistence on retaining their land, their knowledge of the terrain, and their ability to undermine border controls and regulations kept this border rather frail and porous. The 1960s saw significant economic and infrastructure changes in East and West Germany, massive construction of barriers on the Eastern side and investments in industry and the restructuring of agriculture on both sides. These processes all but eliminated most farmers' attachment to their land as an obstacle to border solidification. A growing proportion of the land along both sides of the border was no longer tilled; fewer people lived on it and fewer still worked on it. Physical distance between Eastern and Western frontier residents grew. Their shared commitment to the land faded and with it faded their mutual ability to circumvent regulations. State agents had gradually acquired, through years of patrolling and surveying, much of that same knowledge of the frontier.

A DECADE OF CONFLICT: 1952–61

Many frontier residents regarded themselves as victims of the border and of the conflicting policies of the East and West German state organizations. As discussed in Chapter II, frontier farmers who had lost access to their fields were among the hardest hit. Conflicts over recognition of the GDR had pitted state organizations in East and West Germany against each other, and also put them at odds with frontier farmers. State agencies on both sides of the border tried to win over frontier populations as part of their efforts to enforce authority along the border.

Western Conflicts

Bonn was unwilling to grant frontier farmers full compensation (in alternative land or in cash) for land in the GDR to which they lost access. The West German Federal Government's reasoning was that such compensation would entail recognition of the de-facto confiscation of the land by East German state agencies. West German state agencies also protected the ownership rights of Eastern frontier farmers by allowing its citizens to work fields owned by GDR citizens only as trustees, through private or state-proffered contracts. In practice, this meant that the FRG offered very limited help to its frontier farmers. As mentioned in Chapter II, the only help state agencies offered these farmers during the first year following May 1952, was compensation of up to 50 per cent of lost income on expected harvest sales. In 1952, Western authorities were taken by surprise and had to react quickly to a new situation, which they regarded as temporary. But even with more time at hand, West German state agencies did not change their policy.

As the 1950s progressed, frontier farmers developed more sophisticated and aggressive tactics in their struggle for compensation. They learned to use the explosive conflict between East and West to leverage for attention. As mentioned in Chapter II, of all the border communities in the Western part of the Eichsfeld, Fuhrbach was the one to lose the largest portion of private agricultural land. One hundred and twenty households in the community lost private land, some as much as 80 per cent of their land. In addition, there was no land available to take up in trusteeships near the village.[3] In 1954, the village councilmen, frustrated with the inadequate support, changed the tone of their interaction with state agencies. Rather than simply stressing the losses and difficulties that their community suffered as a result of the border closing, they began to make accusations, expressing bitterness towards their state.

Fuhrbach villagers attacked the contradictions at the heart of the West German state-building project, seeking to exploit the sensitivity to which they gave rise in order to promote their goals. In January 1954, Alfons Hoppmann, Fuhrbach's representative in the district council, wrote to an assistant secretary in the Lower Saxon Ministry of Economy and Transportation. He described in some detail the plight of two farmers in Fuhrbach. In closing, he diverged from the polite language that characterized correspondence on the topic, threatening that the residents of Fuhrbach would not accept being put off much longer. 'Vicious rumors,' he warned, 'maintain that, if practical help would not be allocated in the near future, people will contact the government of the Eastern Zone.'[4]

A private letter from the same month shows that Hoppmann's threat was not an empty one, as some Fuhrbach farmers indeed considered turning to the East German government for help. Fritz Bönning, who had lost some land himself, had asked a cousin of his in the GDR to find out if there was a chance to get some kind of compensation from the East German government. The reply letter was saved in the Duderstadt city archive, testifying probably to Bönning's attempts to use it with the authorities. The letter states that Eastern frontier farmers were compensated by their government with alternative land. Bönning's cousin Willi did not think it wise to turn to his government and replied that Western frontier farmers should get compensation from 'own' government.[5]

---

[3] Landkreis Duderstadt to RP Hildesheim, 17 June 1952, NLA-HStAH, 120 Hildesheim, Acc. 60/78, Nr. 2. Here pp. 21, 25–9.

[4] Alfons Hoppmann to Ministerialdirigent Kleine, 12 January 1954, StADud, Fuhr 326.

[5] W. L. to Fritz Bönning, 28 January 1954, StADud, Fuhr 326.

In his aforementioned letter, district council member Hoppmann added that a representative of the ministry, whom he had recently taken on a tour of the village, had suggested that the federal government would work to solve the problems of the village through reactivation of the KGV.[6] Hoppmann regarded this idea as evasive. First of all, the authorities across the border had already broken down, rearranged, and assigned Fuhrbach plots to other farmers. Secondly, no one could tell how long such new arrangements would hold. Crossing the border frequently to uphold contact with relatives and friends, Western frontier residents witnessed facts being set on the ground. Their government's unwillingness to recognize the new reality entailed a rejection of their demands for compensation. Fuhrbach representatives expected the federal government to realize that their land was gone and they deserved to be compensated for it. They presented East German policy as more realistic and hinted that they were willing to politically embarrass their government by turning to the GDR for help.

Nine months later, the mayor of Fuhrbach summarized the community's grievances once again.[7] He was mostly concerned with establishing Fuhrbach as a unique case requiring extraordinary state intervention. He aimed clearly at deflecting state agencies' claims that the federal government had to see the broader picture and could not treat Fuhrbach as an isolated case. The villagers realized that the money, and the power to decide whether to give or withhold it, lay with the federal government in Bonn.

In early 1956, after another year had passed with no change in relevant West German policy, Fuhrbach villagers tried to circumvent bureaucracy and went directly to the top of the pyramid. Two of their more radical representatives wrote a letter, endorsed by the village mayor, to the chancellor, Konrad Adenauer, with copies to the chairmen of all Bundestag parties and to the Lower Saxon governor.[8] In this letter, the two presented their community not simply as a victim of East German policy but of West German greed as well. The British occupation forces had exchanged territories, which had belonged to Hanover for centuries, they wrote, for the economic benefits they saw in territories they received from the Soviets in return. Specifically, they argued, the British occupation zone had received an economically important strip of land in the Harz region from the Soviets in exchange for the land taken from Fuhrbach.[9] More than three years of frustrated pleading, explaining, and demanding from local and regional state agencies radicalized Fuhrbach's negotiators. In 1956, they directly accused the

---

[6] This was the title given to an array of different arrangements which allowed relatively easy border crossing for routine work purposes from 1946 to 1952. For more details see Chapter II.

[7] 'Die Geschädigten der Gemeinde Fuhrbach fordern', 3 September 1954, StADud, Fuhr 326.

[8] For a copy of this letter, see Fritz Bönning and Willi Eggert im Auftrag der Zonengrenzgeschädigten der Gemeinde Fuhrbach to Bundeskanzler Dr. Konrad Adenauer, 4 March 1956, NLA-HstAH Nds. 120 Hildesheim, Acc. 60/78, Nr. 2. For the short personal appeal to the Lower Saxon Minister President introducing his copy of the letter, see Fritz Bönning and Willi Eggert to Nds. Ministerpräsidenten, Fuhrbach, 4 March 1956, in the same file.

[9] This remains the explanation commonly accepted in Fuhrbach for the loss of the village's land: to date no proof has been found to the existence of a connection between the border changes in these two areas.

federal government of making economic profits on their back, leaving a small community's farmers to pay the price for a deal from which the whole state benefited.

This letter succeeded in drawing state agencies' attention to the village, but all the villagers won was a chance to plead their case again. Two months after endorsing this letter, the village council received a delegation from the county of Hildesheim. For the first time, a state agency above district level directly engaged the village's demands. The visitors listened selectively. The author of the memo summarizing this meeting detailed only those demands of the villagers that he could flat out deny as unrealistic or legally impossible.[10] He did not provide any details about the more moderate financial demands made by the village council, nor did he propose any answers to these demands. He reported the financial support received by the community in previous years (1952–5) and added that 'Because the claimants were not satisfied by these allocations, the matter had been repeatedly taken up, but nevertheless a solution acceptable to the community of Fuhrbach could not be found.'[11]

During the 1950s, Bonn had to deal with the demands of other groups of citizens who suffered economic damages as a result of the GDR's official sealing of the border. For federal officials, Fuhrbach was just one of many such cases. That the Allies swapped land strips between them was beyond the FRG's control. In Bonn, the broader perspective of Western 'German policy' (*Deutschlandpolitik*) as presented in Chapter III, overshadowed any local economic considerations.

A fascinating example of this reasoning and its power was documented in an internal memo of the MfgF from March 1958. It demonstrates how the concentration of resources under state agencies' control allowed them to impose their viewpoints and interests. Recognizing that federal agencies held the power to allocate significant resources, individuals and groups who suffered financially from the process of division turned to these agencies for help. They found that in order to gain access to these resources they had to accept state organizations' assumptions and prerogatives. An anonymous MfgF official summarized a meeting with representatives of an association of West Berlin residents who owned property in the Eastern part of the city.[12] This organization represented roughly 30,000 West Berliners who saw their houses or land confiscated after May 1952.[13] They aimed to unite all citizens of West Germany who had suffered similar problems as a consequence of the GDR's closing of the border in May 1952. The initial demand

---

[10] 'Vermerk über die Bereisung der Gemeinde Fuhrbach', 29 May 1956, NLA-HstAH, Nds. 120 Hildesheim, Acc. 60/78, Nr. 2. For the details behind this reasoning, see Chapter II.

[11] 'Vermerk über die Bereisung der Gemeinde Fuhrbach', 29 May 1956, NLA-HstAH, Nds. 120 Hildesheim, Acc. 60/78, Nr. 2, 4.

[12] The Association of Aggrieved Eastern House and Land Owners, Private Home Owners and Interested Parties (*Vereinigung ostgeschädigter Haus- und Grundbesitzer, Eigenheimer und Eigenheim-Interessenten e.V.*).

[13] 'Vereinigung ostgeschädigter Haus- und Grundbesitzer, Eigenheimer und Eigenheim-Interessenten e.V', Bonn, 19 March 1958, BArch-K, B137, Nr. 3139.

presented in this meeting was for financial compensation for the confiscated property.

The MfgF official gave the answer that Fuhrbach villagers were familiar with: that the FRG did not recognize the confiscation and therefore could not compensate for it; that the federal government's goal, rather, was to achieve a reunification, and with it the return of the property to its lawful owners. The representatives of the organization conceded that legislating such compensation would entail recognition of the 'Soviet occupation zone' as an independent second German state. Unable to counter this political reasoning, they asked for stop-gap assistance (*Überbrückungshilfe*) of up to 1,000 DM for each confiscated property.[14] In rejecting this demand, the official used a combination of administrative, pragmatic, and political arguments. How could the federal government locate all the people who should be included in such a program? How could it verify their claims? The federal government could not simply ask anyone whose property in the 'Eastern zone' had been confiscated to register, because that would evoke expectations for compensation and might be taken as recognition of the confiscation. To undertake a project of this scope, a federal agency or office would have to be created, with a considerable budget, and much time would pass before this agency would even be able to compile a list of potential beneficiaries.

Overwhelmed by these arguments, the president of the organization requested time to prepare an assistance request for West Berlin alone. Like the villagers of Fuhrbach, he too could not counter bureaucratic consideration of the overarching federal perspective and opted instead for presenting a unique case, which should be treated separately.

The two examples show how problems created by the process of division along the border forced frontier residents to interact closely with state agencies. Policies and interests were justified with 'interests of the state', overruling problems and demands of individuals and groups, thus reinforcing the effect of the state. These cases also reveal the interconnection of state-building and border formation. State organizations used their resources to enforce certain priorities within their territorially bound jurisdictions and were unable to effect developments beyond it. Their insistence on de-legitimizing state organizations in East Germany only emphasized the power and independence of these organizations vis-à-vis their Western rivals. Western and Eastern state-building projects thus reinforced each other and the role of the border between them.

The campaigns of Fuhrbach farmers and Berlin homeowners to win federal compensation both failed during the 1950s. West German state agencies found ways to reject demands for greater compensation by different groups of people whose economic position was hampered by the solidification of the border in 1952. They could not, however, placate these populations, giving rise to growing dissatisfaction. By the late 1950s and early 1960s, the sealing of the border seemed less and less temporary and Western state agencies, with more money at hand, searched

---

[14] The representatives of this organization showed no knowledge of the fact that farmers along the border had been receiving such stop-gap assistance since 1952.

for ways to put an end to such grievances. Still tied to the exclusive representation logic, their options were limited.

A correspondence between the Federal, Bavarian, and Hessian Ministers of Agriculture and Forestry from 1959–60 demonstrates the will to find a solution and the inability to achieve this within the existing political and economic framework. In September 1959, the Federal Ministry of Agriculture and Forestry under Werner Schwartz suggested offering generous loans to frontier farmers who owned land across the border so that they could buy alternative land in the West.[15] In his reply, the Hessian minister, Gustav Hacker, argued that this initiative was not only unfeasible but also would not address properly the grievances of frontier farmers, at least in Hessen. In the smallholders' regions (such as the Eichsfeld) land was very scarce, he wrote, and prices for available plots had risen over their earning capacity. Consequently, Hacker added, most frontier farmers who owned land east of the border would not find alternative plots even if they had the money.

But that was only part of the problem. According to the Hessian minister, frontier farmers would not accept loans as an adequate solution to their plight. A loan was not compensation because a loan, even a very convenient one, has to be repaid. Hacker added: 'I am therefore of the opinion, that only real compensation payments should replace the existing financial aid.'[16]

By 1959, the Hessian minister understood the positions of frontier farmers quite well. He realized that they considered their fields in the GDR as lost and therefore were not seeking more stop-gap funds but real compensation. With the passing of time, and with no change in sight, their demands made sense to more people, including within different arms of the state. At that point, the cause of frontier farmers, refugees from the GDR, and other Western citizens who owned property in the East became politically valuable enough to attract the attention of the national parties. In the Federal Ministry for Internal German Relations (*Ministerium für innerdeutsche Beziehungen*, formerly the MfgF) the lights burned late phrasing answers to motions from opposition parties on this subject.

In late 1959, the ministry prepared talking points for the minister in reply to one such motion in the Bundestag.[17] According to this document, the federal government agreed that it was necessary to collect and verify as much information as possible about confiscation of property in the 'Soviet occupation zone'.[18] The federal government, as the text stated, was already doing just that, spending public money on an archive of land holdings (*Archiv für Grundbesitz e. V*), which received and checked claims of FRG citizens to legal ownership of land east of the border. The government also financed the work of the 'investigating committee of free

---

[15] The Hessian minister referred to this idea in his reply letter. See Hessische Minister für Landwirtschaft und Forsten to Bundesminister für Ernährung, Landwirtschaft und Forsten, 9 February 1960, HeHStAW 502, Nr. 3563.

[16] Hessische Minister für Landwirtschaft und Forsten to Bundesminister für Ernährung, Landwirtschaft und Forsten, 9 February 1960, HeHStAW 502, Nr. 3563.

[17] 'Sprechzettel zur Frage der Bundespolitik', 20 November 1959, BArch-K, B137, Nr. 3139.

[18] The text uses alternatively the acronym SBZ and the term Central Germany (*Mitteldeutschland*) to refer to the territory of the GDR. This strategy and its consequences are discussed in Chapter III.

jurists' (*Untersuchungsausschuss freiheitlicher Juristen*) examining other kinds of damages. But the federal government wanted such inquiries to maintain a low profile and opposed attempts to endow them with legal power. This was primarily, according to the document, because of the fear that formal government action might be taken to entail recognition of the confiscation. The second reason was that the information collected by these organizations could not, in Bonn's opinion, be accurate enough to serve as a basis for a just action for the benefit of all Germans. Seventeen million East Germans could not be consulted or asked for information; neither could GDR land registry offices be expected to contribute to the effort. Any attempt to compensate for confiscated property was bound therefore to neglect damages caused to—and therefore discriminate against—millions of Germans whom the federal government claimed to represent. Consequently, the federal government saw the efforts to collect information as important preparatory work to make compensation quicker and easier after the reunification of Germany, which remained, stated the document, the primary goal of the government's policy.

Bureaucrats in Bonn and in the different state administrations invested much thought in this issue throughout the 1950s. Confronted by growing pressure from more and better organized aggrieved groups, they came up with more elaborate arguments and explanations for the FRG's position. From the vantage point of frontier farmers, and others who owned and lost property in the GDR, the bottom line had not changed. Western state agencies insisted on the vague prospect of unification at an unknown future as the primary policymaking anchor. Thus, they were unwilling to compensate property owners for their losses, insisting, in the face of reality, that these were temporary losses. In the eyes of Western frontier farmers, the federal government sacrificed their immediate real interests in order to protect the assumed future rights of Eastern frontier farmers.

Eastern Conflicts

As in the West, so too in the East, state agencies demanded that frontier farmers who owned land across the border pay a price for border formation. GDR leadership circles saw the border as a declaration of independent statehood, and devised border policies that would compel the West to recognize it. The chronological orientation of East German state agencies was exactly the opposite to that of Western ones: they wanted and expected an immediate and irreversible transformation of reality. State agencies wanted to centrally control the use of land along the border for two major purposes: they wanted to secure agricultural productivity in order to feed the population, and they aimed to preclude any challenge to the official view of the border. But in the context of frontier agriculture, these two goals turned out to be contradictory.

Confronted with such contradictions, state agencies prioritized the demonstration of state power over ensuring productivity. In pursuing this goal, state agencies deported many frontier farmers to the hinterland (many others crossed to the West to avoid the risk of deportation) and saw those who remained as suspect due to their cross-border connections. State agencies tried to win over farmers from the hinterland and refugees from the former German territories in Eastern Europe as new frontier farmers. Eastern frontier farmers (those who were not deported and did not cross to the West) received compensation in alternative land for plots they owned in the West. In return, the state demanded that they give up property they held in the West. But many frontier farmers did not view this as a fair deal. They only got alternative land up to ten hectares (approx. 24.5 acres). As state agencies preferred others over them, the plots they received were not in all cases comparable in quality to those they had lost. They also realized that these plots were still claimed by their West German owners and that in the future their hold on them might be disputed. They therefore never officially gave up their property in the West and enjoyed at least part of the income derived from these plots.[19] They were able to do so partly because they enjoyed a strong bargaining position that state agencies had not taken into consideration in advance.

Following the announcement of the new border regime in May 1952, it seemed that East German state agencies had the power to determine property ownership and use along the border. Centrally planned in Berlin, police and party units arrived in frontier communities during the first half of June and deported thousands of residents to the hinterland. Many others left for the West before they could be deported.[20] The land of these people (in the Eichsfeld, mostly smallholding farmers), along with the land of Western frontier farmers, was to be tilled under the authority of district administrations.

Decision makers in East Berlin devised solutions to problems created along the border in early June 1952. The guidelines set by the subcommittee for agriculture and supply covered most of the possible categories of farmers and of plots created by these dramatic processes, and determined general rules and specific procedures for handling them.[21] The legal status of property was not to be changed in any of the cases. The major concern of this document was to ensure that fields would be tended to and harvested, and to guarantee state supervision of the reallocation of land. Legal matters were not of high priority. Frontier farmers who owned land in the West were to be compensated with alternative land from the reservoir of plots along the border owned by farmers from the West. Since the legal status of the land was not to be changed, the farmers who got them were to work them as trustees under the supervision of the district. Plots belonging to farmers who were deported to the hinterland were also to be worked under the supervision of the district, given to responsible farmers who would sign a contract with the district authority. District administrations could also use both types of plots to create agricultural

---

[19] As discussed in Chapter II, West German frontier farmers who worked these fields usually did so as trustees, and part of the profits were saved for the use of the original owners.

[20] See the relevant documents pertaining to the deportations in Bennewitz and Potratz, *Zwangsaussiedlungen*. See also, Rainer Potratz, 'Zwangsaussiedlungen aus dem Grenzgebiet der DDR zur bundesrepublik Deutschland im Mai/Juni 1952', in *Grenzland: Beiträge zur Geschichte der deutsch-deutschen Grenze*, edited by Bernd Weisbrod (Hanover: Hahnsche Buchhandlung, 1993), 57–69.

[21] 'Beschlussentwurf: Richtlinien zur Besetzung von Bauernstellen und gewerblichen Betrieben', 12 June 1952, BArch-B, DE 1, Nr. 6085, 9–13.

collectives or district farms serving the district's economic needs. There were many additional instructions regarding fees, responsibilities, and more.

The refugee influx of previous years and the difficulties of land reform left a strong impression, which informed these guidelines heavily; they assumed a large qualified workforce eager to take on additional land. Planners in East Berlin laid most of the responsibility for regulating the reallocation and production along the border on the shoulders of district administrations. They failed to take into account the mass emigration to the West unleashed by the new border policy. They did not realize that some district administrations would have many more vacant fields to deal with than planned and would need to work them with a smaller population. Above all, the authors of the proposed guidelines had overestimated the control of district-level party organs over the entire process in frontier districts.

In mid-August 1952, the GDR's central board of coordination and control asked the Ministry of Agriculture to explain why many of the fields which 'were made free' ('*frei geworden*') in May and June were still untended. The same document also questioned why frontier districts were missing farmers and agricultural labourers and why there were shortages in supply of fodder in some of them.[22] The internal report produced in the ministry in response admitted that the ministry did not have updated information from much of the area along the border. The tables were based on partial reports from some districts, while other districts did not report at all. There was no data about plots left untended. The report stated that further initiatives could not be considered at that point because data from many districts was still missing.[23]

While the ministry in Berlin blamed the districts for their slow response, district administrations felt that Berlin did not offer enough support. In a memo from late June, a senior party activist in Heiligenstadt (Eichsfeld) wrote that the shortage of agricultural workers in the district was great. The district council could not find people to work all the vacant plots in the district, not while superior state agencies offered only obstructions. The district council pulled whatever strings it could in the party and the workers' union but had so far received no help. In an attempt to get some work done and secure more harvest, the district offered to employ the inmates of a youth prison in agriculture along the border. The police replied that prison inmates of all ages were banned from the restricted zone (*Sperrzone*) along the border. The activist tried to override the police by turning to a secretary in the ministry of the interior but the secretary sided with the police.[24]

Correspondence between the district and its frontier villages on these issues shows that the same pattern of delegation of responsibility worked within districts as well. The district assigned finding farmers for many farms to the communities in which these farms lay. The pressure to find solutions quickly, the lack of advance

[22] Koordinierung und Kontrollstelle to Ministerium für Land- und Forstwirtschaft, 16 August 1952, BArch-B, DK 1, Nr. 137, 84–5.

[23] 'Durchführung der Regierungsverordnung vom 26.5.1952' 23 August 1952, BArch-B, DK 1, Nr. 137, 86–8.

[24] 'Arbeitskräftebeschaffung für die umgesiedelten Betriebe', 27 June 1952, KrAEich, EA HIG, Nr. 192.

preparation and the insufficient agricultural know-how of some mayors and council members at district and village levels led to many problems. In one village, a farm was entrusted to the hands of a person who had no experience in farming and suffered from heart disease. He neglected his farm to the point where his cows ran astray and caused damages in neighbouring farms.[25] From another village came the plea to relieve the council of responsibility for farming. The council members were not experts on agriculture, they wrote, and they could not oversee work on a substantial area of 34 hectares (approx. 84 acres). The village council had not found, until that point, someone to take over this land and asked the district to assume responsibility.[26] No wonder, in this situation, that border districts were willing to go to great lengths to attract farmers from districts in the GDR hinterland. Districts offered to farmers, who were cleared by the police and by their home districts, assistance with moving expenses and in setting up their new farms.[27]

Even so, not enough people (and especially not enough experienced farmers) were won over for frontier agriculture. Some were deterred by the limitations of living on the periphery of the restricted zone or by debts and mortgages on the vacant farms. Others were not cleared by the police. Many feared that the previous owners would reclaim their farms. These concerns, coupled with the long-term trend of migration to industrial centres, made ensuring agricultural production along the border very difficult. In the Eastern Eichsfeld, many fields, especially the less fertile ones, remained untilled for years.

The balance of power between frontier farmers and state agencies, therefore, was not as clearly tilted in favour of state agencies as the decisive policy instructions and the aggressive action of May 1952 might have suggested. To achieve some of their central goals along the border, state agencies depended on the cooperation of frontier farmers, who could easily avoid or circumvent supervision by crossing to the West. In the first postwar years, the influx of refugees from bombed cities and Eastern Europe caused overcrowding in rural areas, and there was more than enough workforce to compensate for the loss of forced labour and of soldiers who did not return from the war. In the early 1950s, many of the refugees who had originally settled in East Germany continued their journey west to the mining and industrial centres. The wave of deportations and the resulting emigration to the West left GDR rural border regions short of agricultural workforce for the first time in years. Faced with this new reality, decision makers in Eastern state agencies realized that they had to conduct their policy with greater care.

State organizations had an asset they could use for this purpose—the land that was 'made free' following the deportation and emigration. Beyond compensating frontier farmers, who stayed and lost access to their land in the West, this reservoir of land was intended to lure loyal and disciplined farmers to settle along the

---

[25] Kellner to Abt. Wirtschaft, 30 June 1952, KrAEich, EA HIG, Nr. 192.

[26] Gemeinde Reinholterode to Landrat Taubert, 8 August 1952, KrAEich, EA HIG, Nr. 192.

[27] See instruction to pay for the move of a family and transport of cows to their new farm: 'Bezahlung des Umzuges', 30 August 1952, KrAEich, EA HIG, Nr. 192.

border.[28] But established farmers from the hinterland did not flock to the frontier. Applicants to move to the restricted zone and accept vacant farms were mostly refugees or those with a history of migration; many of them had no experience in agriculture.[29] Eastern frontier farmers saw many plots in or near their villages untended in 1952. Some of these were coveted, fertile plots. They understood quite quickly that ownership rights of their western neighbours would not be respected, and realized that state agencies did not designate them as the primary beneficiaries of this situation.

During the 1950s, East German state agencies assumed that the best way to improve their position along the border was to promote collectivization of agriculture. Frontier party officials viewed collectivization as a way to gain better control of agricultural production and, at the same time, improve their position vis-à-vis frontier farmers. Collectives would, went the party reasoning, be easier to supervise and more efficient, thus augmenting party power and solving the problem of a diminished workforce.[30] The conditions of workforce shortage and the ease with which frontier farmers crossed to the West, endowed the collectivization campaign along the border with greater urgency than elsewhere in the 1950s. The same causes also undermined this campaign's efficiency.

The favoured solution for working fields which were 'made free' along the border following the summer of 1952 was to allocate them to agricultural collectives. The problem with this solution was that very few such collectives existed in 1952. Those few that did exist were populated mostly by former refugees and agricultural labourers and were too small to assume additional responsibilities. In fact, when the new border regime was announced in May 1952, there were no agricultural collectives in the restricted zone along the border in the Eichsfeld.[31]

Collectivization was bound to be difficult in the Eichsfeld: there were few landless labourers in the region; farmers were mostly medium and smallholders, and the small and dwarf-holding households usually had additional income sources. Former refugees, who received some land during the land reform, were the first to accept collectivization. Their property typically included small, less-fertile plots. Many of them were inexperienced farmers, and their farms were poorly equipped.[32] For these farmers, collectivization offered a way out of a marginalized position as well as support from the state to improve productivity. The established frontier population in the Eichsfeld, on the other hand, was much harder to win over for

---

[28] See the undated and unsigned list of Eichsfeld communities in which such land was available and the suggestions about its usage in the files of the Thuringian Ministry of the Interior, probably compiled in July or August 1952. 'Vorschläge für die Besetzung der Betriebe', ThHStAW, Land Th, MdI, Nr. 3040, 76–8.

[29] There are many such applications in KrAEich, EA HIG, Nr. 192.

[30] 'Örtliche Landwirtschaftsbetriebe', 21 October 1953, ThHStAW, Rat d. Bezirkes Erfurt, L-03, 11–14.

[31] 'Bericht über die Massnahmen zur Festigung', 12 January 1952, KrAEich, EA WBS, Nr. 2216, 1–5; Eichsfeld Aktiv and URANIA-Bildungsgesellschaft Eichsfeld, *Die Entwicklung der Landwirtschaft des Landkreises Eichsfeld im Zeitraum von 1945 bis 2000* (Worbis: S. N., 2003), 30.

[32] Bauerkämper, 'Junkerland in Bauernhand?', 79–86 explains well how this situation came to be. For the same process in the Eichsfeld see Klinge, 'demokratischen Bodenreform',167–92.

collectivization. For them it meant giving up full ownership of plots, which had been family property for generations, and subordinating their work and major source of living to decision makers they did not trust.

But there were temptations as well. Lands along the eastern side of the border owned by Western frontier farmers were one such temptation. State agencies used these plots to persuade frontier farmers to collectivize. A party activist from Heiligenstadt, who played a central role in the collectivization drive in the Eichsfeld, wrote in 1978 about the establishment of the first agricultural collective (LPG) in the district. In the frontier community of Bischhagen (GDR), many farmers had fields across the border. In the summer of 1952, following the sealing of the border, they found themselves in a tight spot economically. Within the territory of their community lay many fields of the large private farm Vogelsang, situated just across the border. These were rich fields, well taken care of, planted, and approaching harvest time, but the owners from the West could not reap the fruits of their work. Bischhagen farmers naturally wanted to have these fields as compensation for the land they had lost in the West.

Those were days of large-scale reorganization and centralization efforts in the GDR. In July 1952, the second party conference of the SED convened in Berlin and adopted collectivization as a major agricultural policy. The LPG founded in the village of Merxleben (Thuringia) was adopted as the model for this campaign and its chairman spoke at the conference.[33] So when the mayor of Bischhagen asked district officials what should be done with Vogelsang's ripe untended fields of canola, wheat, and sugar beets, the answer he got was: 'Do something like they did in Merxleben, then you will get all of it!'[34] It is worth noting here that in this area, the inter-German border overlapped with the border of the Eichsfeld. The frontier residents on the western side of the border were not Eichsfelder. Accordingly, cross-border networks tying villagers from both sides to each other were not very strong. As discussed in Chapter II, taking over land in such cases was simpler. This prompted the establishment of the first LPG in the district of Heiligenstadt on 23 July 1952 and the farmers who joined it indeed counted the Vogelsang fields as their collective property.

From early on, then, border construction and collectivization were closely linked in the Eichsfeld. This was true also in the village of Kella, studied by Daphne Berdahl. As she wrote:

Two events in 1952, often conflated now in the memory of villagers, fundamentally transformed the basis of village social organization and differentiation under socialism. The first was the deportation and emigration of five families in the spring of that year.

---

[33] Barbara Schier, 'Die Ablieferungsgemeinschaft der merxlebener Neubauern als Klassenkampfinstrument? Ein Thüringisches Dorf auf dem Weg zur Kollektivierung', in *Zwischen Bodenreform und Kollektivierung: Vor- und Frühgeschichte der 'sozialistischen Landwirtschaft' in der SBZ/DDR vom Kriegsende bis in die fünfziger Jahre*, edited by Ulrich Kluge, Winfrid Halder, and Katja Schlenker (Stuttgart: Franz Steiner, 2001), 221–2.

[34] Eichsfeld Aktiv and URANIA-Bildungsgesellschaft Eichsfeld, *Die Entwicklung*, 30–1. quote from p. 31.

The second was the collectivization of agriculture that forced the remaining Bauern into the local agricultural cooperative.[35]

Despite the fact that collectivization of agriculture in the village was only completed in 1960 (and even then only on paper), the villagers remember it as connected to deportation and emigration spurred by the new border policy of May 1952. Berdahl's informants did not account for the role of the land that was 'made free' in the collectivization. This land was of course used by the collective, but Berdahl's primary source, the memory of the villagers, left this fact out of the story. The way the story came through memory and generations, collectivization in the village had only progressed through negative pressure.[36]

Collectivization of land ownership and usage was not the only instrument of increasing state control over agricultural production in particular, and work in general, along the border. Agricultural machinery was key to improving efficiency and production. Only successful farmers with fertile medium or large plots could afford a tractor. Those who owned tractors would then increase their income and cement their status through renting it to smaller holders. The tractor thus replaced horses as a primary status marker and a major factor in the resilience of the social structure of village society. Wishing to undermine this structure and bind farmers to the state and party instead of the richer farmers, GDR authorities founded 'machine and tractor stations' (*Maschinen-Traktoren Stationen*, MTS). The idea was to locate such stations near agricultural areas and have the best equipment on hand with professional mechanics to support the work of smallholders, and especially to support agricultural collectives. But the resources of the young state were more modest than its presumptions and the inventory of the MTSs did not create the kind of attraction expected. The insufficient equipping of MTSs was perceived in central party circles as a hindrance to the security of the Western state border.[37]

Six months later, someone in the Ministry of Agriculture had an idea for how to solve this problem without undue spending: privately owned tractors and agricultural machines should be used according to state priorities. According to a memo with instructions to the counties, all owners of agricultural machinery would be required to bring their machines and tractors to the closest MTS for inspection and registration. Once these were registered, the owners would be committed to lend them out for work according to state agencies' instructions.[38] But such plans were much easier to devise than to carry out; in practice, Eastern state agencies were not able to take hold of private farmers' machines, and without these machines they did not have enough to make the MTSs into the major magnet for collectivization. In

[35] Berdahl, *Where the World Ended*, 108.

[36] Berdahl, *Where the World Ended*, 109. See the undated and unsigned document titled 'Vorschläge für Besetzung der freigewordenen Ländereien im Kreis Worbis 1952', ThHStAW, Land Thür, MdI, Nr. 3040, 78 for evidence that state agencies did use the lands of evacuees and migrants to the West to encourage collectivization in Kella.

[37] 'Durchführung der Regierungsverordnung vom 26.5.1952', 16 August 1952, BArch-B, DK 1, Nr. 137, 84–5. Like the collectivization drive in general, the establishment of the MTSs was modelled on the Soviet experience.

[38] 'Maschinen-Traktoren-Stationen', 25 February 1953, ThHStAW, Rat d. Bezirkes Erfurt, L-03, 21.

1959, a security report from one frontier village in the Eichsfeld quoted farmers in the village as saying: 'give us tractors and freedom of movement, but leave us alone with the LPG. Over there [across the border] all the small farmers have tractors and they are doing well without LPG.'[39]

Playing the cards of land and machinery, party functionaries in the Eichsfeld made very modest progress in collectivizing agriculture along the border during the 1950s. The most troubling obstacle in their path was the imminent threat of emigration to the West, which the GDR officially termed *Republikflucht* ('flight from the republic').[40] Time and again internal reports had to acknowledge that the motives of many farmers who moved to the West were connected to pressures for collectivization.[41] This was not unique to the Eichsfeld. Patrick Major, who conducted a meticulous study of '*Republikflucht*', shows a correlation between collectivization pressures and the number of farmers in the entire GDR who opted to move to the West.[42]

During the following four years, collectivization proceeded slowly and attracted mostly the economically weaker smallholders, agricultural workers, refugees, and some industrial workers. The better-off medium holders avoided collectives or, in some cases, formed their own Type I collectives, sharing land but not livestock. Smallholders and workers could only join such collectives and enjoy the higher quality and relative abundance of farmland if they accepted the role of the founders as managers of the LPG. The policy which aimed to restructure rural society failed, then, to undermine traditional village hierarchies.

From 1959, state agencies made full collectivization of agriculture a primary goal. While joining an LPG was still voluntary in principle, state agencies applied increasingly aggressive pressure on private farmers, ushering in a second wave of farmer emigration. Brigades of party activists and workers were sent to the countryside and subjected resistant farmers to 'persuasion talks'. In addition, farming households refusing to join collectives were denied access to rare staples in local stores, necessary fertilizers, and more.[43]

In East Berlin, central offices noted the sharp increase in *Republikflucht* of farmers in late 1959 and early 1960, which clearly resulted from the massive collectivization pressure applied in that period. In an official analysis of this growing flight to the West from rural areas, the GDR Ministry of the Interior noted a

[39] 'Situationsbericht über Lindewerra', 25 May 1959, KrAEich, EA HIG, nr. 402/II.

[40] The term was intentionally reminiscent of *Fahnenflucht*, used for desertion in the military, to denote negative, immoral action.

[41] 'Republikfluchtgrunden Kreis Heiligenstadt 1955', undated, KrAEich, EA HIG, Nr. 319; 'Analyse und Statistik zur Republikflucht Kreis HIG 1959', 28 December 1959, KrAEich, EA HIG, nr. 611; 'Bericht über die Ursachenforschung der Republikflucht', 14 September 1959, KrAEich, EA HIG, Nr. 402/II.

[42] Patrick Major, 'Going West: The Open Border and the Problem of *Republikflucht*', in *The Workers' and Peasants' State: Communism and Society in East Germany under Ulbricht 1945–71*, edited by Patrick Major and Jonathan Osmond (Manchester: Manchester University Press, 2002), 200–1.

[43] Dagmar Langenhan, 'Halte dich fern von den Kommunisten, die wollen nicht arbeiten!', Kollektivierung der Landwirtschaft und bäuerlicher Eigen-Sinn am Beispiel Niederlausitzer Dörfer (1952 bis Mitte der sechziger Jahre), in *Herrschaft und Eigen-Sinn in der Diktatur*, edited by Thomas Lindenberger (Cologne: Böhlau, 1999), 146–58.

50–100 per cent increase in the number of farmers who went to the West between January and April 1960 compared to the previous year.[44] In April 1960, the party announced that full collectivization of agriculture had been achieved. This was not the case in reality, however, and the increase in emigration of farmers to the West, lasting into the following year, was just one indication.[45] Farmers could not, like most workers, intellectuals, or professionals, transfer their primary capital with them. They knew that land in the FRG was scarce and expensive and therefore they were underrepresented in the western emigration throughout the entire period. But in 1952–3 and in 1960–1, their proportion in the total number of '*Republikflucht*' approximated their share in the population.[46]

Forcing collectivization may have been a case of 'flight forward' for SED decision makers. By 1958, collectivization had not achieved what it was designed to. Many collectives were weak and village hierarchies remained almost untouched by the process. Furthermore, state agencies found themselves locked in a protracted conflict with farmers—collectivized farmers expected greater support and more and better land, while independent farmers resented pressures for collectivization.[47]

The Eichsfeld presented a complex set of challenges for the collectivization project. It was primarily a region of small and medium holders, whose self-perception was intimately tied to land ownership. The small number of larger estates that had existed in the region before 1945 meant a relatively small number of agricultural labourers and 'new farmers'.[48] The traditional suspicion of the state, typical of Catholic regions and of small farmers in Germany since Bismarck's 'culture war', exposure to western media, and the ease with which farmers could and did cross to the West combined to make the Eichsfeld very resistant to collectivization.[49] The district of Heiligenstadt was the last district in the county (Bezirk) of Erfurt to report full collectivization of agriculture. In his chapter about the collectivization drive of 1959–60, George Last writes 'In the Eichsfeld district . . . the functionaries charged with advocating collectivization tended either to lack the conviction themselves or simply had insufficient authority within the community to make a convincing case.'[50] In contrast to residents of rural areas further inland, and even more than residents of other border areas, most Eichsfeld

[44] 'Analyse der Republikfluchten in der Landwirtschaft', 12 May 1960, BArch-B, SAPMO, DY 30, IV 2/12/92, 76–8.

[45] For a very good analysis of the different stages of collectivization see Jonathan Osmond, 'Kontinuität in der Landwirtschaft der SBZ/DDR zur Zeit der Bodenreform und der Vergenossenschaftlichung 1945–1961', in *Die Grenzen der Diktatur*, edited byRicharch Bessel and Ralph Jessen (Göttingen: Vandenhoeck and Ruprecht, 1996), 150–9.

[46] Major, 'Going West'. See especially Figure 2 at the top of p. 201.

[47] These conflicts were portrayed beautifully with much of the nuance and complexity of rural life in Ervin Srittmater's novel *Ole Bienkopp* in 1963.

[48] The official party title for refugees and expellees from Eastern Europe who received land under the land reform.

[49] 'Militärgeographische Beschreibung Kreis Heiligenstadt', 1961, ThHStAW, Bezirksbehörde d. Deutsche Volkspolizei Erfurt, Nr. 482, 1–42. See especially the section 'Einschätzung der einzelnen Schichten der Bevölkerung', beginning on p. 14.

[50] Last, *Socialist Spring*, 13.

frontier farmers had good contacts in the West. Quite a few of them could count on a reasonable chance of success in finding work and even land on the other side if they were to move.[51] Many Eichsfeld households held small plots, orchards, and gardens while earning additional income from industrial, construction, or other non-agricultural work, mostly available in the West. GDR regional authorities identified this pattern as a problem after the official sealing of the border in 1952, and tried to solve it by moving industry into the Eichsfeld and reviving the local small-scale tobacco industry. According to their analysis, over 2,000 Eastern Eichsfeld residents worked in the West until May 1952, and they would continue to look for work in the West unless jobs were created for them in the East.[52] Some Western companies, which were forced to close branches in the Eastern Eichsfeld in 1952, were happy to accept their trained workers if they moved to the West, and many Eichsfelder took this route.

There was no need for a risky border escape in such cases. The most common Western migration protocol of the 1950s was through a legal family visit. Family visit permits were given routinely to most people if they had family in the West and acquired the necessary employer approval. The fact that so many Eichsfelder had relatives in the West thus made crossing the border legally the first stage of most cases for *Republikflucht* of those years. In light of this phenomenon, the GDR gradually restricted such permits.[53]

During the full collectivization drive of 1959–60, the Heiligenstadt district department of internal affairs set out to investigate the situation in frontier villages. The team of party functionaries reported on villagers' attitudes towards the state, the work of party organs, and the chances of collectivization in villages along the border. Its reports were not encouraging for collectivization supporters. The overwhelming majority of villagers with whom they spoke had relatives in the West. They resented that these relatives were not granted permits to visit them (reports about Döringsdorf, Asbach-Sickenberg, and Wahlhausen). They also resented that conversing with these relatives across the border fence was forbidden, and that they had to conduct it while avoiding the border guards (Lindewerra, Döringsdorf). They relied on such conversations, Western media, and other sources, to assert with confidence that party functionaries exaggerated in describing the threats from the West (Lindewerra, Döringsdorf). Party and state representatives (mayors, teachers, and border police) were often isolated socially, caught in internal conflicts or dependent on better-off villagers (Asbach-Sickenberg, Bebendorf, Lindewerra). '*Republikflucht*' cases were frequent and collectives were few. Existing LPGs were economically weak and did not include the better-off medium

[51] Last, *Socialist Spring*, 40. See Chapter II for more details about cross-border networks in the Eichsfeld.
[52] 'Analyse über Arbeitskräftelage im Kreis Heiligenstadt 1950–52' (Undated), ThHStAW, Bezirksparteiarchiv der SED Erfurt, Kreisleitung der SED Heiligenstadt 1945–62, IV/4.06/146, 1–4.
[53] 'Betr.: Direktive der Koordinierungs- und Kontrollstelle', 4 October 1954, KrAEich, EA HIG, Nr. 321.

holders (Bebendorf, Wahlhausen).[54] Before 1959, collectivization was very slow in the Eichsfeld as a whole. A detailed report on the economy of the Eichsfeld prepared in Berlin that year stated that over 85 per cent of the agriculturally used land was privately owned.[55]

As in other areas in the GDR, all types of pressure were brought to bear on the more stubborn private farmers during the 1959–60 collectivization drive, aiming to force them into 'voluntarily' joining collectives.[56] Plots belonging to Western frontier farmers, which had not already been taken over by collectives in previous years, were used to create new LPGs or strengthen existing ones.[57] In their haste to show progress and reach full collectivization, district authorities were willing to approve a variety of arrangements. Independent medium holders all over the GDR found ways at that point to retain considerable independence while complying with the formal framework of collectivization. The collectives of Types I and II allowed much flexibility in patterns and measures of collective work. Livestock and machinery remained privately owned and only fieldwork had to be shared according to these models. In the 1959–60 rush to collectivize, functionaries allowed small groups of medium holders to come together and call themselves collectives of Type I. These collectives were managed by the members as they saw fit, and farmers were practically left to work their farms in almost the same way they had before, if they so chose. This way they could rid themselves of further activist brigade visits and enjoy state support in machinery and more. They compromised their nominal ownership but were able to protect and maintain their self-perception as independent farmers rather than workers of a state-owned farm. Senior functionaries at the district level were willing to compromise the rigours of the policy so as to be able to report completion of their mission.[58] Of 190 LPGs in the two districts covering the Eastern part of the Eichsfeld in 1960, more than half were less than a year old, 145 were type I and only 36 were of the fully collectivized Type III.[59]

The collectivization drive marked the end of a decade of conflict between state authorities and frontier farmers in the GDR surrounding questions of land ownership and agricultural work. Despite the declaration of full collectivization, no side had clearly gained the upper hand in this conflict during the 1950s. A compromise seemed to have been reached and a new status quo arrived at, with which both sides

[54] Most of these multi-page reports can be found in KrAEich, EA HIG, Nr. 402/II. See specifically Asbach-Sickenberg, 27 July 1959; Bebendorf, 28 September 1959; Döringsdorf, 28 September 1959; Lindewerra, 27 May 1959; Wahlhausen, 4–5 June 1959. See also 'Einschätzung über die Gemeinde Lindewerra', 24 April 1960, KrAEich, EA HIG, Nr. 394/II.

[55] 'Plan zur Entwicklung des Eichsfeldes (2. Entwurf)', 15 April 1959, BArch-B, DE1, Nr. 5295, 18–85, here especially p. 29.

[56] See a review of such pressure measures in Last, *Socialist Spring*, 18–20.

[57] K. E. papers in private collection of the author. The correspondence was acquired from the daughter of a now-deceased man with the help of the Grenzmuseum Eichsfeld. I thank Margareta Engel and Ben Thustek of the museum.

[58] Langenhan, 'Halte dich fern', 149–64.

[59] Eichsfeld Aktiv and URANIA-Bildungsgesellschaft Eichsfeld, *Die Entwicklung*, 34–8, here especially the table on p. 37.

could live. Officially, all farmers were members of collectives and all agricultural land was cultivated by collectives. In practice, though, farmers, especially the economically stronger medium holders, retained independent control over much of their possession and could hold on to their self-perception as independent *Bauer*.

Frontier farmers found that the state was willing to invest considerable resources and use force in order to make them comply with its policies. They had also learned that by making concessions on the symbolic level, they could retain material assets, so long as they did so quietly. Obstinate evasion, practices typical of what Alf Lüdtke termed *Eigen-Sinn*, proved much more successful than confrontation.[60] Frontier state and party administrations realized that they had not achieved the restructuring of rural society for which they had aimed. They compromised in order to present achievements to their superiors. Both these groups could live with the achieved status quo.

State-building during the 1950s had not progressed as far in East Germany as it had in the West. State organizations had not monopolized resources to the same degree. As the compromises over collectivization demonstrated, the balance of power between state and non-state groups and individuals was not clearly tilted in the state's direction. But Eastern farmers had to accept, at least outwardly, state organizations' definition of reality and play by the rules they made. During the 1960s, collectives were gradually consolidated and party influence on them grew throughout the GDR. Along the rural border, party-state agencies had less patience with gradualism; the next stage began with yet another intensive drive in the fall of 1961.

A DECADE OF COMPROMISE: 1961–70

Frontier farmers and state agencies on both sides of the border learned important lessons during the 1950s. In the following decade, they capitalized on these lessons to find ways to promote their primary interests while reducing the level of conflict. One lesson frontier farmers internalized was the significance of the inter-German border. They learned that on each side of the border different organizations and power structures determined the conditions and rules. Economic growth and stabilization led to major structural changes along both sides of the border. In different ways, policies in both the East and West accelerated significantly the long process of flight from the land, reducing the cultivated areas and the number of farmers along the border. The GDR's massive border build-up transformed the landscape, swallowing up much agricultural land in the East and making cultivation in the West more difficult. The diminishing role of agriculture in the economy of the rural borderlands spelled a transformation in the balance of power between frontier residents and state agencies. It also increased the physical distance between

---

[60] For a short discussion of this term and its applicability see p. 7 in the Introduction.

frontier residents on both sides of the border. As a consequence, the border assumed a much more solid presence.

Border-Land: Changing Land Use along the Border in the East

On the heels of the collectivization drive of 1959–60 came another intensive campaign along the rural border. This campaign was directly linked to the construction of the Berlin Wall on 13 August 1961. After blocking the main channel for illegal emigration to the West in Berlin, GDR leadership sought to tighten its control of movement across the entire length of the rural border. Since the dramatic policy watershed of May 1952, change was slow and uneven. The orders issued by the GDR Ministry of the Interior in August 1961 indicate that the government was aware of its poor control over the border and was determined to alter the situation.[61] But changes took longer along the rural border than they did in Berlin, and did not amount to a border regime nearly as effective as the one established in the capital.

The introduction of new measures for securing and controlling the border bore important consequences for agriculture and property ownership along the border. Private farmers and agricultural collectives alike faced deportation and flight to the West, and more importantly, the massive confiscation of land designated for border construction. Among other things, the new regulations resulted in a significant extension of the limitations on agriculture along the border. All agricultural roads adjacent to the ten-metre strip were to be blocked, no tall growing crops were to be allowed within 100 metres of the border, and all work in the vicinity of this strip was to be carried out only in full daylight and subject to the discretion of border guards.[62]

In practice, GDR border forces confiscated a considerable area along the border. New barracks were built for the National People's Army (*Nationale Volksarmee—* NVA) units stationed along the border, forested plots were taken over and cleared, and many areas were fenced and became minefields or laid fallow. According to a report from March 1962, 831.5 ha (approx. 2,055 acres) were confiscated along the border in previous months in the district of Heiligenstadt alone, of which 476 hectares (approx. 1,176 acres) were cultivated fields and the rest were fruit orchards or unused land. The district authorities had to adjust production estimates and quotas accordingly, reducing them significantly.[63] Units stationed along the border had the authority to limit or ban access to areas along the border as they saw fit. Agricultural work along the border therefore entailed continuous negotiations with NVA officers, who in many cases had no understanding of agriculture.

---

[61] See 'Gewährleistung der Sicherheit an der Westgrenze', August 1961, BArch-B, DO 1, 20.0/643, 173–87 for a final draft of this order.
[62] 'Gewährleistung der Sicherheit an der Westgrenze', August 1961, BArch-B, DO 1, 20.0/643, pp. 173–87, here 174–5.
[63] 'Realisierung der Direktive der ZK d. SED', 9 March 1962, KrAEich, EA HIG, Nr. 305.

As they did during the collectivization drive, state and party organs dispatched activists and experts in great numbers to the rural borderlands. Local party representatives reported that 'in the border communities, a veritable invasion of instructors and committees is registered.'[64] This sudden attention to the border and its management gave rise to fears among frontier residents that a new wave of deportations was in store. Their concerns were justified as deportations were indeed part of the new border measures, but rumours proved much worse than reality. In the Eichsfeld, only 148 people were slated for deportation to the hinterland, and district party committees requested renewed discussion in 35 of those cases.[65] But the fear of deportation and the arbitrary, opaque process made many frontier residents question their decision to stay in the GDR. In the Eichsfeld as in other border regions, illegal crossing to the West rose precipitously in the fall of 1961.[66]

In the most dramatic episode of the period, 55 people—about a quarter of the population of the village of Böseckendorf, including many children and a cartful of belongings—cut the border fence and crossed unnoticed on the evening of 2 October 1961. This case demonstrates how different the build-up of the border had been in the rural borderlands than in Berlin. It was impossible to effectively seal a long, open space overnight; frontier residents could manipulate and circumvent barriers and regulations. Turning the rural border into an iron curtain was more complicated than erecting it in Berlin, and required diverse measures in addition to physical construction.

Almost all members of the Böseckendorf crossing party were collectivized farmers. They were led by the chairman of the collective, an independent farmer who had been 'won over' for collectivization just a year earlier.[67] This was not a coincidence. The reaction of frontier farmers to the new border measures in the fall of 1961 and beyond was directly connected to their experiences during the collectivization drive.

From the frontier farmers' perspective, some aspects of the border build-up beginning in the fall of 1961 seemed a direct continuation of the collectivization drive. In implementing 'security measures', GDR frontier administrations viewed agricultural collectives almost as arms of the state. Collective chairmen received orders regarding the cultivation of plots close to the border. Certain plots became accessible to collective members only. These and other plots were to be used only for certain (low-growing, non-work-intensive) crops and access to these fields would require permits. At this stage, many collectives were such in name only.

---

[64] 'Beratung mit den in den Grenzkreisen eingesetzten Genossen', 26 September 1961, BArch-B, SAPMO, DY 30, IV 2/12 72, 177–80.

[65] 'Beratung mit den in den Grenzkreisen eingesetzten Genossen', 26 September 1961, BArch-B, SAPMO, DY 30, IV 2/12 72, 177–80. See also 'Aktion Kornblume in Kreis Worbis', 6 October 1961, ThHStAW, BdVP Erfurt, Nr. 571, 159–66.

[66] Last, *Socialist Spring*, 41.

[67] 'Aktion Kornblume in Kreis Worbis', 6 October 1961, ThHStAW, BdVP Erfurt, Nr. 571, 159–66. In 2005, the German TV network ARD aired a documentary on the affair. See Peter Adler and Katrin Völker, 'Wir wollten nur noch raus!: Ein Dorf flieht in den Westen.' DVD. ARD, 10 August 2005.

Collective chairmen simply did not wield the kind of authority presumed by the orders.

This became very clear when state agencies tried to enlist frontier farmers to the work of border construction. In this case, the government's newly asserted strictness trapped state agencies into dependence on frontier population. The new security measures along the border required large-scale deforestation, which the regular forester cadres could not carry out on their own. State agencies supplied the required machinery and some expert machinists, but there remained the question of workforce and of horse-drawn carts to clear and transport the felled wood. Were workers to be brought in from the hinterland, each individual would have to first be cleared by the police and receive a permit to enter the restricted zone. This was expected to be a long process, which might delay the work.

To avoid delays, state agencies decided to rely on frontier residents for this work. In January 1962, the district council in Worbis ordered mayors of frontier communities to instruct LPG chairmen to send given numbers of men, horses, and carts to work under the foresters. In early February, a report to the district council found that the deforestation was progressing much slower than expected. Communities sent 0–40 per cent of the workforce they were instructed to send and the foresters could not go any faster without more workers. The district administration sent clear threats down the line—the district Internal Affairs (*innere Angelegenheiten*) department informed LPG chairmen that the full force of the defence laws would be used to punish those who did not comply. The results came within days—LPG chairmen acted swiftly and effectively and managed to produce the full quota of required carts and horses and, in some cases, even more than what was required of them. But, even under threat and having clearly made an effort, most of them could not produce more than 50 per cent of the required number of workers. The district investigation of this situation found several causes for this failure. The most important of them was the obstinate resistance of farmers to do the state's bidding and the limited authority wielded by collectives. In late February, another admonishment was sent to mayors, ordering them to hold assemblies and persuade their communities to meet their quotas. Two weeks later, another reminder was sent to all frontier mayors, stating that their communities had not yet met their quotas.[68]

The GDR's rural borderland was not yet really collectivized: certainly, it was not solidly under party and state control for more than a year after the declaration of full collectivization. In trying to eliminate escapes to the West, East German state agencies applied much pressure to frontier communities. Policymakers in East Berlin relied on the reports of full collectivization, and expected collectives to endorse party plans and help implement them. But they found that they still had to deal with many private, independently calculating farmers.

State agencies were not averse to using the new defence laws to confiscate land, but were nevertheless open to negotiation with frontier farmers for several reasons. They depended on frontier residents to ensure agricultural production and

---

[68] The many reports, complaints from the forester offices, orders to mayors and responses are all in KrAEich, EA WBS, nr. 7241.

cooperation in intensifying border control, and they could use these negotiations to push collectivization further. Once more, as in the 1950s, new restrictive border measures served to further collectivization of agriculture along the border. Border forces restricted work in certain areas near the border and pressured LPG councils to take them over. As mentioned above, LPGs did not prove very disciplined and cooperative in the early 1960s. However, they made it possible for border forces to deal with one person or council instead of many individual owners. In the following years, LPGs became a major channel for party-state work. Party activists and officials put LPG leadership cadres under much pressure, and replaced, threatened, and admonished them often. Advances were slow, but the SED never gave up the collectives as the primary organizational channel in rural areas. By the mid-1960s, land within the 500-metre strip along the border was finally fully collectivized.[69]

State agencies offered cash or land compensation for plots which were confiscated for border construction, but frontier farmers protested the fixed prices or the alternative land. In January 1963, a report to the council of the district of Worbis stated that 128 farmers accepted either cash (92 cases) or alternative land (36) and signed contracts to give up their land along the border. In 219 cases in the district the state confiscated the land using its defence laws because the farmers were unwilling to settle. In some cases, owners had moved to the West but in others 'despite exhaustive discussions, the owners refused to sign a contract'.[70] These farmers might have lost their land with no compensation, but they retained their self-image as the plots' owners and refused to recognize the legitimacy of state organizations' actions.

Frontier farmers resented the state's incursion on their land and how they worked it. They complained and protested and, more effectively, they just did not cooperate. State agencies found it difficult to make frontier farmers work their land according to the plans devised in Berlin. The attempts to seal the border were motivated by state agencies' desire to increase their control over the East German population by eliminating escapes to the West. For frontier farmers, though, these measures were another stage in a long history of attempts to curb their economic freedom. If they could not retain their independent farmer status, they still had several options open to them. They could try to cross the border to the West, and a good number of them did. The risks involved grew as more forces were assigned to the border, but for locals this was still a viable option during the 1960s. But land was harder to get in the West, so unless one owned land across the border, going there to protect one's self-image as an independent farmer did not make much sense. They could try to bargain and many of them did just that—they tried to get alternative land, to get more land or better land, and to improve their working conditions.

---

[69] Last, *Socialist Spring*. For a good example of a part of the conflict between party plans and practices in the LPG and the attempts to make LPGs comply, see pp. 104–10.

[70] The citation and the data are from 'Entschädigung der Ländereien bei der Erweiterung des 10-m Streifen', 17 January 1963, KrAEich, EA WBS, nr. 7241.

In the half-decade following the construction of the Berlin Wall, Eastern frontier farmers continuously negotiated with state agencies for these things. They held to their legal ownership and refused to sign agreements. They registered complaints, obstructed the work of border forces, and, most commonly, refused to play the parts assigned to them. Collectivized farmers proved they could negotiate as well as private owners. Sometimes they negotiated in both capacities at the same time; in other cases, private farmers and collectives negotiated together.

The village of Kella provides a good example. In the spring of 1963, representatives of the local LPG 'Silberklippe' participated in a tour of the border with NVA officers. The officers could not guarantee unobstructed work in parts of the village's lands along the border. Ten private farmers owned four and a half ha (approx. 11 acres) in this area. The LPG council estimated that with such small plots they could not keep up work in these fields if they were limited by the NVA. The officers' solution was to press the LPG into buying this land from the private farmers. Collective ownership would allow more flexibility in cultivation and better discipline in keeping to security regulations. But the collective did not wish to shoulder the burden of building up the border. Its leaders suspected that working these fields might become quite impossible and they turned to the district council. The LPG, they wrote, did not command the resources to rent these fields from their owners, but the district probably did. So it would be best, the letter continued, if the district rented the fields and allowed the LPG to use them. Then the LPG would use these fields for non-critical crops and could be flexible in working them. This would achieve two goals: compensation for the private farmers and cultivation of the fields in accordance with security needs.[71]

As this case demonstrates, private land ownership and agricultural work was still a factor in the Eichsfeld in the age of 'full collectivization'. Private owners, who officially belonged to collectives, still expected to have their income from agriculture protected and could still rent out their land. In addition to their village council, they could also look to the LPG for representation. Private and collective interests coincided in trying to get state agencies to invest more resources in solving the problems created by the new border measures of the 1960s. The LPG emerged thus not only as a vehicle of party and state power, but also as a channel for individual farmers' interests to reach state organizations.

Prolonged negotiations with frontier residents and state organizations' dependence on their cooperation for much of the work made construction of the rural border in the Eichsfeld a complicated and drawn-out project. In stark contrast to the overnight appearance of the Berlin Wall, the rural border was built up gradually during the 1960s and, as shown in Chapter V, was only completed during the following decade. Rather than a dramatic watershed in the history of the Iron Curtain, 1961, seen from the rural border, was one important stage in a long process.

---

[71] LPG Silberklippe to Rat d. Kreises Heiligenstadt, 13 May 1963, KrAEich, EA HIG Nr. 305.

Despite these challenges, the Eastern build-up of the border progressed during the decade, effecting a transformation of frontier agriculture. The confiscation of land following the fall of 1961 was much more extensive than in 1952. This time, there was no longer much alternative land to give away as compensation, because deportation numbers were small and the land owned by Western farmers had already been divided. Throughout the decade, added fortifications, minefields, and barracks took up growing proportions of agricultural land along the border. Restrictions on work hours, numbers of workers, and machinery reduced the productivity of many fields and made cultivating them an economic burden for LPGs. Some NVA border units prevented work in fields along the border for extended periods, and others opened and closed checkpoints on the roads to those fields arbitrarily or without advance notice, making rational planning of agricultural work impossible.[72]

Such widespread restrictions combined with the extensive confiscations of land to reduce greatly the volume and significance of agriculture as a source of work and income for frontier residents during the 1960s. This was another stage in the process of flight from the land, by then more than a century old. Emigration to industrial centres and a gradual transition from sole reliance on agriculture to mixed household economies were part of a well-established pattern in the Eichsfeld. The acceleration of this trend during the 1960s had an important effect on the conflicts surrounding land ownership and agriculture along the GDR side of the border. With significantly less agricultural land and increasing limitations on cultivating it, growing proportions of working-age men and women found employment outside the restricted zone. Quite a few young men, traditionally the most mobile and ambitious group, still opted for the West. Others found work in the developing industry in the few towns in the Eichsfeld (all outside the restricted zone) or commuted to cities further in the GDR hinterland.

This was no simple coincidence, but, rather, the result of a concerted, centrally planned effort. The Eichsfeld had been for many years regarded as economically backward. The first analysis produced in the GDR declared the Eichsfeld an 'emergency area' (*Notstandsgebiet*) in need of radical structural transformation.[73] More reports and analyses of the Eichsfeld economy followed throughout the 1950s, which, however, toned down the emergency. One of them even directly attacked the 'emergency area' definition, writing that 'under socialist production relations in the GDR there are no emergency areas . . . The most we can observe in the GDR as inheritance from capitalism are less developed areas or areas which are behind in development.'[74] But all county- and state-level analysts agreed that the state needed to invest in the Eichsfeld, improve infrastructure, and bring industry to it.[75] During the 1950s, these efforts did not achieve much, partly because the

---

[72] See examples in 'Rat der Gemeinde Neuendorf', 23 November 1963, KrAEich, EA WBS, Nr. 7241; 'Rat der Gemeinde Böseckendorf', 24 November 1963, KrAEich, EA WBS, Nr. 7241.

[73] Staatliche Plankommission, 'Das Notstandsgebiet Eichsfeld' (undated), BArch-B, DE1, Nr. 5296, 24–37. This report is almost certainly from late 1950 or early 1951.

[74] 'Die Landesplannung und das Eichsfeld', 10 January 1956, BArch-B, DE1, Nr. 5295, 12–17.

[75] See BArch-B, DE1, Nr. 5296, 6–22, 70 for different ideas and efforts in this vein.

resources invested were limited. In 1959, a very detailed analysis showed clearly that the Eichsfeld was behind on most parameters of economic progress.

This analysis was produced as part of an ambitious seven-year plan prepared by the county planning office in Erfurt and approved in Berlin in 1959, usually referred to as the 'Eichsfeld Plan'.[76] As part of this plan, state agencies invested considerable resources in the Eichsfeld during the first half of the 1960s, which greatly increased the accessibility of non-agricultural work. State agencies improved transportation infrastructure in the Eichsfeld, as bus lines connected all but three communities and a fast train connected the towns to industrial centres, enabling daily or weekly commutes to work.[77] Great care was taken to ensure that frontier residents would be able to get to work and back. For example, one report found that in order to get to work in Nordhausen on time villagers would need a train to leave Zwinge, a small frontier village, at 4:48 a.m. and return at 6:12 p.m., travelling about an hour and a half in each direction. For workers spending a full week in further cities, the report stressed it would be important to maintain the Friday train arriving in Zwinge at 11:07 p.m.[78]

The decline in the proportion of frontier residents engaged in agriculture also meant, then, a decline in the total number of frontier residents and a decline in the length of time frontier residents spent along the border. Better infrastructure transported frontier farmers away from the border for growing portions of their days and weeks. Industrial or construction work concentrated them in towns and cities of the hinterland, neutralizing the advantages they possessed (and the threat they posed) when they worked their fields along the border. Through negotiations, pressures, and the accessibility of new alternatives, the border measures of the sixties swallowed more land, resulting in an ever broader 'no-man's land'. Agriculturally cultivated land along the eastern side of the inter-German border diminished markedly during the decade. Only LPG members were allowed to work it, and they, too, could only work under severe constraints. In the most concrete sense, frontier farmers were turned away from the border. The physical distance which separated East German frontier residents from the West gradually increased during the 1960s.

East German state agencies related to Eichsfeld frontier farmers during the 1960s on two fronts, both of which affected their relationship with the land: collectivization and border build-up. Both campaigns required extensive engagement with local conditions, traditions, and structures. Frontier farmers' attachment to their land was a stumbling block to both processes, and much flexibility and patience

---

[76] 'Plan zur Entwicklund des Eichsfeldes,' 15 April 1959, BArch-B, DE1, Nr. 5295, 18–85. For the purpose of this chapter, the 'Eichsfeld plan' is important because of the implications it had on the role of agriculture and land in the Eichsfeld.

[77] See Rat d. Kreises Worbis to Kreiseinsatzleitung Worbis, 12 April 1962, KrAEich, EA WBS, Nr. 7241.

[78] Rat d. Kreises Worbis to Kreiseinsatzleitung Worbis, 12 April 1962, KrAEich, EA WBS, Nr. 7241. For more details about the lines added during the first half of the 1960s see 'Bericht der Bezirkplankommission über die Erfüllung des Eichsfeldplanes 1966', ThHStAW, Rat d. Bezirkes Erfurt, Nr. W-101.

were demanded of state agencies. The compromises negotiated in each case were not stable, final conditions, but stages in the processes. State agencies progressively pushed the compromise further and further. Eastern frontier farmers thus lost more and more ground, both literally and figuratively, as the decade wore on. By the end of the sixties, frontier farmers hardly challenged the GDR's border regime anymore. Crossing the border to the West was still an option, but one which was chosen almost exclusively by young men. Some land was still held privately along the border, but within at least 500 meters from the border-line very little land was still used for agricultural purposes and no land was cultivated privately.

Land-Marks: Capital and Compromise in the West

West of the border, there was no dramatic change in border policy throughout most of the 1960s. If anything, the construction of the Berlin Wall, another example of the real power held by the GDR over millions of Germans, only reinforced Adneauer's insistence on ignoring the East German state. But the decade did see a steep rise in the resources that the FRG marshalled for the solution of such conflicts. The West German 'Economic Miracle' (*Wirtschaftswunder*) was already apparent from the mid-1950s, but it had only gradually begun to affect life in the rural frontier provinces during the following decade. Because of the poor transportation and trade conditions in regions that became the end of the road, private money did not flow into most of them. The growing capital reserves found their way into these regions primarily through public channels. The federal government operated aid programmes for border areas in the 1950s as well, but the number of programmes available to frontier farmers and their combined volume grew exponentially from the late fifties. Without giving up their symbolic opposition to compensation for land in the East, Western state organizations in fact compensated frontier farmers during the sixties well beyond the monetary value of their losses.

The fast-paced economic growth in the West German hinterland accelerated, more dramatically than in East Germany, the process of 'flight from the land'. Some found non-agricultural sources of income that capitalized on the existence of the border, offering different services to the growing number of border tourists. The trickle of border tourism, which began in the mid-1950s, turned into a steady stream from the early 1960s onwards.[79] These developments coupled with the large investments to smooth the rough edges of the conflicts with state agencies surrounding land ownership.

In 1960–1, another round was played in the conflict between the worst-hit frontier farmers from Fuhrbach and their state on the question of compensation for the land they owned in the East and had lost access to since 1952. The main protagonists had not been replaced and the issues at hand had not changed, but this round proceeded differently, underscoring the shifts of the intervening years. In 1960, another accusatory letter was sent from the village of Fuhrbach, this time to

---

[79] For more about the development of border tourism in West Germany, see Eckert, 'Greetings'.

the president of the Federal Republic, Heinrich Lübke, demanding that the state not neglect the farmers of the community.[80] As in 1956, Friedrich Bönning signed this letter, but this time he was the sole signatory. The village council did not endorse his letter. The most telling shift was in the position of the district administrator, Matthias Gleitze, which reflected the development of Western state-building and its connections to border formation. As the chief administrator of the border district, Gleitze was a civil servant, member of a state organization, and the top representative of the state in his region. On the other hand, he was an Eichsfelder who was born and raised less than five miles from Duderstadt and earned his doctorate studying Eichsfeld agriculture. He spoke the local dialect, shared the Eichsfeld Catholic tradition, and began his political career, as a good Eichsfelder, in the Center Party.

In 1952, Gleitze championed the cause of the farmers from Fuhrbach and tried to assign them as trustees for fields owned by Eastern frontier farmers, absolve them from paying rent, and get state organizations to cover their losses. In 1956, the protest letter to the chancellor resulted in sending the county president to the village to discuss the matter, because the district administrator sided with the village. But in 1961 the affair ended with Gleitze inviting Bönning to his office and setting him straight.[81]

According to Gleitze's letter to the county president summarizing the meeting, there was nothing that state agencies could do at that point, and Bönning's demands for compensation had, in any case, little to do with his land. Bönning and his wife, Gleitze explained, had given up agriculture altogether in 1958 and therefore had not received even the compensation for lost harvest income since then. The small patch of 1.2 ha (approx. three acres) that they owned across the border did not interest them anymore. They were in a hard spot economically, he wrote, because Bönning's health had deteriorated and he could not work full time as a plasterer, as he had done for many years. He had in mind to open a plastering business in Cologne with his three sons and needed the money for that purpose; this was his motive to revive the compensation demands.[82] Gleitze repeated the need for compensation in this letter and also the reasons making compensation impossible. But he also indicated that the real problem was no longer land or compensation for it; the real issue was cash flow and that could be solved with cash.

Cash offers were indeed the manner in which West German state agencies approached conflicts with frontier residents during the 1960s. In September 1964, the Federal Minister for All-German Affairs reviewed in a cabinet meeting the economic situation of the *Zonenrandgebiet* (zonal border area). In a 12-page

[80] Before being elected as President of the Federal Republic, Lübke served six years as Minister of Agriculture. It is possible that Fuhrbach farmers turned to him because they thought he would see their plight in a favourable light.

[81] Oberkreisdirektor Dud to RP Hildesheim, 20 April 1961, NLA-HStAH, Nds. 120 Hildesheim, Acc. 58/78, Nr. 6.

[82] Oberkreisdirektor Dud to RP Hildesheim, 20 April 1961, NLA-HStAH, Nds. 120 Hildesheim, Acc. 58/78, Nr. 6.

document, he enumerated the different programmes through which state money was directed to this area in the preceding decade, the sums invested, the methods used, and the results achieved.[83]

The border area was first defined as an area in need of special state support by a joint committee of the four frontier federal states, Schleswig-Holstein, Lower Saxony, Hesse, and Bavaria, in 1952.[84] Not surprisingly, the representatives of the states who hoped to benefit from federal investments defined the affected area broadly. They did not define it by distance from the border or by conditions of economy or infrastructure, but according to administrative units. The entire territory of every district bordering on the GDR was included in this definition, stretching to an average distance of 40 kilometers from the border. The outcome was a very diverse region including different economic conditions and needs. Alongside some of the poorest agrarian provinces of the FRG, like the Eichsfeld and the Bavarian forest, it encompassed some major industrial and commercial centres such as Lübeck and Wolfsburg. Border areas enjoyed not only direct benefits; some districts and communities were also eligible, as special development areas, for several federal assistance programmes (*Fördergebiete, Ausbaugebiete, Sanierungsgebiete*). Many millions of Marks were poured into these areas through different state channels. These measures were only partly successful. The document described many unresolved problems and complaints and tasked the cabinet to invest more thought and greater resources into solving them.[85]

The regional distribution of the benefits from such diverse programmes was determined to a large extent by market dynamics. Even with inducements and tax reductions, few entrepreneurs chose to invest in remote rural provinces with poor infrastructure and insufficient manpower. They could enjoy at least some of the same benefits when investing in cities such as Braunschweig, Göttingen, or Wolfsburg included in the border areas, and so they did. Consequently, poorer border districts saw very little industry settling in them, and the decrease in unemployment was mainly due to emigration. This emigration, the federal minister emphasized, could only be halted through changing the economic conditions in these regions.[86]

Duderstadt, the only town in the Western part of the Eichsfeld, was a good example. It was viewed as a 'regional centre' and picked for several government aid programmes in the hope that it would draw up the economy of the entire Western Eichsfeld. In 1961, federal offices declared Duderstadt to be 'saturated' with state funds from different programmes, and reduced the investment in the town from the regional development programme. However, two years later a report from the

---

[83] MfgF, 'Memorandum über die Lage im Zonenrandgebiet', 1 September 1964, BArch-K, B126, Nr. 51699.

[84] 'Denkschrift über das Ostgrenzgebiet der Bundesrepublik', 15 May 1952, NLA-HStAH, Nds. 120 Hildesheim, Acc. 55/78, Nr. 393. The response of the federal government and the ensuing conflicts over this issue in 1952–3 are discussed in Chapter II.

[85] MfgF, 'Memorandum über die Lage im Zonenrandgebiet', 1 September 1964, BArch-K, B126, Nr. 51699.

[86] MfgF, 'Memorandum über die Lage im Zonenrandgebiet', 1 September 1964, BArch-K, B126, Nr. 51699.

Lower Saxon Employment Bureau (*Landesarbeitsamt*) maintained that this was mistaken. Indeed, some businesses could be won over to relocate to Duderstadt, stated the report, but at the same time others closed and moved out. The bottom line was that many Eichsfelder, like Fritz Bönning, found their livelihood outside the region. The report recommended that federal agencies extend Duderstadt's eligibility in the regional development programme, originally scheduled to expire in 1961, at least until 1965.[87]

One issue which none of these federal aid programmes addressed was agriculture. West German economic planners did not regard existing private agriculture as an economic engine any more than their counterparts in the East. As in the East, restructuring land ownership was deemed an essential step en route to the rationalization and modernization of agricultural production. The progress from 1955 towards a (West) European common market, including a joint regulation of agriculture in the six member states, made modernization a pressing matter. Kiran Patel writes that in the mid-1950s, there reigned a rare consensus among 'important parts' of all major German parties, including the agriculture minister Lübke, that modernization and rationalization of agriculture was essential.[88]

Rather than collectivization, West German policy saw consolidation of large plots in private hands as the way to achieve this end. The Land Consolidation Act (*Flurbereinigungsgesetz*) came into effect in January 1954 and was revised many times during the following decades.[89] It aimed to induce landowners to organize, swap, and sell land between them to create large, consolidated holdings. This reorganization was to allow for the laying of good roads and clear, angular field borders suitable for mechanical cultivation. State funds and support were allocated for the work involved, and the amounts allocated increased with the years. The implementation of this reform depended on landowners' willingness to embrace it. In each community, a critical mass of landowners was required in order to form the 'community of participants' (*Teilnehmergemeinschaft*) responsible for planning and carrying out the reform in the village or town.[90]

The Western Eichsfeld, an area with mostly smallholders following many generations of fracturing of family plots through inheritance, was a natural candidate for land consolidation. But the reform was very slow getting off the ground in the Eichsfeld. In March 1957, the district administrator from Duderstadt reported that:

---

[87] Landesarbeitsamt Niedersachsen to Präsident d. Bundesanstalt für Arbeitsvermittlung und Arbeitsversicherung, 7 February 1963, BArch-K, B102, Nr. 43372. See also Landkreis Duderstadt, 'Übersicht über die Gewährung von Darlehen und Zuschüssen für öffentliche Vorhaben', undated, NLA-HstAH, Nds. 120 Hildesheim, Acc. 8/87, Nr. 597.

[88] Kiran Patel, *Europäisierung wider Willen: Die Bundesrepublik Deutschland in der Agrarintegration der EWG 1955–1973* (Munich: R. Oldenburg Verlag, 2009). This consensus was causal, according to Patel, in the relatively light-hearted West German approach in those years to the negotiations of agricultural unification in the European Economic Community (EEC). See p. 111.

[89] Erich Weiß, *Zur Entwicklung des Flurbereinigungsgesetzes der Bundesrepublik Deutschland in den Vergangenen 6 Jahrzehnten* (Butjadingen-Stollhamm: Agricola, 2009) reviews the law in all its versions.

[90] Hans-Günther Bothe, *Landwirtschaft und Flurbereinigung* (Stuttgart: Eugen Ulmer, 1963), 21–6.

Unfortunately, the efforts of the local agricultural trade association representatives, as well as those of the district authority and not least of the Land Consolidation Office remain unsuccessful, because, at this time, most of the owners of agricultural enterprises view the Land Consolidation Act with hostility.[91]

The land consolidation reform indeed did not play any role in land ownership and agricultural work in the Western Eichsfeld during the 1950s and 60s. As argued above, land's significance for frontier farmers' economy had gradually diminished during those years, but it was still important enough to a large enough group of them to resist ownership reform. Keeping the ownership but neglecting to actually work growing portions of the land along the border, frontier farmers in the Eichsfeld thus left much of this land fallow and spent much less time on their plots along the border. So long as the Land Consolidation Reform did not make any headway in the Eichsfeld, state support for agriculture in the area was very limited.

The expanding federal budget was nevertheless used directly during the 1960s to quiet the concerns of frontier farmers who had lost access to their fields across the border. In the village of Fuhrbach, ten farmers signed forms in August 1966 stating that they received that year sums equal to ten times the yearly compensation for lost harvest income, and committing themselves to reporting what they did with the money.[92] Offering such exceptional cash grants to farmers changed the relations between the farmers and their state agencies. The sums paid were calculated on the basis of the yearly compensation for lost harvest income, thus adhering to state agencies' refusal to compensate for property. At the same time, the multiplication by ten was tantamount to admitting that the regular compensation was not enough.

Another channel directing both public and private capital to the Western border areas, which had turned from a trickle during the 1950s into a veritable flood in the 1960s, was border tourism. The phenomenon of private West Germans taking day trips to see the Iron Curtain had begun already in the mid-1950s, but the numbers, so far as we know, were not significant. At any rate, they did not lead to any institutional response in the frontier economy or administration.[93] Beginning in 1960, Western state agencies along the border identified a growing tide of border tourism, first as a challenge and gradually also as an economic resource and a lever for federal investments. Visitors from the hinterland had been a source of concern along the border since the late 1950s. As outsiders to border areas who did not know where exactly the border path was, they were liable to cross it by mistake and be taken in ('kidnapped' in Western jargon) by Eastern border guards. As the years went by, the fence constructed in 1952 and the ten-metre strip were neglected in many areas, making unintended border crossings by visitors a growing concern.[94]

[91] 'Aktuelle Fragen der Landwirtschaft d. Kreises Duderstadt', 29 March 1957, NLA-HStAH, Nds. 120 Hildesheim, Acc. 60/78, Nr. 1.
[92] The identical forms follow each other in StADud, Fuhr 160.
[93] Eckert, 'Greetings', 1–3.
[94] For example 'Witzenhausen Nr. 697', 28 April 1958, HeStAM 401/13a, Nr. 99; see similar cases in HeStAM, 401/13a, Nr. 37.

The number of visitors and incidents grew rapidly from the late 1950s. In May 1960, the Federal Minister of the Interior decided that this has gone too far. He wrote that in the span of five weeks, 12 West German citizens had been detained by Eastern border guards after having crossed the border. Such incidents caused unnecessary tension, he wrote, and instructed the Federal Border Guard (*Bundes-grenzschutz*) to conduct a widespread operation to clearly mark the border with warning signs.[95]

When large numbers of tourists began to arrive in the border areas, Western border guards and customs officers were tasked with supervising and directing them. Quite quickly they found that, especially on weekends, this task consumed all their resources. In 1962, an internal memo of the customs service in Frankfurt stated that during weekends and holidays, customs officers along the inter-German border turned into tour guides and traffic controllers and could not perform their real tasks properly. The memo suggested contacting a non-governmental organization to take over these assignments.[96]

Border tourism offered not only risks and challenges but also potential benefits. The Western part of the Eichsfeld offered very few traditional tourist attractions and none of the instant border attractions such as a divided house or village or wall. It therefore lagged somewhat behind other border areas in seeing, and responding to, growing numbers of border tourists. In 1960–1, some of the communities noticed the potential and began trying to attract tourists based on their proximity to the border.[97] District authorities reacted more slowly. The impetus for engaging border tourists in a more organized fashion, encouraging and regulating their visits, actually came to the Western Eichsfeld from above. In late 1963, the federal government and the Lower Saxon government initiated a project aimed at harness-ing border tourism for 'all-German public relations work' (*gesamtdeutsche Öffen-tlichkeitsarbeit*). In January 1964, the Lower Saxon Minister for Expellees and Refugees convened a meeting of the chief administrators of all frontier counties and districts with representatives of the Federal Ministry for All-German Affairs.[98] The convened were called to discuss how to better inform and educate border tourists. The representatives of the Federal Ministry committed their budget to financing a central office to coordinate this project in Lower Saxony as a whole. One of the office's tasks would be to direct tourists to those districts in which existing facilities were not yet overburdened, such as the rural district of Duder-stadt. In addition, frontier districts were urged to improve the infrastructure for

[95] Bundesminister d. Innern, 'Verhinderung von Grenzzwischenfällen', 25 May 1960, HeHStAW, 531, Nr. 126. See also 'Markierung d. SBZ.- Demarkationslinie', 25 September 1961, KrAGö, LKGö, A32, Nr. 4.

[96] Abt. Leiter Z, 'Zunahme d. Besichtigungen an d. SBZ-DL', 25 June 1962, HeHStAW, 531, Nr. 79.

[97] 'Markierung d. SBZ.- Demarkationslinie', 25 September 1961, KrAGö, LKGö, A32, Nr. 4.

[98] 'Schaffung eines gesamtdeutschen Zonenrandwerkes im Lande Niedersachsen', 27 January 1964, NLA-StAW, 90N, Nr. 1.

tourists by constructing observation towers and roads. Lower Saxon and federal officials promised to take care of the bills for such works from their budgets.[99]

Indeed, district offices began receiving money for hosting and leading tourist groups during 1964, something they had done for free until then. With the money, they improved tourist infrastructures and printed brochures. Observation points and visitor centres were established in many frontier villages, and visitors were encouraged to dine and spend their nights in local establishments. The number of visitors kept growing and so did the business they brought with them.[100] Guiding, hosting, and feeding tourists gradually evolved into a significant income source for many frontier residents, bringing both private and public resources into their pockets (see Figure 4.1). Tourism provided more than just income, however. Representing the border to the visitors from the hinterland and from other countries, frontier residents came to occupy an important symbolic position. Not marginal and forgotten, in these interactions they were rather guardians of national values. They showed visitors where and how division took place, and helped them relate to it.[101] They could and did also try to use this symbolic position in their bargaining with state agencies. When the federal railway company announced the planned closure of the bus line leading to several border villages in the Eichsfeld in 1968, the district authorities appealed to Lower Saxon superiors, asking to undo this decision. Among other arguments, the appeal mentioned that every year 25–30,000 tourists visit the hill overlooking the border. These tourists could see the bustling railway station at the Eastern side of the border. The run-down rail-bed, exposed of its rails that they saw on the Western side, reflected negatively on Western state agencies' claims to improve the economy of border regions.[102]

At the same time that income options from various sources became more accessible, working the land along the inter-German border became more challenging. Border construction in the GDR affected agriculture on the other side as well. As detailed above, increasing proportions of the land along the Eastern side of the border was left untended and fell fallow. In the early sixties, frontier farmers in the West noticed that pest weeds, which multiplied in these neglected plots, migrated into adjacent plots on the Western side in growing volume and became very tough to eradicate. In the summer of 1963, as mentioned in the opening of this chapter, a regional farmer's association wrote to the district authority in Göttingen warning of this problem.[103] The other nuisance to Western frontier agriculture coming from

---

[99] For more on this meeting see Sagi Schaefer, 'Re-Creation: Iron Curtain Tourism and the Production of "East" and "West" in Cold War Rural Germany', *Tel Aviver Jahrbuch für Deutsche Geschichte* 40 (2012): 116–31.

[100] For the development of border tourism facilities along the Eichsfeld border with resources supplied by county and state see 'Niederschrift über die Besprechung am 16. Dezember 1964', undated, KrAGö, LKGö, A32, Nr. 52. See programmes for group visits in the district of Duderstadt, which were all directed to local restaurants and hotels in KrAGö, LKGö, A32, Nr. 43.

[101] Schaefer, 'Re-Creation', 128–30.

[102] Landkreis Duderstadt, 'Beabsichtigte daurende Einstellung der...', 27 September 1968, StaADud, Fuhr 142.

[103] Vereinigung Landwirtschaftlicher Ringe to Verwaltung d. Landkreises Göttingen, 28 August 1963, KrAGö, LKGö, A32 Nr. 14.

Fig. 4.1. A sticker/shirt print for border tourists from the private collection of Siegfried Schmidt. Reading only the large print would spell 'I was in the GDR', but adding the small print the sticker reads 'I was in Duderstadt'.[104]

across the border was herbicide. Eastern border forces did not mind the weeds on most neglected fields, but they did attempt to keep a strip along the border weed-free so that they could track footprints. This cleared strip immediately along the borderline grew broader during the 1960s. To cover the length and width of this strip, Eastern border guards used large-volume spraying, and since they wanted to destroy everything that grew on that strip, they used very strong poison. When the wind blew in the wrong direction, spraying caused the destruction of crops on the Western side as well.[105]

A combination of push-and-pull factors worked during the 1960s to reduce the number of frontier residents engaged in agriculture along the border in the Western Eichsfeld. An ever-greater proportion of the land along the border was left untended or was used for wood or other less demanding work. Western state agencies'

[104] I thank Siegfried Schmidt, a long-time official of the district of Duderstadt, for allowing me to copy this and some other documents from his private collection. I thank also the Grenzlandmuseum Eichsfeld, and especially Ben Thustek, for facilitating the contact with Herr Schmidt.
[105] 'Unkrautbekämpfung im Bereich der Zonengrenze durch das ostzonale Grenzkommando', 30 May 1968, KrAGö, LKGö, A32, Nr. 2. The same file holds also the press release announcing in 1970 that frontier farmers were eligible to apply for federal compensation if their crops were damaged by East German herbicide.

concerted efforts to develop commerce and industry contributed to this process, as did the accompanying perception of small-scale agriculture as unfit for the market, especially in the evolving EEC. The important battles of the agricultural lobby revolved in those years around the transfer of the agricultural planning authority to the EEC. Despite their success in influencing West German positions in the negotiations, the agriculture lobbyists failed to halt the process, and the power over some of the crucial decisions for agricultural production moved to Brussels during the first half of the 1960s. The contradictions in West German policy, and the lack of long-term planning ability they gave rise to, in and of themselves became obstacles for efficient agricultural production.[106]

Some factors were more clearly related to border formation. Transportation to and from frontier villages deteriorated because it was not profitable. With the closure of bus and train stations, workers who still kept a kitchen garden or a small plot in a frontier village had to give them up. For the younger generation, the end-of-the-road village with not even a bus stop was no match for the attraction of the quickly expanding towns and cities of the hinterland. From one frontier village came this allegation to the regional branch of the federal railway:

> Judging by the current transportation conditions, one could get the impression, and this appears to be the case, as if the plan is to leave the border communities to die as far as transportation is concerned and declare the area as no-man's land.[107]

When the Federal Railway Company decided to discontinue the line connecting a number of frontier villages with the nearby towns, the rural district of Duderstadt protested to the Lower Saxon parliament. Closing this service would have severe economic and even harsher psychological effects on the villagers along the border, stated the letter.[108] Among those who stayed in the region, growing numbers made their living in commerce, service, and light industry in Duderstadt. With no land consolidation, agriculture's role in their economy diminished. As in the East, fewer people spent time working along the border, and those who still did worked shorter hours and fewer days and cultivated smaller proportions of the land along the border. The physical distance between residents of the two sides of the border grew and their economic and emotional ties to the land that they used to share weakened.

Under these conditions, conflicts over property rights and land ownership cooled. Frontier farmers were not as dependent on land for their income. Those of them who still worked the land received aid in sums much greater than the value of their plots across the border. They did not have to officially give these plots up in return for the money and no longer minded keeping up the pretence that the confiscation was not final. But everybody recognized that it was pretence, and that the border was an established fact.

[106] Patel, *Europäisierung*, 282–7.
[107] Gemeindedirektor Hilkerode to Bundesbahnverkehrsamt, 26 June 1963, StADud, Bro 22.
[108] Landkreis Duderstadt, 'Beabsichtigte daurende Einstellung', 27 September 1968, StaADud, Fuhr 142.

Towards the end of the decade, under Willy Brandt's chancellorship, this recognition became official federal policy as well. Accepting division liberated state agencies from self-imposed limitations regarding the regulation of land ownership. In 1969, the Lower Saxon Minister of the Interior initiated a legislation that would entail an implicit acceptance of the finality of division.[109] In the territory of Lower Saxony, there were 80 plots of land, totalling 15 square kilometers (approx. 3,707 acres), which were registered in the books as being under the municipal authority of communities in the GDR. For more than two decades, residents of these areas could not vote for their local government, and authorities could not tax the land in question. The Lower Saxon minister thought that the time had come to legally reassign these areas to the closest communities west of the border. His fellow ministers had no objections, and Bonn too approved the idea.

CONCLUSION

The solidification of the inter-German border was closely tied to the changing status of agriculture and land ownership along both sides of the border. Changes in land use and border formation affected each other: the emergence of division constrained agriculture along the border, and reduced its significance for frontier economy; at the same time, the marginalization of agriculture enabled more effective policing and disciplining of the borderlands. Frontier farmers' attitudes toward state agencies and the policies both states applied to this border changed significantly over the two decades from 1952 to 1972. The transformations in land use and ownership and the related shifts in attachments and orientations of frontier residents were an important chapter in the history of the inter-German border. They were instrumental in solidifying the control of both German states over this border and in their ability to impose their authority along it. These transformations also played an important role in the related process of social division of German society.

During the 1950s, West German state agencies were in a better position than their East German counterparts to enforce policies over frontier residents. Thanks to their successful state-building, Western state organizations were less dependent on mobilizing frontier farmers than were Eastern ones. Eastern frontier farmers had more leverage than their Western counterparts because they could emigrate to the West and because their state agencies needed their work in order to fortify the border.

Intense interactions between frontier farmers and state agencies during the 1950s enhanced the effect of state on both sides of the border. They established the territorially bound, separate jurisdictions of East and West German state agencies as the only relevant frameworks for political, legal, and economic practices for frontier

---

[109] Niedersächsiche Minister d. Innern, 'Diesseits d. Zonengrenze liegende vormalige Gebietsteile von DDR-Gemeinden', 17 November 1969, NLA-HstAH, Nds. 600, Acc. 2000/001, Nr. 50. See the rest of the correspondence in the same file.

farmers. Frontier farmers' failures during the fifties taught them not to expect much in the way of policy changes.

From the final years of the 1950s, and increasingly from the early 1960s, state organizations on both sides of the border invested growing resources in their border areas. During the 1960s, the GDR set to transform agriculture through collectivization and at the same time invested in improving infrastructure and establishing industry. Simultaneously, Eastern forces were busy from 1961 constructing border barriers and claiming ever-growing areas along the previously modest border strip.

The FRG's economic resources expanded exponentially during the 1950s and 60s, and the federal government often opted to spend money as the easiest solution to problems. The Western Eichsfeld, one of the poorest regions even among the rural peripheries of the republic, was targeted by several aid programmes. The results were mixed and could not undo the ever-growing gap between the economy of the region and that of the industrial centres in the hinterland. The government did not invest directly in agriculture in the Eichsfeld because most farmers in the region opposed the restructuring of land ownership. Partly as a result, cultivating many plots in the framework of the new EEC-coordinated agricultural policy became economically unjustifiable. Some consequences of the border construction in the GDR 'migrated' into Western frontier fields as well, making these fields even less viable economically.

The combined effect of these developments on both sides of the border was to reduce significantly the role of agriculture in the economy of frontier residents and shorten the time residents spent working fields along the border. Much of the land along the border was no longer cultivated from the mid-1960s onwards, or was only used for fodder crops and wood. In the areas immediately adjacent to the border, fewer people walked and worked daily who shared a connection to the land and a regional and religious affiliation. Cross-border contacts and communities had not completely disappeared, but they were weaker and functioned primarily in the memories of frontier residents.

Uniformed personnel, drafted and appointed by state agencies, arrived in increasing numbers to the borderlands. They came primarily from the hinterland and they viewed the borderland from the perspective of their tasks as defined by state agencies. For them, frontier farmers were trouble: they needed permits, demanded protection, interfered with border-guarding work, and disobeyed instructions. Most troubling was the threat that their work and their presence along the border posed for the border guards' control of this crucial signpost of state authority. Frontier farmers knew the physical and social terrain on both sides of the border well, and they used their knowledge to resist and undermine regulations. When their numbers declined and the time they spent on the land along the border decreased, state agencies' control over the borderlands tightened. Frontier farmers themselves were attached to the border area and to the cross-border community of the Eichsfeld through their land and their work. Drawn in greater numbers and for longer periods to the hinterland and to non-agricultural work in frontier towns, their attachment to the area and to the community, which previously shared it, grew weaker. These trends can be seen more clearly when viewed over the generational divide. The postwar generation came of age from the late 1950s on. Most of them migrated away from the border and among those who stayed even fewer worked the land as a primary or secondary source of income. With them, frontier agriculture ceased to be a shared, cross-border infrastructure for a regional community.

Land along the inter-German border had become bounded, limited, and controlled; more solidly integrated into two separate political and economic systems; less the farmers' and more the state's land; less of a frontier and more of a Border-Land.

V

Divide and Rule
The Openly Negotiated Border and Its Demise

> A stubborn rumor is circulating in the Upper Eichsfeld that soon visitors from the Federal Republic would for the first time be allowed to visit communities directly along the border, and the restricted zone along the inter-German border would be abolished. Officers of the Border Guard have received during the last couple of days, consentient indications from visitors and migrants from the GDR. In the large demonstrations in Heiligenstadt and Neuhausen, SED representatives have repeatedly suggested that such relaxations [of the border regime] are planned.[1]

Less than fifteen hours after a local newspaper in Göttingen printed these words, the inter-German border opened. This text reveals how beyond belief a complete opening of the inter-German border had been, even in full awareness of the defensive position of the GDR's ruling party and Moscow's announcement that it would not interfere in the Warsaw Pact countries' efforts to reform.[2] Later on that fateful 9 November, the ill-informed speaker of the GDR government, Günter Schabowski, mishandled press questions and West German television hyped his half-baked announcement on freedom of travel. That evening, guards at the Brandenburg Gate succumbed to pressure from the crowds and allowed free passage to the West.[3] On the morning of 9 November, however, the inter-German border still appeared quite permanent.

By that time, this border had a stranglehold on the minds and lives of people on both its sides. Previous chapters charted the trajectory of the development and solidification of the border under parallel, conflicted, state-building projects in East and West Germany. Battles over recognition and legitimacy dictated the framework of border-related interaction during the 1950s and 60s. This final chapter will focus on the changes to this trajectory under a very different set of circumstances during the 1970s and 80s.

---

[1] Hessisch Niedersächsische Allgemeine, 'Hinweise aus Obereichsfeld: Sperrzone bald offen?', *Hessisch Niedersächsische Allgemeine*, 9 November 1989, StAGö, Ztg. 910.

[2] This policy is commonly referred to as the 'Sinatra Doctrine'. It replaced the interventionist approach usually referred to as the 'Brezhnev Doctrine'. The phrase, alluding to Sinatra's famous 'My Way', was popularized after a Soviet government spokesperson used it on a US talk show on 15 October 1989.

[3] Mary Elise Sarotte, 'How an Accident Caused the Berlin Wall to Come Down', *Washington Post*, 1 November 2009, www.washingtonpost.com/wp-dyn/content/article/2009/10/30/AR2009103001846. html, accessed 3 July 2013.

A major stage of border-solidification and state-building followed close on the heels of the mutual recognition of East and West Germany. The two states joined forces in bringing about the final cementing of the divide between them. This chapter investigates the uneasy cooperation between rival state agencies in achieving a stabilization of the border that became important for both states. Historians have long debated the merits of *Ostpolitik*, Willy Brandt's course towards compromise with the FRG's eastern neighbours, including the celebrated Basic Treaty (*Grundlagenvertrag*, or *Grundvertrag* for short) from December 1972 with the GDR. The contribution of *Ostpolitik* to the demise of the GDR and to the reunification of Germany remains an open question.

Little scholarly attention has been paid to the treaty-driven transformation in the development of spatial division between East and West, that is, in the development of the inter-German border. After more than two decades of unofficial and denied negotiations and the ad-hoc problem solving required by such circumstances, the inter-German border became for the first time a subject of official cooperation between the two German states. With the basic treaty, UN membership, and mutually regulated border, the state-building processes of both German states overcame the main obstacles before them.

It is a major contention of this book that from the mid-1970s German division and both German states stabilized and attained legitimacy and an air of permanence that they lacked theretofore. Consequently, both states significantly improved their position vis-à-vis the populations under their power, and especially frontier residents. The dynamics of border construction and especially the power balance between state and non-state actors around the border changed markedly. The transformation is reflected in this chapter, which engages a different set of sources and highlights different interactions and dynamics than the ones foregrounded in previous chapters. With their new-found coordination, East and West German state agencies managed to limit frontier populations' capability to manipulate border regimes. To compensate for the sparser availability of state-archival materials for the 1980s, this chapter complements those sources with more media and with documents from Stasi archives.

Following the history of the inter-German border between the Basic Treaty and the collapse of the border, this chapter argues that Brandt's strategy worked in unexpected ways to solidify the border in the short term and to undermine it in the long. *Ostpolitik* contributed both to a deepening of physical division and a stabilization of the GDR and to impulses that spelled the end of the East German regime. This chapter will demonstrate how policy changes and enforcement framed patterns of interaction along and across the border, and will analyse how these patterns, in turn, affected practices and perceptions of different populations in frontier areas.

Open negotiation in the joint Border Committee allowed, for the first time, an effective border seal. Hence, the border became in the 1970s the ominous instrument of division and control that Western authorities had claimed it to be since the late fifties. At the same time, the treaty kick-started dynamics around the border that led to friction within East Germany and pressure on its regime, warming a tinder box that ignited in the 1980s. Mobility and migration lay at the heart of all this. Therefore, this chapter will extensively examine patterns of border crossing—both legal and illegal—in this period. Growing mobility across the border, a direct result of the Basic Treaty, set processes in motion that strongly influenced the attitudes of frontier residents and other citizens in East and West Germany.

The development of the border had wide-ranging repercussions. This chapter will explore changes in agricultural practices along the border, with considerable space devoted to the question of cross-border coordination. Previous chapters showed that local and regional authorities maintained their contacts across the border throughout the 1950s. These contacts were vital for the maintenance and regulation of many aspects of life along the border. Such lines of communication fell under growing pressure from the mid-1950s due to the heated conflict over recognition of the GDR. By the end of that decade, regional- and local-level cross-border contacts had been attenuated to such an extent that coordination efforts were rendered useless, even before the construction of the Berlin Wall.

Surprisingly, the mutual recognition and state-level coordination born of the Basic Treaty did not lead to a revival of local and regional administrative contact. In fact, this chapter argues, regional administrations remained largely detached from the process of inter-German détente until the late 1980s. Cross-border coordination was monopolized by state-level central authorities. Local administrators in frontier areas had not communicated with their counterparts across the border since the late fifties in most cases, and the new regulations following the Basic Treaty actually contributed to this status quo. The treaty did, however, offer opportunities for (especially, but not only Western) frontier residents to extend their social networks across the border by rekindling old contacts and forming new ones.

State-building progressed, albeit at different rates and under different conditions, on both sides of the inter-German border during the postwar decades. The West German state, previously shackled by physical and economic destruction and haunted by the atrocities committed under the Nazis, had won, thanks to its economic ascendancy, internal legitimacy, and international standing during the 1950s. The GDR followed a more tortuous path to legitimate statehood, partly due to the policies—and partly to the mere existence—of its Western rival state. The much smaller and economically weaker East German state faced greater limitations on internal legitimacy of rule and international power. These limitations were heightened by the Soviet occupation, which entailed a large-scale dismantling of industrial plants and infrastructure and a strict regimentation of the political system. The 1960s saw a gradual economic stabilization and political dominance of the ruling SED within East German society, attained gradually, thanks partly to the Berlin Wall. Its advances in state-building lent credibility to the East Berlin government's claim to independent statehood. The ability of the communist leadership to construct and maintain with increasing efficiency a long, contested border further boosted this claim.

By the early 1970s, the GDR had turned into a stable reality, especially, but not exclusively, in the eyes of younger Germans who grew up with division. Many of them perceived West Germany's refusal to recognize its neighbour state as pointless, backward-looking stubbornness. Recognition of the GDR became a bone of contention in West German politics, and an important element in the political transformation of the country during the second half of the 1960s.[4] The chief instigator of this change in inter-German politics was the mayor of Berlin and frontrunner of the Social Democratic Party (SPD), Willy Brandt, who made a revision of West German policies towards the Eastern Bloc his foremost political agenda. His advancement in West German politics attests to the shift in popular opinion in the country. Compromise with a communist-ruled East German dictatorship and recognition of the 'Yalta borders' became an acceptable idea in West German public discussion in the mid-1960s, and by the end of the decade it proved to be a winning electoral formula.

Brandt's new *Ostpolitik* and the controversy to which it gave rise, reached their zenith in 1972 during the negotiations with East Germany. Brandt barely survived a 'no confidence' vote in the Bundestag and was forced to announce early elections, revealing the strength of the sentiment against accepting division. Uncertain about the fate of the coalition government in elections, Brandt and his chief advisor, Egon Bahr, pushed negotiations with the GDR and managed to initial the treaty—though not to officially sign it—two weeks before the elections. The November 1972 elections proved that the future-oriented acceptance of Cold War realities on the ground had a strong popular appeal. In these elections, broadly perceived as a referendum on *Ostpolitik*, the SPD achieved its best electoral result in the postwar years, making it the biggest party in the country. Brandt and Bahr interpreted the results as a green light, and within a month signed the treaty between the two German states, commonly known as the Basic Treaty.[5]

The West German government committed itself to support the GDR in various ways, and the GDR agreed in return to relax limitations on inter-German travel and discuss issues such as the environment and human rights. Wielding its economic advantage and its diplomatic edge with the international community, the Federal Republic managed to avoid explicitly retracting some central tenets of its long-standing 'German policy' (*Deutschlandpolitik*).[6] As much as Brandt and Bahr were eager to do away with the rigidities of the Hallstein Doctrine, neither was keen on openly recognizing the legitimacy of the SED regime, or relinquishing the prospect of reunification and the claim of the FRG to represent the entire German nation. They were able to keep all these elements pretty much intact, at least on paper, in their negotiations with the GDR. The treaty involved a de facto-only recognition of the GDR. The emissaries exchanged after the treaty entered into force were not granted the title 'ambassador'. The West Germans also succeeded in warding off pressure to change the articles in the West German Basic Law that mentioned the exclusive representation of the German nation and

[4] Hans Magnus Enzensberger, 'Bin Ich Ein Deutscher?' *Die Zeit*, 6 May 1964, sec. kultur, www.zeit.de/1964/23/bin-ich-ein-deutscher, is a very early example of this. Accessed 23 July 2013.
[5] Arnulf Baring, *Machtwechsel: die Ära Brandt-Scheel* (Munich: DTV, 1984), 491–8.
[6] The central elements of this policy and their development were discussed in Chapter III.

created a quick path for future integration in the Federal Republic of all East Germans.[7]

Such an impressive feat of 'having one's cake and eating it too' could not be repeated when discussions turned to the border between the two states. Yet, agreement on the border path was necessary for a stable new *modus vivendi* between the two states. The treaty therefore established a joint Border Committee, which met regularly, beginning in January 1973. This committee brought together for the first time high-ranking representatives of Eastern and Western state agencies to discuss, decide on, and demarcate the border between the two states.

OPEN NEGOTIATION: THE BORDER COMMITTEE

Much of the work entrusted to the Border Committee was technical in nature. There were few significant material disputes between representatives of the two states regarding the path of the border. Every small change in the location of visible border markers was of symbolic significance and at least some Western committee members thought such changes could spark public protest. In practice, public interest at most stages of the Committee's work was limited. The Basic Treaty was generally seen as covering the most important political-symbolic issues by recognizing the existence of the GDR and opening diplomatic channels between the two states. Tensions and heated debates surrounding symbolic issues such as the size and shape of letters spelling FRG and GDR on border stones made sense only to state officials who had been immersed in the legal-symbolic conflicts of recognition for years.

The Committee charged professional teams from both states with the technical work of measuring the exact path of the borders agreed upon in the inter-Allied London conference in 1944. Those borders between projected occupation zones in Germany relied on the old administrative and state borders, such as the borders between Hanover and Saxony. The most complicated challenge was reaching compromises on the border path in areas in which the Allies themselves did not stick to the London conference maps but exchanged territories and changed the borders between occupation zones. Some of these agreements were well document-ed, while others had not been recorded by regional commanding officers who made them in 1945.[8]

But even in those more difficult cases of border strips lacking a reliable map to work with, the sides were usually able to reach a compromise. The technical work

[7] M. E Sarotte, *Dealing with the Devil: East Germany, DéItente, and Ostpolitik, 1969–1973* (Chapel Hill, NC: University of North Carolina Press, 2001), 164–70. The articles in the Basic Law remained a bone of contention between East and West German governments until unification. See for example 'Auch SPD lehnt DDR-Forderung zur Staatsbürgerschaft ab', *Göttinger Tageblatt*, 1 February 1985.

[8] Klaus Otto Nass, *Die Vermessung Des Eisernen Vorhangs: Deutsch-Deutsche Grenzkommission Und DDR-Staatssicherheit* (Freiburg: Centaurus, 2010), 35–7; Bundesminister d. Innern to Auswärtige Amt, 26 April 1973, 'Grenzkommission' BArch-K B137, Nr. 6002; 'Zusammenfassung des Überprüfungsergebnisses über den Verlauf der Demarkationslinie und deren Abweichungen von der ehemaligen Landesgrenze', undated, BArch-K, B369, Nr. 79.

progressed very quickly, partly because searches for stones, triangulation, and mapping were carried out by teams of professionals who had been given the go-ahead to set aside conflicts and supply data to the Committee. Initially, the number of open cases and disagreements about paths was daunting; there were as many as 25 short strips of unclear border path along the Lower Saxon border with the GDR alone, just over a third of the total length of the border.[9] However, the sides typically reached quick compromise, in most cases relying not so much on precise detail as on established practice. The 'habitual border' (*Gebrauchsgrenze*), the one that border guards from both sides had been patrolling for decades, was usually adopted as the final line of demarcation.

This was, for example, the case with the border on the grounds of the domain of Paterhof. The former state domain fell victim to division: most of its fields lay in Thuringia and became part of the Soviet zone and of the GDR, where they were taken over by the state and divided between agricultural collectives. The dispute from then was about the path of the borderline vis-à-vis the core farm buildings. When preparing files for the Border Committee's discussion on the area, the Western delegation pulled out the report by a Western customs officer from 1952, explaining how the habitual borderline had been established.[10] The line had been determined by one-to-one negotiations between border guards on the ground, approved by Soviet officers, and adhered to ever since despite the absence of any official document to support its legal validity. By late 1975, 23 of the 25 cases on the Lower Saxon portion of the border had been settled in similar fashion.

Questions of little or no material significance but heavy declarative-symbolic consequence were much harder to handle. Such, for instance, was the issue of exchanging land registry documentation. Recall West German bureaucrats' objections to handing over even copies of land registries to their East German colleagues, discussed in Chapter III. The problem arose because of the above-mentioned area exchanges between the Allies in 1945. The occupiers did not think about transferring relevant documentation with the areas and populations they exchanged between them. As a result, court files and land registry documents were kept across the border from the populations and areas to which they pertained. To legally validate property inheritance or sale, state offices on both sides of the border had to rely on border-crossing communication, which became increasingly problematic during the 1950s and impossible in the following decade.

The Border Committee dealt with the border path going from north to south, beginning therefore with the border of the GDR with Schleswig–Holstein. Not two months into the discussions, the GDR presented a draft for an agreement to include an exchange of land registry documentation for areas which had been exchanged along the border. The Western response was generally positive, but

---

[9] See the 25 small booklets, one for each of these strips, prepared under the titles 'Grenzverlauf bei...', BArch-K, B137, Nrs. 6414 and 6415.

[10] Zollgrenzkommissariat Duderstadt to Hauptzollamt Northeim, 25 June 1952, BArch-K, B137, Nr. 6414.

stated that the Eastern draft was so vague as to require new legislation in the FRG. The motion could only be entertained, it was declared in the counter-draft, if it was limited to specific areas in Schleswig–Holstein.[11] This draft attracted the attention of the (West German) Federal Minister of the Interior, who did not know the history of this issue and decided to check with the relevant states. He directed representatives of the four border states in the Committee to produce official position statements from their states.[12]

The Lower Saxon Minister of Justice, Hans Schäfer, prepared a detailed reply, pointing out that such an exchange might have adverse consequences for landowners in the GDR and for the struggle for private property in Germany more generally. Schäfer, member of the Lower Saxon SPD, who served in this capacity from 1970–6, presented a series of objections to an exchange of land registry documents in the framework of the Border Committee.[13] He reminded his colleagues that land registry offices in Schleswig–Holstein already in 1945 had ceased to update their registers on lands that were transferred to the Soviet zone. Their books were therefore free of information that would be damaging to GDR citizens. This was not the situation in the other three *Länder*.

In Lower Saxony, Hesse, and Bavaria, many land registry offices, adhering to the claim for exclusive representation, tried to keep their books up to date. They accepted new entries over the years, especially by landowners who either migrated to the West or visited (legally or illegally) and appealed to change the status of their plots in the books. For GDR citizens and for those who chose to leave the East German dictatorship for the West, these new entries in the land registry were a means to keep their claims to confiscated or collectivized land. Such claims had become illegal in the GDR and therefore could not be entered into GDR records. Schäfer warned that such information might be used against landowners who counted on West German land registries to safeguard their rights and secrets. And of course, in Schäfer's view, handing historical legal documentation of the land registry to GDR authorities would only help them create a legal façade for what he considered illegal confiscation of land for collectivization. Very soon thereafter, Schäfer could point out that there was popular support for this claim. It came in the form of a political campaign by one man and an organization he founded, the 'Alliance of Zonal Border Victims in Lower Saxony' (*Notgemeinschaft Zonengrenzgeschädigter in Niedersachsen*). A letter campaign under this title reiterated many of Schäfer's reservations regarding the exchange of land registry documents.[14]

---

[11] 'Protokollvermerk über den gegenseitigen Austausch von Grundbüchern, Grundakten und Vermessungsdokumenten für die durch den britisch-sowjetischen Vertrag vom 13. November 1945 betroffenen Gebiete...', undated, NLA-HstAH, Nds. 380, Acc. 2003/066, Nr. 6. The draft treaty was submitted by the GDR delegation during the meeting of 28–29 March 1973.

[12] 'Bundesminister d. Innern to Ländermietglieder d. Grenzkommission, persönlich/vertraulich! VS-nur für den Dienstgegrauch!', 9 May 1973, NLA-HStAH, Nds. 380, Acc. 2003/066, Nr. 6.

[13] Nds. Minister der Justiz to Nds. Minister des Innern, 'Grenzkommission nach dem Zusatzprotokoll zum Grundvertrag. Hier: gegenseitiger Austausch von Grundbüchern, Grundakten und Vermessungsdokumenten', 17 May 1973, NLA-HStAH, Nds. 380, Acc. 2003/066, Nr. 6.

[14] See for example Badekov to von Wrangel, undated, 'Grundvertrag - Aufgaben Der Grenzkommission', 28 May 1973, NLA-HStAH, Kleine Erwerbungen, Acc. 2000/002.

These letters also reflected a concern regarding the process of settling the border between the two states via the Border Committee. The letters demanded full disclosure of Border Committee discussions on all matters affecting land owner-ship, and direct involvement of the affected individuals, municipalities, and organ-izations in forming West German positions. The letters claimed that Western frontier residents in Schleswig–Holstein had been kept in the dark about discus-sions which directly pertain to their livelihood and private property and expressed concern that this could happen in Lower Saxony as well.[15]

Knowing that there were many cases in which territories were swapped between the occupiers and land ownership was contested, state agencies along the border worried about popular reaction to the settling of the border in frontier areas. In the winter of 1974–5, the work of the Border Committee progressed apace, and officials planned to begin posting the newly agreed-upon border stones in Hesse the following spring. In December 1974, the Hessian Minister of Economy and Technology informed all land registry offices in the border districts of this expected development.[16] He directed state agents in border areas on how to explain the new agreement to frontier residents, especially farmers with plots along the border who might raise objections. The major design of this planned public opinion campaign was to prevent legal action by aggrieved frontier residents against the newly agreed-upon borderline. The minister instructed land registry offices to approach in advance those farmers whose fields near the border might be diminished through changes to the border path and those who owned fields on the other side of the border, before making border marking public. State officials were to make sure the farmers realized that the FRG had no choice in the matter, that it was legally bound to approve the borderline and powerless to affect changes on the other side of it.

This was understood as a hard sell because, as discussed above, the federal government had been telling the same frontier farmers just the opposite for many years. Since 1952, West German state agencies had based the Western border regime on the rejection of this border and of the state on its other side. The West German state, therefore, had refused demands of frontier residents who had lost access to their lands in the GDR for full compensation on their lost property, reasoning that such compensation would entail recognition of the division of Germany and of the legality of the GDR's actions. Now, after two decades, the same federal government asked that frontier farmers accept a joint demarcation of the border.

As mentioned above, West German negotiators managed to steer the Basic Treaty away from explicit, full recognition of the GDR. Negotiating the location of agreed-upon border stones betrayed the pretense of non-recognition. The placing of stones that bore the initials DDR and declaring thus the territorial

---

[15] Badekov, 'Vertrag über die Grundlagen der Beziehungen Zwischen der Bundesrepublik und der DDR - Aufgaben der Grenzkommission', undated, NLA-HStAH, Kleine Erwerbungen, Acc. 2000/ 002.

[16] Hessische Minister für Wirtschaft und Technik to Hessische Landesvermessungsamt. Wiesbaden, 10 December 1974, HeStAM, 610 Nr. 111.

jurisdiction of the previously denied state—in full view of the people most affected by division—was not a moment of pride for West German state agencies.

Throughout two years of discussion, West German delegates on the Border Committee tried to improve their position, or at least their public image, in this foreseen but dreaded situation. From the early phases of discussion of the *Grundvertrag*, Western delegates repeatedly suggested establishing some sort of coordination regarding the protection of property rights, in the hope of achieving at least a measure of influence on the legal status of land in East Germany. Time after time, the GDR rejected it as interference in its internal matters. In October 1974, Western delegates presented a draft resolution to bind both states to entering information from the other state into its land registry records, hoping thus to legalize property transactions of land in the GDR, which were only entered into Western records. Like previous attempts, it failed. The East German counter-draft suggested that reason demanded that ownership of each plot of land would be determined according to the laws of the state in which the plot was found. In other words, 'Don't interfere with our land regime and we won't interfere with yours.'[17]

At the time of the Lower Saxon minister's directive to land registry officers to update frontier farmers, West German officials already realized that they would not make much progress in this area. As a final face-saving move, the West Germans suggested that the borderline markings include a renewal and validation of existing field border stones. Such stones existed along the border, marking places in which plot borders cut through state borders. The committee was able to reach a quick agreement on a joint decision, representing a compromise. The decision authorized both states to place plot border stones on their side of the border (as opposed to directly on the border as the West Germans wanted) after the proper marking of the line. This was a purely symbolic decision, as clearly each state could place such stones on its own side without having to consult the other. But West German delegates could at least use this statement to prove to their frontier farmers that they had not given up the fight for their property rights.[18]

This issue was important enough that the FRG pushed it despite the certainty of Eastern refusal, and it was important enough that the GDR countered any such attempt and made sure that the status quo remained intact. Both states had been through long and difficult negotiations with frontier farmers on issues concerning land ownership around the inter-German border in the 1950s and early 60s. The institutional memory of Western state agencies prepared them for a bitter public, and possibly legal, struggle. After two decades of efforts to assert this border as final and enormous investment in its physical construction, Eastern state organizations were attached to the image of the 'state border west' as final and impenetrable.

As it turned out, representatives of both states on the Border Committee overestimated the level of interest of frontier farmers and landowners in the final

---

[17] The FRG draft: 'Vorschalg zum Problem der Grundbuchumtragung', 11 October 1974, HeStAM, 610, Nr. 110. The GDR reply: 'Niederschrift d. Staatpunktes der DDR zum Problem der sogenannten Grundbuchumtragungen', 3 December 1974, HeStAM, 610 Nr. 111.

[18] HeStAM, 610, Nr. 111.

border demarcation. In 1974, frontier farmers in Eichsfeld accepted this as a primarily symbolic and political act and were more interested in other aspects of the inter-German compromise, such as the opening of a local border checkpoint.

NEW CHECKPOINTS AND NEW PERMITS

As part of the *Grundvertrag*, the GDR agreed to open several new border-crossing checkpoints and established a new category of Western visitors specifically designed for the needs of frontier population. The *Grenznahverkehr* (roughly 'border area traffic', henceforth GNV), was a system which allowed residents of the border areas in West Germany to apply for periodic crossing permits, first for three months at a time, and later for six months. These permits enabled their holders to cross the border for one-day visits, returning by midnight, as many as nine times every three months (up to a maximum of 30 times per annum). In the Eichsfeld region, these two parts of the *Grundvertrag* caused excitement. One of the new border checkpoints agreed upon was planned on the road, which until 1952 connected Duderstadt and Worbis. Ever since 1952, when the KGV arrangements were terminated,[19] frontier residents who wanted to cross this border legally had to take a long detour southeast, turning a ten-minute bus ride or a reasonable walking and cycling distance into a major half-day journey, including several changes of trains and buses. Under these circumstances, even those Eichsfeld residents who could get permits—GDR pensioners since 1964, West Germans with family in the GDR—found it quite difficult to visit and only did so infrequently. The prospect of doing away with this discomfort created many expectations in Eichsfeld.[20]

Enthusiasm was naturally much greater in the Western part of the Eichsfeld than in the Eastern. For East German frontier residents, the new agreement did not entail a change in the range of persons allowed to travel to the West. Travel permits were issued to pensioners and for important family occasions before 1972 and continued to be issued to these categories thereafter. The only real and immediate improvement in mobility of East German frontier residents was that pensioners from frontier areas would be allowed to cross the border through the new GNV checkpoints, thus saving time and trouble. In fact, as the parts of the Basic Treaty dealing with the GNV became public during the summer of 1972, East German frontier residents felt as if their situation would actually worsen under this treaty. For over a decade up to that point the border was officially closed, preventing regular travel and contact across it. The GNV had made it clear that the border was only closed to working-age East Germans and relatively open for all West Germans from the border areas. Furthermore, the restricted security zone of five kilometers

---

[19] The GDR's one-sided revocation of these border-crossing arrangements in May 1952 is discussed extensively in Chapter II.

[20] 'Um 0.00 Uhr soll sich der Schlagbaum an dem neuen Grenzübergang heben', *Göttinger Tageblatt*, 19 June 1973; 'Verkehr wird morgen aufgenommen: erster Bus rollt über die Grenze', *Göttinger Tageblatt*, 7 April 1973; 'In Omnibussen von Duderstadt nach Worbis', *Südhannoversche Volkszeitug*, 16 June 1973, KrAGö, A32, Nr. 25.

along the border was declared out-of-bounds to Western visitors. In practice, this meant that residents of dozens of communities along the border would not be allowed even to host family and friends from the West in their homes. They would be forced to travel and meet their visitors in a hotel. During the second half of 1972, therefore, SED officials in border districts found themselves inundated with tough questions regarding travel arrangements.[21]

In an attempt to shape the perception of the treaty as a victory for the GDR, and in order to gauge popular opinion on this matter, the SED held 'residents' forums' (*Einwohnerforen*) in many communities, especially in border regions. This was a well-tested party strategy in East Germany: let the public be heard and vent complaints and at the same time spread the party line and 'explain' the reality as it should be perceived. In Erfurt county activists of the National Front, an SED- controlled federation of parties and organizations, reported many positive reactions to the treaty as a whole. On the other hand, they noted, that 'Once again, we witnessed the appearance of illusions and speculative wishes regarding travelling options.'[22] Such wishes centred, of course, on the possibility of travel to the West and changes in border regulations, especially regarding entry to the restricted zone. But there was also a general sense of resentment towards a government that did not trust its citizens and extended relative generosity to Westerners.[23]

The checkpoint was not ready to be opened in 1972 as the optimists in one local newspaper had predicted.[24] But as summer approached, the building work progressed on the checkpoint between Gerblingerode and Teistungen. More details about the planned regulations of border crossing were made public as East German offices began to coordinate the nitty-gritty of the GNV in the region with their Western counterparts. The checkpoint would not allow pedestrians or bicycles crossing at all, and only on rare cases would private cars be allowed across. Generally speaking, crossing would take place via public transportation. Visitors would use a specially-established bus line connecting Duderstadt and Leinefelde. A West German bus operator would be in charge of the part between Duderstadt and the checkpoint and halfway between the West and East German toll bars the passengers would change to an East German bus. These regulations were designed to prevent Westerners from visiting the five-kilometer restricted security zone along the

[21] Nationale Front Bezirksausschuß Erfurt, 'Aktuelle Information laut Informationsbeschluß d. Sekretariats d. Nationalrates', 31 October 1972, BArch-B, DY 6, Nr. 4913; Nationale Front Bezirksaussschuß Erfurt, 'Wertung der am 21. Juni 1972 in 20 Grenzorten des Kreises Heiligenstadt durchgeführten Einwohnerforen', 30 June 1971, BArch-B, DY 6, Nr. 4913; Nationale Front Bezirksaussschuß Erfurt, 'Erste Wertung der Einwohnerforen, die durch das Bezirksreferentenkollektiv am 30.5.1972 im Kreis Worbis durchgeführt wurden', 6 February 1972, BArch-B, DY 6, Nr. 4913.
[22] Nationale Front Bezirksausschuß Erfurt, 'Stimmung und Meinung der Bürger zu den Verhandlungesergebnissen, bzw. über der Vertrag über die Grundlagen der Beziehungen zwischen der DDR und der BRD', 15 November 1972, BArch-B, DY 6, Nr. 4913.
[23] Nationale Front Bezirksausschuß Erfurt, 'Stimmung und Meinung der Bürger zu den Verhandlungesergebnissen, bzw. über der Vertrag über die Grundlagen der Beziehungen zwischen der DDR und der BRD', 15 November 1972, BArch-B, DY 6, Nr. 4913.
[24] 'Grenzübergang Noch Vor Weihnachten?', *Göttinger Allgemeine*, 5 December 1972, StAGö, Ztg. 204.

border, which remained out of bounds for Western visitors until 1989. The rigidity of this regulation exposes East German authorities' defensive position vis-à-vis the new border crossing arrangements drafted in the Basic Treaty with West Germany. The single-route bus, making only one stop in the GDR, made it easy to control Western visitors.

> The forty police officers stationed in Duderstadt for the weekend had their hands full. 20,000 people in 6,000 vehicles flooded Duderstadt and Gerblingerode on Sunday. The private cars of curious sightseers, who came to see the border checkpoint, parked along the entire road from the checkpoint . . . A similar volume of traffic is expected for next week as well, and thereafter begins the period of travel into the GDR. Duderstadt's sleeping beauty time is finally over.[25]

As this news story shows, Western excitement reached fever pitch when the checkpoint finally opened, following the entering into effect of the Basic Treaty, on 23 June 1973. There was very little actual border crossing during the first weeks, as application forms had been made available only several days earlier and processing applications took several weeks. But even the promised sight of vehicles crossing the border on this road, which had been severed for two decades, drew enormous crowds to the small town, more than trebling its population for the weekend. It was not just curiosity. As soon as they could, residents of the Western (Lower) Eichsfeld crossed into the GDR and pensioners from the Eastern (Upper) Eichsfeld enjoyed doing their shopping in Duderstadt. GNV regulations stipulated that crossing into the GDR must take place at the checkpoint closest to the destination. The Eichsfeld checkpoint quickly became the busiest of all eight checkpoints along the border, claiming a third of the total GNV traffic, and thus proving the attraction that the larger Upper Eichsfeld still held for residents of the Lower Eichsfeld. After a slow start in July, numbers grew by the month, especially after the GDR agreed to add two stops to the bus line and even more importantly, to open the checkpoint to private cars. With experience, GDR authorities became less concerned about Western visitors. They could see that the GNV traffic was touristic or personal in nature, and supervising it was not very difficult since everyone crossing it had to continue on the same narrow road, even by private car, until leaving the restricted zone. Of course the additional stops were not in the restricted zone, and cars were also strictly forbidden from making any stops in it. By October 1973, more than 20,000 Lower Saxons were crossing the border every month under the GNV.[26]

GDR restrictions resulted in traffic flow that was overwhelmingly West-to-East and whose numbers rose steeply on weekends and holidays. Under the previous system, travel was time-consuming, and the difficult-to-secure visit permits were

---

[25] 'Duderstadts Dornröschenschlaf ist vorbei', *Südhannoversche Volkszeitug*, 25 June 1973, KrAGö, A32, Nr. 25.

[26] 'Übergang stark genutzt', *Göttinger Allgemeine*, 15 September 1973, StAGö, Hauptamt C14, Nr. 78; '60,000 Bewohner Niedersachsens waren in der DDR', *Göttinger Tageblatt*, 3–4 November 1973, StAGö, Hauptamt C 14, Nr. 78; 'Grenzlagebericht für die zeit vom 1.10. bis 31.12.73', NLA-HStAH, Nds. 1150, Acc. 108/92, Nr. 184 T. 1.

issued for between one and three weeks. Western visitors to the GDR, therefore, usually had to spend their annual vacation or parts thereof across the border. The GNV turned visits to the GDR into a simple and flexible enough affair that visiting could fit into one's weekend and holiday schedule. Application processing for the permit could still take up to six weeks, but once in possession of a three-month permit, a person could choose to cross the border at any given date for up to nine single day visits during that period. Consequently, most GNV visiting happened during weekends and summer and major holidays. Such was the case during Easter of 1975: over the Easter weekend, more than 26,000 people in 7,700 vehicles crossed the checkpoint into the GDR. In freezing weather and intermittent snow storms, passengers waited as long as seven hours just to get to the checkpoint. The municipality of Duderstadt teamed up with the Red Cross and the police to try and alleviate their suffering, offering hot tea and selling sausages to those who were not lucky enough to find a chair in one of the few restaurants near the checkpoint.[27]

PERMANENT NEGOTIATION WITHOUT REGIONAL ADMINISTRATIONS

Negotiating disagreements, and comparing measurements to delineate the precise path of the border, took a long time. After years of work on this project, however, it became obvious that this was not the most complicated task on the road to reducing tension and improving quality of life along the border. The Basic Treaty had only charged the Border Committee with demarcation of the border, with the idea that coordination could be left to lower-level authorities. For this purpose, Border Information Points (*Grenzinformationspunkte*, henceforth GIPs) were installed along the border from 1973. The GIPs were direct phone connections between border-guarding units in East and West Germany, which covered parallel areas. These units were tasked with spreading information to the relevant authorities along the border and facilitating coordination through the GIPs. But the communication afforded by the GIPs proved insufficient to deal with the many elements of cross-border coordination necessitated by routine life along this border. The rigidity of GIP-based coordination under military discipline led to the development of two other channels of coordination: the permanent, state-level Border Committee and the re-emergence of individual action via personal networks. Notably absent from the developing system of cross-border coordination were local and regional administrations; these had served as the bedrock of coordination prior to 1945 and continued to play that role until at least the mid-1950s, as discussed in Chapter III.

By the end of 1976, the Border Committee had decided upon and marked 1,298 out of a total of 1,393 kilometers of border. The remaining 95 kilometers of disputed border stretched almost entirely along the river Elbe. Both sides agreed, as had

---

[27] Stadtdirektor Duderstadt to Landkreis Göttingen, 8 April 1975, KrAGö, A32, Nr. 4.

the Allies, that the Elbe would function as the border, but the maps provided by the Allies were not accurate enough to indicate if the borderline was drawn on the eastern bank or in the river itself. This question was of great consequence, as control over the river hinged on the answer. Could the GDR, for example, search boats on the river? Who would receive fishing rights? Critically, were East German border guards permitted to open fire at people who tried to escape while they were in the river?[28] The issue of the Elbe border remained unresolved until 1990, with many fluctuations in levels of tension and cooperation along the river.

This sticking point did not prevent the Border Committee from declaring its job done. The sides 'agreed to disagree' on the Elbe, or as the internal memoranda on the topic stated, to parenthesize (*ausklammern*) it. In internal discussions, GDR government officials voiced concerns that the West Germans were behaving evasively and the East Germans therefore insisted that a treaty over the border path would have to include an explicit statement that negotiations, especially regarding the Elbe, would continue.[29] The treaty was finally signed in Bonn on 29 November 1978.[30] With its mission accomplished, it seemed as if the Border Committee could be dissolved, six years after its establishment.

However, life along the border gave rise to problems that required coordination and negotiation. In six years of work, Committee members and their superiors came to value the Committee's role in both maintaining the border and facilitating communication between the two governments. A joint team to oversee mainten-ance work for the border marking would need to be established. The Border Committee had become the address for many of these issues. In addition, there was the Elbe issue, which the GDR insisted be handled by a known organ.[31]

Thus, with the initial border marking work almost complete, it turned out that high-level inter-state coordination was still required. The Border Committee then became a permanent coordinating body, that is, a conflict resolution mechanism, for the two German states. It served in this capacity until the GDR ceased to exist in 1990. Local and regional coordination across the border had broken down during the 1960s, as described in Chapter IV, yet there were many routine problems and quite a few emergencies that required such coordination. Some of the most frequently arising issues involved the maintenance of riverbeds, management of fires, and return of lost livestock. Pollution in border-crossing waterways was a

[28] Nass, *Vermessung*, 35–8, 141–2. See also Ministerrat der Deutschen Democratischen Republik, 'Konzepzion für das weitere Vorgehen der DDR-Delegations in der Grenzkommission DDR/BRD', 21 June 1976, BArch-B, DC 20 I/4/3585; for the position of Lower Saxony on the issue see 'Unterrichtung Über den Stand der Verhandlunge in der Grenzkommission', 11 November, 1974, NLA-HStAH, Nds. 380, Acc. 27/98, Nr. 37.

[29] W. Stoph, 'Konzeption für das Vorgehen der Delegation der DDR in der Grenzkommission DDR/BRD zum Abschluß der Vereinbarung der Regierung der DDR und der Regierung der BRD . . .', 21 June 1978, BArch-B, DC 20 I/4/4109.

[30] Nass, *Vermessung*, 125–44.

[31] 'Ordnung für die Arbeit der Kommission aus Beauftragten der Regierung der BRD und der Regierung der DDR 1978', 1 June 1978, NLA-HStAH, Nds. 380, Acc. 27/98, Nr. 49 is a draft of the final treaty (re-)establishing the Border Committee in 1978.

major concern for Western authorities. For example, in July 1969, the communities drawing water from the river Leine decided to stop pumping after a large number of dead fish were found in the river between the GDR border and Göttingen. The city of Hanover, further downstream, also issued a warning to its citizens about the possibility that poisoned water from the Leine would contaminate water supply in the city.[32] Authorities in these border districts as well as the municipality of Göttingen immediately attempted to contact their East German colleagues in order to determine the source of the pollution. Only the next day, however, was contact made by a water expert from Hanover, who got someone on the line at the district of Heiligenstadt, only to receive the laconic answer that for such issues he should contact the government of the GDR in Berlin. In the meantime, water testing had proven that the pollution was not as dangerous as suspected, and the alarm bells were silenced.[33]

GIPs were meant to supply the infrastructure for building the cooperation required to deal with situations like the pollution of the Leine. They were installed quite quickly following the establishment of the Border Committee itself. They proved themselves to be rather efficient channels of information exchange in cases where information was available and readily provided. The municipal and district office files in which GIP notifications were collected serve as an interesting record of the number and diversity of activities which took place in the immediate vicinity of the border. The files include notifications regarding, among other things, maintenance of roads and forests, hunting, herbicide spraying, clearing of riverbeds, political demonstrations, and official visits.[34]

GIPs were far less effective at resolving cases where information was unavailable or concealed, and had the least success at resolving cases that required actual coordination and negotiation, especially such that were time-sensitive. There were many border incidents with little or no political significance which demanded a measure of good will and coordination beyond a simple exchange of information. Since the information exchanges were formalized under a treaty and consisted of short phone calls between border guards who did not know each other, little, if any, good will surfaced in this mechanism. For example, on 15 April 1976, a hunting dog dug under the border fence near Wustrow and ran into the GDR. The forester to whom the dog belonged managed to have his district use the GIP, and three hours after the dog had escaped, the GIP operator in the West asked his East German colleague for help in retrieving the dog. The reply was short: 'I took notice of your message. It does not fall under the agreement over joint damage control along the border.'[35]

---

[32] 'Giftalarm in Niedersachsen: auch in der Leine Massensterben der Fische', *Göttinger Presse*, 7 February 1969, StAGö, Ztg. 196.

[33] 'Giftalarm aufgehoben Leine-Verpestung unter Kontrolle', *Göttinger Presse*, 7 May 1969, StAGö, Ztg. 196.

[34] 'Informationsaustausch in Schadensfällen gem. der Vereinbarung zwischen der BRD und der DDR', 18 August 1982, KrAGö, A32, Nr. 1 is just one example. The whole file is (and many files in other archives are) full of similar telegrams sent to local authorities from their GIPs.

[35] Vorkommnis Grenze am 15.4.1976, 22 April 1976, NLA-HStAH, Nds. 1150, Acc. 108/92, Nr. 227.

Such issues could have been easily resolved via direct coordination between community and district councils on both sides of the border, as they indeed were frequently solved during the 1950s. But, contrary to the expectations of at least some frontier residents, the process of compromise through the Border Committee did not lead to re-establishing these contacts. Most of the mayors and district administrators had been replaced during the intervening decades, and there existed an almost complete lack of communication across the border. Local politicians along the border did not make use of the new opportunities to cross the border in order to establish contact with their colleagues. When the forester turned to his district to retrieve the dog, it turned out that the frontier administration depended on the federal armed forces for cross-border communication.

This remarkable transformation within a relatively short time span is noteworthy. During the early 1950s, as demonstrated in Chapter III, frontier politicians and functionaries on both sides of the border entertained lively contacts with 'the other side'. In fact state agencies on both sides had to work hard during that period to control such contacts. Only two decades later, the process of division had made strangers of frontier administration in East and West Germany, with border-crossing communication monopolized by state agencies.

There were exceptions to the rule though, especially when the issue at hand was of a private and politically insignificant nature, such as the aforementioned case of the runaway hunting dog. The GNV opened a channel for easy, unplanned passage of Western frontier residents into East German frontier districts (excluding the five-kilometer restricted zone). This enabled Western frontier residents to form—or renew—contacts across the border. Such contacts were perforce limited in coordination capacity, being informal and devoid of legal or administrative power. And yet, the incident of the runaway dog highlights their potential. After the district administration (via the GIP) failed to produce the hoped-for result, the frustrated forester received some unexpected help. Georg Lampe, a member of the local German Shepherd Association, heard about the incident and offered his assistance. He had good contacts across the border and his three months' crossing permit was valid. He set out for the nearby town of Salzwedel (GDR) on the morning of 19 April, a trip of about 50 kilometers via the closest GNV checkpoint. At Salzwedel he was shunted from one acquaintance to another, but when he got to the town hall he found a sympathetic ear. The person who received him there was also a hunter and dog lover and he promised to help. Lampe produced the international vaccination certificates of the dog and it took the municipal employee all of several hours to track the dog down. Together they went to a local dog kennel and retrieved the dog. Though he was not asked to do so, Lampe paid the kennel owner some money for taking care of the dog and then took it back with him.[36]

While local and regional administration had gradually given up on border-crossing contacts, and under the new system was unable or unwilling to re-establish them, frontier residents capitalized on the GNV to form connections and pursue

---

[36] 'Vorkommnis Grenze am 15.4.1976', 22 April 1976, NLA-HStAH, Nds. 1150, Acc. 108/92, Nr. 227.

coordination. These newly founded border-crossing networks were sometimes based on pre-division ones and often on kinship ties. A 1983 Stasi report on the district of Worbis (East German part of the Eichsfeld) suggested that the most important channel for Western subversion in the district was 'traditionally existing kinship ties in the border area'. These were upheld and used for the spreading of Western propaganda through the GNV.[37] Lampe's first visit in Salzwedel was to a forester whom he knew from way back when. But he returned from the 'dog-finding mission' with two new friends in the persons of the town clerk and the kennel owner. In this case, the Western frontier district turned to the border guards and the GIP because the border with East Germany had severed all other administrative contacts.

A SITE OF WEST GERMAN INSUBORDINATION

During the 1970s and 80s, West German border forces frequently found themselves in an awkward position, trying to enforce the inter-German border despite its lacking legal standing within West German law. In 1976, the BGS unit stationed in Duderstadt asked the rural district of Göttingen for help with one such case. The farmer Bernhard Hartenkopf was renting several fields situated directly on the border path, and had been tilling land on these fields several meters into GDR territory since at least 1971. He declared in hearings not to have known that he had overstepped the borderline, and yet repeated the same 'mistake' every year. BGS officers time and again warned and instructed him, but Hartenkopf proved himself incorrigible (*unbelehrbar*).[38] The BGS command expressed frustration in this letter that:

> Due to the legal positions of the federal government, the only action that can currently be taken against a farmer who plows land beyond the border is to instruct him about the dangers that his actions give rise to. In the mentioned case of Mr. Hartenkopf, this has been undertaken keenly enough.[39]

To prevent inadvertent violation, the BGS placed large warning signs along the border. In hearings with BGS officers, Hartenkopf denied any knowledge of damages caused to BGS border signs placed over the years along his fields and the BGS had no evidence to connect him or his workers to these damages. West German border-guard reports reveal that this was hardly an exceptional case. In many cases, West German farmers who tilled fields, felled trees, and grazed livestock along the border, crossed the borderline and utilized land, grass, and trees east of the line.[40]

---

[37] 'Erhebungsprogramm Kreis Worbis Mai 1983', BStU Aussenstelle Erfurt, MfS, BV Eft Abt. Kusch, Nr. 1878.

[38] Grenzschutzabteilung III/5 to Landkreis Göttingen, 11 September 1976, KrAGö, A32, Nr. 4.

[39] Grenzschutzabteilung III/5 to Landkreis Göttingen, 11 November 1976, KrAGö, A32, Nr. 4.

[40] 'an der deutsch-deutschen Grenze herrscht ein korrekter Ton vor', *Göttinger Tageblatt*, 3 January 1985; Witt, 'Aktenvermerk', 10 October 1978, NLA-HStAH, Nds. 1150, Acc. 108/92, Nr. 229.

One might expect that this phenomenon would have been of greater concern to East German than West German authorities. After all, those farmers violated GDR sovereignty regularly and used East German resources without paying rent or taxes. And yet, to the dismay of West German border guards, their Eastern colleagues did nothing to prevent the violation. This was the result of the closely related processes of inter-German compromise and GDR border construction measures, both of which gained momentum during the 1970s.

The 1970s saw intensive border fortification by the GDR. Growing portions of the land along the border path were swallowed up by double and triple fences, minefields, dog runs, patrol roads, and 'no man's land'. Border build-up is identified in literature and popular imagination with 1961 and the Berlin Wall. But along the rural border, fortification was a prolonged process. Lower Saxony shared the longest border with the GDR of all West German *Länder*, 525 kilometers in total. The yearly BGS reports meticulously detailed the progress of fortification works along this border. At the beginning of 1972, there were only 209km of double fences, the new third fence had not been started yet, and automatic firing devices were mounted along 42km of fence.[41] By the end of 1979 the numbers were 545km, 436km, and 187km respectively.[42]

These gradually spreading installations swallowed ever-greater swaths of land east of the divide. In a process which began in 1952 and gathered momentum between the late 1960s and the end of the 1970s, arable land along the border was taken over by various facilities and construction, or fell under restrictions and was eventually left fallow. Border construction thus pushed East German farmers away from the immediate vicinity of the border along most of its length.[43] This partly accounts for Hartenkopf's ability to usurp land unchallenged by farmers on the Eastern side. Forbidden from tilling these plots, East German farmers never bothered to approach the relevant authorities in East Germany to protest Hartenkopf's unilateral annexation. It is even unclear whether any of the owners of those plots ever knew that their land had been taken over.

The question remains, though, why East German authorities, who clearly knew of such highly visible routine violations, did not act to prevent them. East German border guards—since the late 1950s soldiers in the National People's Army—were aided by ever-more sophisticated technology and were instructed to avoid unnecessary interaction with Westerners. To reduce the temptation to desert to the West,

---

[41] Bundesgrenzschutz Kommando Nord, 'Lageentwicklung im Jahre 1972 an der Demarkationslinie zur DDR im Bereich des GSK Nord', 8 January 1973, NLA-HstAH, Nds. 1150, Acc. 108/92, Nr. 184 T. 2, 231.

[42] Bundesgrenzschutz Kommando Nord, 'Lageentwicklung an der Grenze zur DDR im Abschnitt GSK Nord im Jahre 1979', 15 January 1980, NLA-HstAH, Nds. 1150, Acc. 108/92, Nr. 186, 75. The 545km length of the double fence appears in this report. I can only surmise that it could be longer than the actual border because the fence took extra turns in some points.

[43] Many land transactions in those decades were explained in the official land registry entries as necessary for grounds of 'border security'. See, for example, the official transfer of land from an agricultural collective in the village of Asbach to the district authority of Heiligenstadt in 1986: 'Antrag auf Fortführung des Wirtschaftskatasters - Änderung des Nutzungsverhältnisses', 24 February, 1986, ThHStAW, Katasteramt Heiligenstadt- Witschaftskataster Gemeinde Asbach Bl. 1r.

their command reduced their presence in the immediate vicinity of the border-line. The double metal mesh fences were built anywhere from ten to 500 meters east of the actual border-line. They came to demarcate the eastern-most line of operation for the majority of East German border guards most of the time.[44] Patrols west of the fence became sparse. The territory between the fences and the border-line could be supervised from the new watchtowers, hundreds of which were built along the border in the same period. By 1978, the GDR border strip with Lower Saxony had on average a watchtower for every 2.5km of border.[45] Soldiers in the towers were mostly preoccupied with watching the areas east of the fence, from where potential '*Republikflucht*' attempts were expected to come. Nevertheless, upon identification of a border violation, patrols could quickly cross the fence and approach violators by opening fence sections that were equipped with quick-release screws.

Thus, the procedural and theoretical apparatus was in place for East German border guards to efficiently manage most kinds of border violation. But their border-guarding strategy had a weak spot that Western residents of the border areas learned to leverage. East German state organizations had a very difficult time defending their sovereignty against *willful* crossing of the border, so long as the persons crossing remained very close to the border-line. Eastern border guards could quite easily make people who accidentally crossed the border retreat by shouting or discharging warning shots. But what were the options open to East German border guards when a Western citizen worked several meters inside GDR territory and did not retreat when warned? A patrol could be sent across the fence, but that would leave the 'provocateur' enough time to take the few steps back to the FRG. Shooting at him from the tower was technically possible but politically very risky because that would by definition entail shooting at the territory of the FRG, which counted as a severe border incident. A more benign solution, such as spraying herbicides on the fields, would have created fodder for Western propaganda against the GDR. I do not know if these were even considered, but it is clear that border-guard command instructed units in the field to let these farmers be.

I suggest that GDR authorities had strong incentives, especially after 1976, to turn a blind eye to Western farmers' usurpation of land. GDR authorities documented these cases carefully, and laid them before the Border Committee as border incidents blamed on the West. This was precious currency in the developing dynamics in the Committee. The Western delegation, eager to avoid dealing with the problem of the border path along sections of the Elbe river, tried to direct discussions to what it presented as practical affairs, especially towards environmental issues and increased options for inter-German travel. The GDR delegation wanted to open as little as possible its borders for Western intervention and so raising complaints about border violations by Western farmers came in

[44] Göttinger Tageblatt, 'Bald sind alle Minen gesprengt: viele Flüchtversuche in der DDR scheitern weit vor der Grenze', *Göttinger Tageblatt*, 27 June 1985, describes the spread of double fences and sophisticated electronic devices along the border of Lower Saxony with the DDR.

[45] Bundesgrenzschutz Kommando Nord, 'Lageentwicklung an der Grenze zur DDR im Abschnitt GSK Nord im Jahre 1978', 15 January 1979, NLA-HstAH, Nds. 1150, Acc. 108/92, Nr. 186 T. 2, 210.

handy. While Western representatives submitted complaints about the poisoning of waterways, explosion of mines, and more, the GDR delegation could this way produce numerically equal or superior lists of '*Grenzverletzungen*' that the West had not solved.[46] At the annual press conference held by the BGS unit in Duderstadt to summarize 1984 the unit commander reportedly stated that:

> Quite a few farmers were caught red-handed, having extended their fields into GDR territory. They plowed up to two meters on the other side of the border. Such incidents [are so important that they] are sometimes discussed even in the German-German border committee.[47]

West German farmers along the border routinely exploited the GDR border guarding's 'weakness' and got hold of free, untaxed land, wood, and pasture, a bonus courtesy of German division. The dynamics of the inter-German compromise made this free pass a problem for the federal government of West Germany. And so, indirectly, protecting the sovereignty of the GDR, the absolute inviolability (*unverletzlichkeit*) of its border became a priority of Western border guards, and authorities more generally.

On the night of 30–31 July 1978, three two-meter-high GDR border posts with the emblem DDR were vandalized. The top 30cm of each of the solid concrete-over-metal constructions was broken to bits and the cast iron emblems were stolen. GDR border guards heard the hard pounding noise from afar but did not get to the spot on time. When they did get there, they established that the culprits had come from the West and that their Western colleagues from the Federal Border Guard and the police were also examining the scene.[48]

Farmers' obstinacy and cool economic calculation were not the sole sources of frustration for West and East German border guards. During the 1970s, they had to deal with border incidents involving growing numbers of West German men using the negotiated, marked, and sealed border for night-time pranks, displays of courage or stupidity, and violent aggression. These violations generally fell into one of two categories: attacks against symbolic elements of the border marking or barrier,[49] and attempts to climb fences into the GDR under the influence of alcohol.[50]

Beyond damages to property and health, such acts were a nuisance to border guards and other state agencies. They spelled full-scale alarm along portions of the border, night service for many guards, officers, and policemen on both sides, and

---

[46] Nass, *Die Vermessung*, 38.

[47] Göttinger Tageblatt, 3 January 1985, 'an der deutsch-deutschen Grenze herrscht ein korrekter Ton vor'.

[48] Referatsleiter SK Major Schleicher and Leiter der Abteilung IX Oberstleutnant Thiele, 'Information', 30 July 1978, BStU, MfS, BV Suhl, Abt. IX, nr. 187. See also other incidents reported in the same file.

[49] Der Kommandeur, Grenztruppen der DDR, Grenzregiment 1, 'Protokoll der Beratung des Zusammenwirkens des Kommandeurs Grenzregiment 1 mit den Leitern der anderen Schutz- und Sicherheitsorgane der...', 12 April 1985, BStU, MfS, BV Erfurt, KD Langensalza, Nr. 68.

[50] 'Lageentwicklung im Jahre 1973 an der Demarkationslinie zur DDR im Abschnitt des GSK Nord', 17 January 1974, NLA-HStAH, Nds. 1150, Acc. 108/92, nr. 184 T 1.

later interrogations and much paperwork. Some of these incidents landed their instigators under East German border-guard custody, and some of them were only released to the West ('pushed back' was how most reports put it) days later, after they were investigated and paid a fine. This, for example, was the case of the miner T. F., married and father of three, from Kronach in the Bavarian frontier area. He drank alcohol and had a fight with his wife. Wanting to frighten her, he declared 'I'm leaving', and rode his bicycle to the nearby border fence. He proceeded to climb the fence and immediately turned himself in and asked to be sent back to the West. He explained that it was a sentimental act of a drunken man and no more. Two days later he was 'pushed back' to the West. Like the farmers who usurped borderland, so too these border violators became grist for the GDR complaint mill in the Border Committee.

BORDER CROSSING AFTER OSTPOLITIK

Ironically, the same mutual recognition that increased the West German ability to legally cross the border functioned as a spur to the final push in this border build-up, ultimately making illegal crossings nearly impossible. Following the Basic Treaty and the Border Committee's work, the inter-German border solidified in a manner that had not been theretofore possible. Other than the Elbe, there were no longer areas of disputed border path. Furthermore, international recognition, and especially West German commitment to respect GDR sovereignty along the border, enabled East German state agencies to extend border fortifications systematically and to guard the border more effectively than ever before.

The Basic Treaty with West Germany fuelled the East German border- construction project of the 1970s. The border reached its most ominous form in the latter half of the seventies specifically because important limitations on border construction were lifted by the Border Committee and the *Grundvertrag* more generally. It is well documented that the GDR dramatically changed its attitude to the inter-German border in the autumn of 1961. Following the construction of the Berlin Wall in August of that year, Berlin was transformed from an almost unprotected opening in the border into its most guarded section. Consequently, as discussed in Chapter IV, the number of illegal crossing attempts along the rural border grew, and with them the determination of central agencies in East Berlin to improve their control over the border. This project was not completed in 1961, or even by the end of that decade. Partly, the length of the process was due to the enormity of the task and the limited means at hand. But it was also held back because it brought to the fore conflicts with West German authorities—over the exact path of the border, for example, and over land and water rights. Under the new reality of compromise, East German decision makers no longer felt an urgency to worry about West German reactions. The work of the Border Committee, eliminating disputes and demarcating separate sovereign territories, endowed GDR state agencies with the confidence to push this prolonged project to its completion.

The decade of *Ostpolitik* and the Basic Treaty was also the decade of final bordering and division. The physical transformation of the border accelerated parallel to the work of the Border Committee. Along with the double and then triple fencing, minefields were extended, automatic firing devices were installed, dog runs, bunkers, and watchtowers spread along the entire border. The result was that illegal border crossing became significantly more perilous during that decade, even for frontier residents and border guards. Though it never became impenetrable, the inter-German border certainly earned its renown as the best-guarded border in the world in this period. Along the rural border, the percentage of successful escapes out of total attempts (which never went below 20 per cent prior to the Basic Treaty) dropped to single digits by the early eighties. The total annual number of successful escapes to the West over the GDR border with Lower Saxony (constituting over a third of the length of the border and the site of more than half the number of successful escapes) dropped from a bit over 300 in 1969 to only 11 one decade later, representing the trend for the entire border.[51]

Already in 1972, some Western observers noted that the GDR's actions along the border did not demonstrate greater permeability of the border, nor did they reflect closer relationships between the people or the governments of West and East Germany. Expectations in the West that the treaty would lead to greater openness in a variety of East–West relations were dashed when a series of new regulations by the GDR government demonstrated its own perspective. State employees in different offices, for example, were instructed to report all manner of contacts they had in the West and were reminded that, as bearers of secrets, they were forbidden from entertaining such contacts. Critique in the Bundestag forced the West German coalition into a defensive stance, and the federal government announced that it would protest.[52] The fact was that the Basic Treaty and the traffic treaty which preceded it had not given the West German government much influence over East German border policy beyond the letter of the agreement itself. The GDR was still wary of border-crossing travel and still sought to limit it as much as possible. It agreed to the GNV not as part of a new-found willingness to open the border, but, rather, in order to win the political and financial benefits of the treaty.

GDR leaders expected the work of the Border Committee to allow for a hermetic sealing of the border and reduce uncontrolled interactions across the border. Their approach to the work of the Committee itself was telling: to prevent fraternization or temptations from Western participants, secret service personnel supervised the

[51] Grenzschutzkommando Nord, 'Lageentwicklung in Jahre 1970 an der Demarkationslinie zur DDR im Bereich des GSK Nord', 8 January 1971, NLA-HStAH, Nds. 1150, Acc. 108/92, Nr. 183; Grenzschutzkommando Nord, 'Lageentwicklung an der Grenze zur DDR im Abschnitt des GSK Nord im Jahre 1978', 15 January 1979, NLA-HStAH, Nds. 1150, Acc. 108/92, Nr. 186 T2, 207–11. The Stasi also collected this data. See for example 'Protokoll der Beratung des Zusammenwirkens mit den Schutz- und Sicherheitsorganen der Grenzkreise . . .', 22 May 1985, BStU, KD Mühlhausen, Nr. 38 and similar reports in the same file.

[52] 'DDR Bremst Westkontakte', *Göttinger Tageblatt*, 12 July 1972; 'DDR errichtet Drahtzaun', *Göttinger Tageblatt*, 12 July 1972; 'Kritik an DDR-Vorgehen dauert an', *Göttinger Tageblatt*, 11 September 1973; 'Behinderungen im Besuchsverkehr bestätigt', *Göttinger Tageblatt*, 21 December 1972.

works of all GDR teams on the ground. The name chosen for the Stasi's operation to secure the Border Committee's work was symbolic—'*Beton*' (German for concrete).[53] While the treaty itself and the Border Committee offered East German state agencies the prospect of legitimacy and efficient border control, the GNV was perceived as a threat. The opening of new checkpoints and the influx of Western visitors in border areas elicited, therefore, not a relaxation of border regulation, but, rather, precisely the opposite.

At least in the short term, then, the Basic Treaty led to an imposition of stricter discipline on the border. It made it easier for Westerners and privileged East Germans to receive a crossing permit, but at the same time it brought this border the closest it ever got to being impenetrable for illegal crossing. The years immediately following the signing of the treaty saw a tightening of regulation and control, along with the above-mentioned build-up of border fortifications. The German–German compromise thus solidified both states' control over the border between them, endowing state agencies on both sides with greater leverage vis-à-vis their respective citizens.

Illegal border crossing had become perilous, even for frontier locals and border guards, as the above-noted numbers show. What the numbers don't reveal, however, is the excruciating nature of even successful escapes. The story of the East German border guard Hans-Jürgen Pflug, who escaped to the West on 7 April 1978, is a good example. Pflug served as a guard in the unit stationed not far from the new checkpoint. He knew the terrain and guarding routine and prepared his flight well. He chose a spot where he knew he could reach the fences without walking through minefields. He crawled to the fences unnoticed and climbed the first one successfully. While climbing the second fence he was not careful enough and activated the automatic firing device, wounding both his calves badly. He still managed to fall to the Western side of the fence and drag himself a further hundred meters before collapsing. Doctors at the hospital in Duderstadt, to which the West German border guards brought him, took more than a hundred metal splitters out of his legs. He was hospitalized for several weeks while local media celebrated his heroism and highlighted the cruelty of the East German border policies.[54]

Pflug's hardships seemed be over after he left the hospital. To local media and politics, Pflug symbolized the victory of free human spirit over oppressive communist dictatorship; a victory, in other words, of West over East Germany. He was not an Eichsfelder and had no local connections (or relatives in West Germany), but having become a popular figure in the Lower Eichsfeld during his recovery, he

[53] See for example Bezirksverwaltung für Staatssicherheit Suhl SR III, 'Auskunftsbericht über Handlungen gegnerischer Kräfte im Rahmen der Aktion 'Beton' im Jahre 1974', 21 February 1975, BStU, MfS, BV Suhl, Abteilung III, Nr. 756; Nass, *Die Vermessung*, 248–88 reprinted a copy of Erich Mielke's command framing 'operation concrete' and announcing its name.

[54] Zollkommissariat Duderstadt, 'Grenzgänger Ost-West am 7. April 1978', 8 April 1978, NLA-HStAH, Nds. 1150, Acc. 108/92, Nr. 9; see also Ute Rang, 'auf dem Kolonnenweg: Mutter holt Sohn zurück in DDR', *Thueringer Allgemeine Online Edition*, 9 March 2011, www.thueringer-allgemeine.de/startseite/detail/-/specific/Auf-dem-Kolonnenweg-27-Mutter-holt-Sohn-zurueck-in-DDR-935791181, accessed 26 June 2013.

was 'adopted' by Duderstadt. Local businesses collected money and favours for him. The 21-year-old was immediately given a job at a car factory, an apartment, and a small sum in a bank account. Quite quickly it turned out that that same free spirit who had beaten Eastern oppression could not find his way in Western freedom and plenty. Pflug found it hard to make a new life in the West. He could not hold on to a job, did not become part of any social circle, spent a lot of time drinking and soon began accumulating debts. Before Christmas, his mother came from Stansdorf near Potsdam to visit him in Duderstadt. Within a few days, they sold the few belongings he had and went back to Stansdorf together, leaving disappointed creditors behind.[55]

In East Germany, Pflug turned from (yet another) example of the allure of the West into a relatively rare exemplar of the cold, materialistic reality greeting crossers. The once-uniformed border guard who became a border violator returned home a penniless criminal and was sent to prison. In West Germany, he started out as a local celebrity demonstrating the positive human qualities of East German citizens, and ended as a shameful story about lazy and incapable products of East German education. From dramatic, near-death escape to low-profile bus ride back across the Iron Curtain, Pflug's eight-month-long border-crossing experience tells much about the progress of German division by the late 1970s.

Pflug was not the only East German refugee who chose to repatriate. Of the 19 West Germans who crossed the border into the territory of the county of Suhl (GDR) during the second half of 1974, five were former GDR citizens.[56] He also was not the only one who had a hard time achieving economic solvency in the West and who returned to East Germany to avoid his creditors. In July 1974, West German border guards picked up a man who had crossed the border from the GDR. The escapee refused to produce identifying documents and was taken to the police station to check his identity. It turned out that he had already migrated to the FRG ten months earlier, but had run into debt and gone back east.[57] His failed attempt to return to the status of newly arrived refugee, receive a new welcome packet and a fresh start with the authorities, would probably have found sympathy with Pflug.

From 1952, the GDR made efforts to bring back *Republikflüchtige*, and the western press was probably accurate in assuming that Pflug's mother only received a permit to visit her son because she had made some kind of deal with the Stasi to convince him to return. During the first three months of 1987, for example, the Erfurt Stasi branch managed to 'win back' (*rückgewinnen*) three GDR citizens who illegally left for the West during the preceding year. In all three cases this success was

---

[55] 'Nur Schulden blieben hier: In die DDR zurückgekehrt', *Göttinger Tageblatt*, 2 February 1979; 'Rückkehr des ehem. Soldaten der DDR-GrTr Pflug (Fluchtdatum: 7.4.78) in die DDR', 2 June 1979, Nds. 1150, Acc. 108/92, NLA-HStAH; Rang, 'auf dem Kolonnenweg'.

[56] Abteilung IX/4, Bezirksverwaltung für Staatssicherheit Suhl, 'Analyse der ungesetzlichen Grenzübertritte BRD-DDR im Zeitraum vom 01.07.1974 bis 31.03.1975 im Bereich der Staatsgrenze des Bezirkes Suhl', 4 October 1975, BStU, BV Suhl, Abt. IX, Nr. 1123.

[57] 'Grenzlagebericht für die Zeit vom 1.7 bis 30.9.1974', 10 November 1974, NLA-HStAH, Nds. 1150, Acc. 108/92, nr. 184 T 1.

brought about through the cooperation of family members.[58] But as much as the GDR was concerned about the public relations battle with the West, it was not willing to simply accept anyone who was disappointed by the 'Golden West'. G. I. was one such case. As recorded by the Stasi, he had tried to move to the West since 1970. He was twice caught attempting to illegally cross the border. The second time was in January 1972. After a year in prison, his request to be released from his GDR citizenship was granted and he was deported to West Germany just three days after the signing of the Basic Treaty. In the FRG he managed to get work as an unskilled labourer. The Stasi record from July 1974 documents his interrogation following his third attempt in 18 months to return to the GDR. He was pushed back after short detainments in May and June 1973. In February 1974 he lost his job in the West and subsisted on charity. In July he managed to cross the border unnoticed into the GDR but was caught by the police in a nearby town. He stated that he wanted to get back to living with his family and hoped to get a steady job. He was fined for damages and pushed back to West Germany.[59]

The broader picture of border crossing helps us understand these men—and many other East–West migrants in the 1970s and 80s. Whereas moving from East to West Germany until the mid-fifties was not much different from moving between different cities or regions within a single country, by the late seventies it had become much more complicated. With the exceptions of language, weather, and food, the stark differences between the states demanded a period of adjustment. Finding and holding on to a job was not a skill that East Germans were required to develop; most GDR emigrants to the West had not reckoned in advance that it might be difficult to pay rent, insurance, and food (let alone shiny consumer goods) on a low-level worker salary. Migration confronted them with life behind the shopping windows of the post-oil-crisis West. Eight of the 21 people who were caught entering the territory of the County of Suhl from the West in the second half of 1974 stated that they had failed to find steady employment.[60] Like Pflug and G. I., B. M. also was disappointed by his new life in the West after he managed to cross the border illegally. The trained dairy-farm worker was initially hired as unskilled labourer by Volkswagen in Wolfsburg but was unhappy there and resigned. He did temporary work on different farms but found that he had to work long hours for meagre wages. Disillusioned, he decided to return to the GDR, where he was sure that his profession would ensure a secure existence.[61]

---

[58] 'Lagecharakterisierender Erscheinunge und Arbeitsergebnisse zur Einschätzung der politisch-operativen Lage im Verantwortungsbereich der Bezirksverwaltung Erfurt im Monat März 1987', 4 October 1987, BStU, BdL 1409.

[59] Abteilung IX/4, Bezirksverwaltung für Staatssicherheit Suhl, 'Analyse der ungesetzlichen Grenzübertritte BRD-DDR im Zeitraum vom 01.07.1974 bis 31.03.1975 im Bereich der Staatsgrenze des Bezirkes Suhl', 4 October 1975, BStU, BV Suhl, Abt. IX, Nr. 1123. The same file holds reports of other similar cases. See also Major Meyer, 'Antrag auf Reisesperre', 23 January 1973, BStU, KD Heiligenstadt, Nr. 60.

[60] Major Meyer, 'Antrag auf Reisesperre', 23 January 1973, BStU, KD Heiligenstadt, Nr. 60.

[61] Major Meyer, 'Antrag auf Reisesperre', 23 January 1973, BStU, KD Heiligenstadt, Nr. 60. The same file holds reports of many similar cases, all based primarily on information given by the people themselves in Stasi interrogations.

The experience of many Westerners visiting the GDR for the first time through the GNV was also that of travelling to a foreign country. For some of them, this was actually the point of attraction—finding cheap wares and services or enjoying certain kinds of food and cultural activities that were not available in the West.[62] Some West Germans went to the GDR because it offered a political alternative to what a growing number of young West Germans perceived as an oppressive conservative regime in the West. W. J. declared in his Stasi interrogation that he was a Baader-Meinhoff supporter and had brought documents of his arrests in West Germany to prove it. He also brought an unemployed friend with him, promising that in the GDR they would both have regular jobs.[63] Edith Sheffer argues convincingly that the growing number of border-crossing visits under the GNV from 1973 brought about a recognition of the differences and distance to which the border had given rise over two decades of division, and even contributed to a deepening of this perceived divide between relatives and neighbours.[64]

CHANGE THROUGH RAPPROCHEMENT? REFLECTIONS ON OSTPOLITIK AND REUNIFICATION

Brandt and Bahr had not relinquished the aspiration for a reunification of the two German states. As they presented it to the West German public, the goal of their new policy was to breathe life into the prospect of unification by enabling livelier contact and exchanges on many levels across the border. The story told so far in this chapter suggests that this aim was not fulfilled as hoped. But the 'change through rapprochement' (*Wandel durch Annäherung*) strategy as it emerges from the files is far from being that of a straightforward failure. There is no doubt that the Basic Treaty led to a gradual increase in the volume of contact between West and East Germans. It is also clear that at least as a broad phenomenon, this contact contributed to East Germans' knowledge of life in the West and their tendency to 'grumble' at their own situation and their leadership.

This was identified early as a threat by the East German Ministry for State Security, the Stasi, and taken very seriously. Of course, the Stasi had been monitoring GDR citizens' contacts with West Germany long before the Basic Treaty. Influence of the 'Western enemy' was considered a primary cause for East Germans' insufficient support of their regime, as well as for a host of other problems. This scapegoating was partially related to a refusal to acknowledge governmental failures, guideline inadequacies, or pressure from Soviet overlords. Exposure to the West was probably not the cause—or not the most important one at any rate—of East Germans' complaints regarding issues such as the disrepair of roads or the quality of consumer goods available in stores. But even if we clear Stasi newspeak of its

---

[62] Sheffer, *Burned Bridge*, 225–9. Her findings on this were reinforced by accounts of Eastern and Western Eichsfelder I spoke to about such visits.
[63] 'Analyse der ungesetzlichen Grenzübertritte', 10 April 1975, BV Suhl, Abt. IX, Nr. 1123.
[64] Sheffer, *Burned Bridge*, 225–9.

paranoid and jargon-laden apologetics, its reports indicate a direct relationship between contact with the West and citizen disaffection.

Stasi reports also demonstrate the kind of channels opened for contact across the border after the Basic Treaty and the manner in which these channels influenced East Germans. The Stasi recognized 'adversarial contact-politics' (*gegnerische Kontaktpolitik*) of the West as a rising problem and tried to marshall forces to combat it.[65] The detailed reports deal with individual as well as institutional contacts, which Stasi operatives and informants dug up in conversations, by reading mail, and monitoring the activities of certain groups and individuals. The GNV was considered most susceptible to personal-type contact-politics. A 1983 report from the Stasi office in Worbis specifically stated that Western GNV visitors influenced people who sought emigration from the GDR towards illegal border crossing. The same report cautiously proposed that historical kinship networks did not affect members of GDR security organizations, but expressed certainty that they penetrated all other state agencies in the district, which therefore required strict surveillance.[66]

A Stasi report from 1976 mentioned three major areas of activity of *Kontaktpolitik*: health, church, and sport. Under each of these titles, the reporters highlighted recent trends related to changes following the Basic Treaty, explaining how growing exposure to Western contacts created problems for the GDR. Under the rubric of 'Church' the report reviewed many kinds of activities by individual ministers and priests and by religious organizations. The report showed that individual clergymen from West Germany had been making use of the single-day visiting permits to establish relationships with colleagues in East Germany. In conversations they had in the GDR, these Western priests raised ideas of more political engagement of Christians, greater protection of Christian faith in public life and more. Among other things, the report discusses a high-school reunion in the town of Schalkau (Thuringia, GDR) close to the western border. In his speech, the local priest warmly congratulated the graduates who came from West Germany, asserting that their participation demonstrated the strength of German unity beyond divisions and expressed his hope that the younger generation would find ways to bring about a true reunification.[67] Supporting reunification was a clear statement of opposition to the GDR government, and in the Stasi's book such utterances were clearly caused by increased contacts with the West.

The primary issue in the 'Health' category was a hoary one: trained physicians who wanted to emigrate to the West in order to enjoy the higher salaries, access to

---

[65] For example: Leiter der Abteilung XIX Major Wolf, 'Berichterstattung Kontaktpolitik/ Kontakttätigkeit', 14 September 1976, BStU, MfS BV Suhl, AKG 73, Bd. 4; Leiter der Abteilung XX oberstleutnant Heinz, 'Berichterstattung über weitere Erkenntnisse und Erfahrungen zur gegnerischen Kontaktpolitik/- Tätigkeit...', 14 September 1976, BStU, MfS BV Suhl, AKG 73, Bd. 4.

[66] 'Erhebungsprogramm Kreis Worbis', May 1983, BStU, MfS, BV Eft, Abt. Kusch, 1878.

[67] Oberstleutnant Heinz, 'Berichterstattung über weitere Erkenntnisse und Erfahrungen zur gegnerischen Kontaktpolitik/- Tätigkeit...', 14 September 1976, BStU, MfS, BV Suhl, AKG 73, Bd. 4, here pp. 5–10.

184 *States of Division*

better technology, and research facilities that the West offered. Alongside this traditional concern of the GDR, the report mentioned that in the mid-1970s there was a growing phenomenon of medical practitioners who requested permits to emigrate following love affairs that they had had with Westerners. Such affairs had their roots, according to the report, in tourism. The growing number of Westerners who visited the GDR created the major channel for these relationships. Other couples found each other during coterminous visits in one of the Eastern Bloc countries, where GDR citizens increasingly spent their vacations.[68] As for sports:

> individuals and clubs from West Germany increasingly pursue sport-contacts in lower levels to similarly positioned institutions in the GDR. As a result of these efforts to establish contacts we must note that...there are more discussions among sports-functionaries, athletes, and other people regarding the establishment of sports-relations. In these discussions, the following problems are mentioned...[69]

The 'problems' listed were actually forms of protest against the GDR sports authorities' prohibiting lower-level sports matches with the FRG. The last of the items on the list stated that: 'The SED apparently does not trust the Republic's athletes, and presumably will only allow sports-relations on lower levels after the construction of socialism will be finished.'[70]

The Basic Treaty did not empower local authorities to form official contacts and did not remove the obstacles for regional cooperation across the border, as discussed in Chapters III and IV. The GDR insisted on politicizing cross-border meetings, and the FRG stuck to its guns and forbade the broaching of political or otherwise controversial issues. But the new mobility of Westerners across the border led to many initiatives for exchange and cooperation by East and West Germans, especially in border areas. These initiatives flew in the face of GDR policy, exposing it as the force against greater contact and cooperation. In the atmosphere of the Helsinki era of the Cold War, with *Ostpolitik* having become the mainstay of West German politics even after Brandt's demise, this reflected badly on the GDR. Growing numbers of East and West Germans sought and found channels for increased contact and many of them realized that despite its pretentions to the contrary, the GDR government opposed and tried to curb such contacts. East Germans involved in such initiatives understood also that their regime distrusted them and sought to limit their mobility and social horizons. The Basic Treaty put the GDR leadership in a defensive position, forcing it to both formally accept and in practice act against border-crossing contact.

---

[68] Oberstleutnant Heinz, 'Berichterstattung über weitere Erkenntnisse und Erfahrungen zur gegnerischen Kontaktpolitik/- Tätigkeit...', 14 September 1976, BStU, MfS, BV Suhl, AKG 73, Bd. 4, here pp. 11–12.

[69] Oberstleutnant Heinz, 'Berichterstattung über weitere Erkenntnisse und Erfahrungen zur gegnerischen Kontaktpolitik/- Tätigkeit...', 14 September 1976, BStU, MfS, BV Suhl, AKG 73, Bd. 4, here p. 15.

[70] Oberstleutnant Heinz, 'Berichterstattung über weitere Erkenntnisse und Erfahrungen zur gegnerischen Kontaktpolitik/- Tätigkeit...', 14 September 1976, BStU, MfS, BV Suhl, AKG 73, Bd. 4, here p. 15.

TRAVEL AND MOBILITY: THE INSOLUBLE PROBLEM

The SED worked on many parallel fronts to attain internal and external legitimacy. It is infamous for operating a huge repressive apparatus spearheaded by the all-pervasive Stasi, with its numerous informants. But the GDR regime attempted to win support and legitimacy not only—and arguably not even primarily—through negative means. The regime made regular efforts to address the complaints of its citizens, borrowed heavily to improve living standards and levels of supply, and compromised on many practical issues. At the same time it crafted a network of organizations and ideas aiming to mobilize the population, promoted popular culture, and offered platforms and visions for common identification with an East German imagined community.[71]

But the issue of travel remained a constant source of internal discontent and external critique that forced the regime into defensive postures, improvised policies, and abrupt changes. This was the case ever since the GDR's first attempt to seize control over cross-border movement in the summer of 1952. The building of the Berlin Wall serves as a dramatic example. Following the new options for border-crossing travel opened through the Basic Treaty, East Germans, especially frontier residents, were confronted with their state agencies' contradictory policies regarding travel. Consequently, their willingness to accept such regulations declined and their focus on travel opportunities as a measure of satisfaction with the regime intensified.

Freedom of travel became the cornerstone of Western Cold War propaganda because the subject so acutely embarrassed Eastern Bloc countries, especially the GDR. It was recognized as a basic human right already in Article 13 of the Universal Declaration of Human Rights from 1948, which stated that, 'Everyone has the right to freedom of movement and residence within the borders of each state' and that, 'Everyone has the right to leave any country, including his own, and to return to his country.'[72] Like other statements in this document, it carried very little clout and was rarely treated seriously in the first two decades following its UN ratification, especially in Eastern Bloc countries. But in the age of détente, espe-cially following the Helsinki accords, human rights and the right to travel became a major rallying cry of dissidents throughout Eastern Europe. East Germany was admitted to the UN following the Basic Treaty, and signed the Helsinki accords shortly thereafter. It had thus internationally committed itself to the freedom of travel, but no one in the SED leadership (as in other Eastern Bloc communist parties) had any intention of actually modifying travel regulations.

Inter-state travel was a core negotiation point in the lead-up to the Basic Treaty. A major goal for Western diplomats in these negotiations was to provide access to

---

[71] The SED's positive mobilization strategies and practices have been the subject of growing scholarly interest in the past decade. See Palmowski, *Inventing a Socialist Nation*; Ross, *Constructing Socialism*; Mary Fulbrook, *The People's State: East German Society from Hitler to Honecker* (New Haven, CT: Yale University Press, 2005); David Tompkins, 'Orchestrating Identity: Concerts for the Masses and the Shaping of East German Society', *German History* 30 (2012): 412–28.

[72] See full text at the UN's website, www.un.org/en/documents/udhr/, accessed 11 August 2013.

border-crossing travel to as many East and West Germans as possible. The GNV, whose relevancy was limited almost exclusively to West Germans' travel, was the best they could accomplish. However, the treaty did create a new channel for East German travel to the West.

A nearly unnoticed and initially insignificant improvement in East German travel to West Germany, agreed to by the GDR during the negotiation of the Basic Treaty, was the 'family emergency visit' (*Dringende Familienangelegenheit*). I follow Patrick Major in referring to it as 'compassionate leave'.[73] Under this rubric, East Germans of every age could get permits to visit first-degree relatives for such events as terminal illness, birth, confirmation, wedding, jubilee birthday, and death. Compassionate leave was not a very important category of travel initially, primarily because GDR regulations stipulated that only (biological) parents, children, or siblings could count as first-degree relatives. There were also whole categories of citizens, those who served in the army for example, or others who were considered at risk of not coming back, which were excluded from obtaining compassionate-leave permits. And yet, as Major shows, the number of applications for compassionate leave rose steadily during the seventies, and the average annual number of approved trips was 40–50,000.[74]

This new channel instantly became a source of worry and a target of surveillance for the Stasi. The title given to the Stasi's internal correspondence on the efforts to prevent emigration after the Basic Treaty was typical: 'Guaranteeing the inviolability of the state border, under conditions of the battle for implementation of the peaceful coexistence.' Reports bearing similar titles detailed the multi-front efforts of the Stasi to identify persons suspected of planning emigration through compassionate leave and making sure their applications were denied.[75] Informants were sent to speak with applicants and their acquaintances, background checks were conducted, and any suspicion of abuse of the mechanism was sufficient for denial of an application.[76] Every approved compassionate leave that ended in illegal emigration was noted and reported as a failure of the authorizing office which, naturally, worked to reduce the percentage of approvals.[77]

The story does not end there: the Stasi identified denied applicants for compassionate leave and emigration as a high-risk group. Its members were considered prone to developing negative attitudes towards the state and were seen as at-risk of attempting to escape to the West. In an attempt to deflect complaints and placate this population, operatives offered explanations for the rejection of applications that

[73] Major, *Behind the Berlin Wall*, 198–9.

[74] Major, *Behind the Berlin Wall*, 198.

[75] BStU, MfS, BV Suhl, AKG 73, bds. 4–6 contain many such reports from the years 1974–87.

[76] See for example major Mangold, Leiter der KD, 'Berichterstattung zum Schreiben des Genossen Minister 'Verstärkung der pol.-op. Arbeit aller operativen Linien und Diensteinheiten'...', 21 October 1974, BStU, MfS, BV Suhl, AKG 73, Bd. 4.

[77] For example 'Lagecharakterisierender Erscheinung und Arbeitsergebnisse zur Einschätzung der politisch-operativen Lage im Verantwortungsbereich der Bezirksverwaltung Erfurt im Monat März 1987', 4 October 1987, BStU, BdL, 1409; Major Rudloff, Leiter der BKG, 'Analyse zum ungesetzlichen Verlassen der DDR durch Bürger des Bezirkes Suhl über die Staatsgrenze in anderen Bezirken der DDR...', 3 February 1981, BStU, MfS, BV Suhl, AKG 73, Bd. 5.

were meant to direct the applicants' anger away from the state. Stasi offices invented tales to cover up for the fact that application denial was often based on very slim evidence. Officials of the police and other state offices were encouraged to visit these people and make them understand the (sometimes trumped-up) reasons for the denial.[78] Preventive work in such cases also included surveillance through informants, monitoring of contacts to the West, and strict examination of all travel requests.[79]

Initially, only a small number of eligible applicants applied and was granted permission for compassionate leave and emigration. The ebb and flow of those numbers during the 1980s reflects the fluctuations in the SED regime's confidence. Border-crossing travel and emigration became the crux of conflict between the ruling party and the citizens of the GDR during the 1980s. Compassionate leave, with its built-in flexibility, attracted the brunt of attention. Internal and external pressures on the GDR government created considerable shifts in regulation regarding emigration and compassionate leave in particular. These shifts indicate that the SED was losing ground all through the 1980s.

The first major change in the original regulation pertaining to compassionate leave came in February 1982.[80] This regulation extended the categories of eligible applicants by adding grandparents and half-siblings and increasing the number of events which could merit a compassionate leave permit. The 1982 regulation maintained the framework and rationale of the original policy and did not spur a significant change in the number of applications. The next revision of this regulation three years later reflected a true break from the strict position about border crossing that the GDR had held since 1961. The 1985 revision came from the top. Egon Krenz, then member of the *Politbüro* of the SED, received Erich Honecker's blessing for the reform he prepared following a decision by the party's central committee to increase travel options.[81] Approximately 30 per cent of all rejected applications, wrote Krenz, could be approved upon closer examination.

Some of the suggestions in this document spelled far-reaching transformations in policy. Rejection by category (that is, because the applicant belonged to a category such as 'bearers of secrets' or 'relatives of defectors'), the most common reason given for denial of application, was practically abolished. Officials handling such requests would need to exercise greater flexibility and evaluate requests on a case-by-case basis. This flexibility would extend also to local offices' broader authority to grant exceptional permits to citizens who were considered 'politically responsible' even in cases that did not match the regulations very well. The list of compassionate-leave-

---

[78] For example Hauptmann Knespel, Leiter der Abteilung VI, 'Berichterstattung Zum Schreiben des Genossen Minister 'Verstärkung der pol.-op. Arbeit aller operativen Linien und Diensteinheiten'...', 21 October 1974, BStU, MfS, BV Suhl, AKG 73, Bd. 4.

[79] For example Oberst Höfer, Leiter der AKG, 'Rückinformation Nr. 3/85 über die Einschätzung der Wirksamkeit der politisch-ideologischen Diversion unter übersiedlungsersuchnden Personen...', 5 August 1985, BStU, MfS, BV Suhl, AKG 73, Bd. 6.

[80] 'Anordnung über Regelungen zum Reiseverkehr von Bürgern der DDR', 15 February 1982, BArch-B, DY 30/IV 2/2.039, Nr. 306.

[81] Egon Krenz to Erich Honecker, 12 November 1985, BArch-B, DY 30/IV 2/2.039/306, 3–15.

Table 5.1 Numbers of compassionate leaves from the GDR in 1985–7

	Compassionate Leave[82]			
Period	Applications			Did not come back
	Total	Approved	Denied	
1985	160,739	139,012 (87%)	21,727 (13%)	282 (0.2%)
1986	565,666	525,265 (93%)	40,401 (7%)	1,112 (0.21%)
Jan–Aug 1987	756,526	695,336 (92%)	61,190 (8%)	1,594 (0.23%)

justifying events was extended to include religious ceremonies, and rejections of applications now required approval by heads of departments who would, ideally, specify grounds for rejection.[83]

The consequences of this revision, which entered into force in February 1986, transformed compassionate leave into a major channel of border-crossing travel. The amendments were not officially published, but the change in application approval rates were quickly disseminated by word of mouth and picked up by the West German media. Rumours almost immediately brought a dramatic rise in the number of submitted applications, including a rise in standard applications, which would have been approved even before the revision, testifying to a public notion of greater leniency regarding travel. Even the number of applications that clearly fell beyond the lenient regulations such as visits to old school friends increased at this time. Such applications notwithstanding, the percentage of denials declined markedly. The lower denial rate seems to be strongly related to the flexibility suggested by Krenz, which allowed local offices to weigh applications according to intangibles of the applicant.[84] As Table 5.1 shows, more than half a million compassionate leaves were granted in 1986, almost four times as many as in the preceding year. Rather than a new plateau, this jump signalled the first stage in a graph of acceleration: the year 1987 closed with over a million compassionate leaves.[85]

GDR authorities did not expect the massive response to the revised regulations. It was not only a matter of numbers. Central authority reports on travel applications reflect a gradual shift in relations between applicants and officials. The reports never convey a complete turning of the tables, but some officials, including some very senior, feared such a development. As an examination of the changes following the revision of travel regulation put it in 1986:

[82] Data from 'Übersicht über Reisen in dringenden Familienangelegenheiten', BArch-B, SAPMO, DY 30/IV 2/2.039, Nr. 306, 147.
[83] Egon Krenz to Erich Honecker, 12 November 1985, BArch-B, DY 30/IV 2/2.039/306, 9–12.
[84] 'Bericht über die Untersuchungen durch die Abteilung für Sicherheitsfragen des ZK hinsichtlich der Reisen in dringenden Familienangelegenheiten...', undated, BArch-B, DY 30/IV 2/2.039, Nr. 306, 78–86.
[85] Major, *Behind the Berlin Wall*, 205.

We have noticed that during the submission [of applications] and interviews, some citizens' attitude was demanding. They perceive their requests not as exceptions to the legal regulation, but as rights they are entitled to.[86]

The flexibility of categories and the personal inclinations of different branch heads of the Ministry of the Interior and the Stasi resulted in inconsistent application decisions, leading to many complaints. By 1988, it was not uncommon for applicants to curse, threaten, and personally insult visa officials and even police officers if their applications had been denied. Stasi officials from the town of Gotha in Thuringia reported that year that none of the several dozens of denied applicants accepted the rejection as final. Even those who kept calm and refrained from abusing the officials said that they would find a different channel to get an approval.[87] Visa offices were inundated and were forced to recruit workers and expand rooms. The sheer volume of daily meetings, interviews, decisions, and form completion overwhelmed the staff of local and regional visa offices who were 'at their physical and psychological performance limit'.[88]

Pressure from would-be emigrants was not just internally problematic; it was also internationally embarrassing. The policy changes in 1985 should be seen in the context of a changing international environment following the appointment of Mikhail Gorbachev as the new leader of the Soviet Union in March of that year. The influence of Gorbachev's change of course is undisputed and well studied. As mentioned above, the GDR was committed by then through membership in the UN and the Commission on Security and Cooperation in Europe (CSCE, the organization founded by the Helsinki conference) to articles of human rights, including freedom of movement. A growing number of applicants cited such international agreements in appeals following application denials.[89]

Some emigration seekers took the next step and tried to involve Western powers or public opinion directly. The best-known incidents were those in which GDR citizens sought asylum in West German embassies in Prague, Budapest, and Warsaw. While on approved vacations, East Germans simply entered the FRG embassies in these countries and refused to leave until they were granted a visa to West Germany. The first large number of such cases came in late 1984. It began with 50 asylum seekers in the Prague embassy in mid-September, and the number reached 160 by November. German state agencies in both East and West found themselves between a rock and a hard place. West German authorities hosted under

---

[86] 'Bericht über die Untersuchungen durch die Abteilung für Sicherheitsfragen des ZK hinsichtlich der Reisen in dringenden Familienangelegenheiten...', undated, BArch-B, DY 30/IV 2/2.039, Nr. 306, 81.

[87] 'Information über erste Reaktionen von Übersiedlungsersuchenden,... die Ablehnung ihres Übersiedlungsersuchens ausgesprochen wurde', 11 April 1988, BStU, AKG 223, Bd. 2. Reports from 19 April and 13 May follow in the same file. Note that such follow-up conversations were in themselves a new policy designed to mollify the denied applicants.

[88] 'Bericht über die Untersuchungen durch die Abteilung für Sicherheitsfragen des ZK hinsichtlich der Reisen in dringenden Familienangelegenheiten...', undated, BArch-B, DY 30/IV 2/2.039, Nr. 306, 84.

[89] Major, *Behind the Berlin Wall*, 208–17.

their jurisdiction individuals who, under FRG law, were not foreign citizens and could legally become West German citizens upon request. But they had no realistic way to transport them to West Germany without stirring up a great deal of trouble, not just with the GDR, but with Czechoslovakia as well. East German state agencies were asked to give up one of the most basic prerogatives of a sovereign state, to compromise the legitimacy of its rule under pressure from individual citizens. Negotiations between the two German governments proved fruitless. GDR negotiators were willing to promise only that the emigration seekers would not be arrested upon return and that their applications would be examined. After a prolonged impasse, the last of the asylum seekers gave up and in mid-January returned to the GDR.[90]

The leadership of the GDR gradually relaxed travel regulations, accommodating ever-more requests and complaints. The SED thus tried to contain emigration and travel pressure within state-sanctioned and controlled channels. But every relaxation brought with it growing pressure. The next revision took place in 1988. It was discussed internally for the better part of the year before being adopted by the *Politbüro* in November and published a month later. The 1982 regulation was officially replaced. All the leniencies from the 1985–6 revision remained in place (this time they were made public), but the flexibility introduced to the practice in 1985 was reduced in order to prevent inconsistencies between offices and regions. In addition, the condition of a formal authorization for vacation from the employer was abolished for most workers.[91]

This time, security and party organizations prepared for the occasion, and on the day the new policy was made public, reviews began of its reception and effects. Ten weeks later, an initial summary of this monitoring conveyed very limited success. The report could only quote positive comments from people who were granted travel permits thanks to the new regulations. But, as in 1985–6, the first noted effect was a sharp rise in submitted applications for emigration and compassionate leave, leading to a corresponding rise in rejection and resentment. Denied applicants were even more adamant in their rejection of the decision than those in the Gotha reports from 1988. The reporters were under the impression that all applicants were expecting a further relaxation of travel regulations soon and made their plans accordingly. They also noted clear signs of coordinated action across regions. There were many cases of non-violent protest which demonstrated organization and planning.[92]

The rising number of emigrants—both legal and illegal—since 1986 did not, as some decision makers had expected, exhaust, or even reduce, emigration pressure.

[90] Tyller Marshall, 'Last 6 E. Germans End Asylum Vigil in Prague', *Los Angeles Times*, 16 January 1985, http://articles.latimes.com/1985-01-16/news/mn-8501_1_asylum-seekers, accessed 15 August 2013; '17 DDR-Flüchtlinge verließen Botschaft in Prag', *Göttinger Tageblatt*, 3 January 1985.
[91] 'Information und Schlußfolgerungen zur Durchführung des Beschlusses des Politbüros vom 9.11.88...', 28 February 1989, BArch-B, DY 30/IV 2/2.039, Nr. 307, 51–63.
[92] 'Information und Schlußfolgerungen zur Durchführung des Beschlusses des Politbüros vom 9.11.88...', 28 February 1989, BArch-B, DY 30/IV 2/2.039, Nr. 307, 51–63.

On the contrary, it created a strong 'pull factor' for emigration. Recent emigrants spread 'illusions about life in the West' and became the relatives which other GDR citizens applied to be united with, or at least visit. In January 1989 alone, over 164,000 applications for compassionate visits were submitted, along with over 76,000 applications for permanent emigration.[93] This was the last time that the GDR government could pretend to control migration. In May 1989, the Hungarian government began to open its border with Austria and from September the border was officially open. Another swarming of West German embassies in Warsaw, Prague, and East Berlin by East German asylum seekers unfolded. This time the GDR could not hold its ground, and thousands were shuttled by rail through GDR territory to the West in September. The inter-German border remained almost as well guarded as it had been a few years earlier, but it ceased to effectively enforce GDR jurisdiction.

FROM BARRIER TO BRIDGE: LOCALIZING UNIFICATION IN THE EICHSFELD

The conflicts regarding travel were of great concern in the top echelons of the SED during the eighties. Surprisingly, it was much less of an issue on the local level in the Eichsfeld. In fact, after the excitement of the first couple of years, the border and the act of crossing it became routinized. Many Western Eichsfeld residents continued to use the GNV throughout the 1980s as they had since 1973, but their visits were no longer of interest to Western media. Border crossing and contact across the border remained in the realm of family or individual networks. Coordination of anything beyond these realms was monopolized by state-level organizations. During the late seventies and early eighties, local press in the Western part of the Eichsfeld only wrote about the inter-German border as a national, not a local, issue. When it printed local or regional information about the border, these were reports by the Federal Border Guard unit stationed in Duderstadt. Once a year, the unit commander held a press conference and published a summary of the work of his unit and any incidents along the section it covered. Other than that, the border was represented in the papers only through events in Berlin, diplomatic statements, and political debates.[94]

The GNV remained isolated from the travel and emigration conflicts of the eighties in the GDR until very late. As it did not involve travel for East German citizens, it did not figure into that particular battle. East German frontier residents who wanted to travel to the West applied like the rest of the population via compassionate visits, emigration requests, or as pensioners or disabled persons.

---

[93] 'Information und Schlußfolgerungen zur Durchführung des Beschlusses des Politbüros vom 9.11.88...', 28 February 1989, BArch-B, DY 30/IV 2/2.039, Nr. 307, 51–63.

[94] Based on scanning microfilmed issues of *Göttinger Tageblatt*, *Göttinger Presse*, *Göttinger Allgemeine*, and the local section of *Hessisch-Niedesächsische Nachrichten* at the Göttingen City Archive and the State and University Library in Göttingen.

Lively traffic continued to characterize the routine work at the Eichsfeld check-point, and the volume of traffic grew, along with policy changes in the GDR. The proportion of GNV traffic had always been high at this checkpoint, but as growing portions of the population gained access to travel, more non-locals crossed the border through the Worbis–Duderstadt road. GNV traffic increased continuously, despite consecutive increases in the minimal exchange sum per traveller, which began at 5 Marks in 1973 and had climbed to 25 Marks ten years later. During 1984, checkpoint personnel handled more than 400,000 border crosses. Of this total, 31,560 were GDR citizens. Eighty per cent of them came with the public bus for a single-day shopping visit in Duderstadt, using the 55 Mark 'welcome money' from the federal government automatically distributed to every visitor from the GDR up to twice annually. West Germans crossing for single-day visits in the framework of the GNV numbered 56,048 and there were many school classes and other kinds of groups as well. Lively indeed, but routine. The 'exciting' story at the annual press conference was about a 70-year-old with a forged driver's license.[95] There were no border incidents to report, and even the busiest days did not come close to seeing the traffic of the first Easter weekend of the open checkpoint.[96]

The political conflict surrounding migration from the GDR reached the Eichsfeld relatively late and remained a contained issue of internal East German politics. It was registered through the growing number of legal emigrants and compassionate visitors who passed through the checkpoint. Western authorities noted in 1988 that many visitors' and emigrants' applications would not have been approved in previous years and divined the relaxation of policy before it was officially announced.[97]

Local and regional authorities remained uninterested in border-crossing cooper-ation or even contacts. Judging by the history of border-crossing cooperation in the Eichsfeld discussed in Chapters II and III, one would have expected to find much border-crossing activity in the tumultuous days of September–October 1989, but there was surprisingly little of that. On 8 November 1989, the day before the border collapsed, the mayor of Heiligenstadt sounded skeptical about the idea of a twin-city alliance with Duderstadt. Günther Mock, who was appointed to the position in 1971, was positive about creating neighbourly relations with the Lower Eichsfeld, but did not seem to consider contacting his Western colleagues a viable political option.[98]

---

[95] '249 Übersiedler registriert: Grenzschutzstelle legt Jahresbilanz 1984 vor - 400,898 Reisende', *Göttinger Tageblatt*, 4 January 1985. 1985 was the first year in which no civilian managed to escape the GDR along the border of Lower Saxony. According to the report of the BGS unit in Duderstadt, only three border guards succeeded in escaping during that year. See 'Nur dreien gelang der Sprung in die Freiheit. BGS Duderstadt legt Jahresbericht vor', *Göttinger Tageblatt*, 20 February 1986.

[96] '8,000 Reisten Ostern in DDR', *Hessisch Niedersächsische Allgemeine*, 29 March 1989, StAGö, Ztg. 910.

[97] 'Grenzübergang zur DDR bei Duderstadt: Deutlich mehr Reisende', *Hessisch Niedersächsische Allgemeine*, 15 March 1988, StAGö, Ztg. 910.

[98] 'Duderstädter gern gesehen: Telefoninterview mit Heiligenstats Bürgermeister', *Göttinger Tageblatt*, 8 November 1989.

Given this background, it is quite understandable how, even the next day, no one in the Eichsfeld reckoned that the border between the two parts of the region could ever be completely open for all, let alone that same night, as the quote opening this chapter demonstrates. But, then it did. On screen, through West German television filming at the Brandenburg Gate. This is how the border opened for most Eichsfelder, including those who could see the border installations through their windows. Even border guards on both sides of the border received information about the new situation from the television, like millions of awe-struck viewers worldwide.

It did not take long before jubilation spread from the television to fields and village squares throughout the Eichsfeld. Within a few hours, makeshift openings were made in the fence and neighbours exchanged hugs and tears. The first East German car without permits crossed the Eichsfeld checkpoint a bit after midnight and by dawn the road leading to the checkpoint was packed with Trabants heading for Duderstadt. The euphoria of unification swept through the Eichsfeld as it did in all corners of the (then still) two states and around the globe. Enthusiasm radiated from every encounter and report during the following months. Carried forward by the jubilation, thousands of Eastern Eichsfelder crossed the border, rushing to see the wonders of the West. They were met by equal curiosity and excitement. Western Eichsfeld administrations, organizations, and individuals volunteered, contributed, cheered, and assisted visitors from the East. They showered official 'welcome money', private gifts, free bananas, and simple generosity on their 'sisters and brothers'.[99]

The period after the collapse of the border was special; time itself was experienced differently. Traffic sped through the Eichsfeld day and night, Western public services were open around the clock, special prices were offered, and there was much free sausage and beer to be had. During the first three days, 140,000 people passed through the Eichsfeld checkpoint from East to West and Duderstadt distributed 11 million Marks in welcome money. The festive atmosphere extended beyond Christmas and New Year's Eve. Every day saw another ceremony, another reunion, and another new road opened for traffic.[100]

The *Wende* was emotional in the Eichsfeld, as it was elsewhere along this border, perhaps more emotional than most places. Reunions of old friends and relatives, the

[99] 'Besucherstrom hält weiter an', *Göttinger Tageblatt*, 15 December 1989; 'DDR-Besucherservice weiter rund um die Uhr: "Mal wieder Ausschlafen"', *Hessisch Niedersächsische Allgemeine*, 14 November 1989, StAGö, Ztg. 910; Rüdiger Reyhn, 'Ein Paar Tropfen aus dem Strom: DDR-Bürger am Freitag Abend in der göttinger Innenstadt', *Göttinger Tageblatt*, 11 November 1989; Christina Hövener-Nolte, 'Euphorie über offene Grenze hält an: ein erster Plausch mit Vopo in der Mittagssonne', *Hessisch Niedersächsische Allgemeine*, 13 November 1989, StAGö, Ztg. 910.

[100] 'Diese Freiheit lassen wir uns nicht mehr nehmen', *Göttinger Tageblatt*, 11 November 1989; 'Eichsfeld rechnet mit Besucher-Rekord: Grenze nach Ecklingerode morgen geöffnet?', *Hessisch Niedersächsische Allgemeine*, 17 November 1989, StAGö, Ztg. 910; 'Grenzübergang Duderstadt mit Abstand die meisten DDR-Besucher: 11 Millionen DM Begrüßungsgelder ausgezahlt', *Hessisch Niedersächsische Allgemeine*, 14 November 1989, StAGö, Ztg. 910; 'Nach Zwinge und nach Böseckendorf', *Göttinger Tageblatt*, 15 December 1989; 'Vor 28 Jahre war es anders: bei Böseckendorf ging die Grenze für einen Tag auf', *Göttinger Tageblatt*, 18 December 1989.

opening of roads connecting neighbouring villages and towns, meetings between mayors and administrators, the establishment of regional societies and networks and more, were common.[101] The religious component, so crucial to the identification of Eichsfelder and still central to the daily lives of many of them in 1989, added a further layer to the experience of unification in the Eichsfeld. Catholic priests were prominent in most ceremonies and receptions. For residents of the East German part of the region, the re-assertion of religiosity in the public sphere was a crucial aspect of the peaceful revolution. In Sunday rallies in Heiligenstadt, demands for Catholic kindergartens and schools accompanied the more common freedom of movement and democracy slogans. For Upper Eichsfeld Catholics, reconnection to the Western Catholic establishment was a source of support in their quest to regain the ground they had lost under years of dictatorship. And West German Catholics experienced a new sense of mission and the prospect of invigorating the community and power of political Catholicism.[102]

In December 1989, the CDU unsurprisingly won the first free elections for the district council in Heiligenstadt, making the inexperienced 33-year-old Eichsfeld native Werner Henning chairman of the district council. The CDU had been the bastion of political Catholicism in West Germany and assumed that role in the Eastern Eichsfeld as soon as independent parties were established. Henning almost immediately started a campaign to reunite the Eichsfeld by transferring his district to Lower Saxony. While his motives for this campaign were probably of a pragmatic-political nature, it is clear that Henning's strategy sought to capitalize on the euphoric atmosphere of those months in the Eichsfeld. His arguments leaned heavily on the notion of the historical unity of the Eichsfeld.[103]

CONCLUSION

Werner Henning was 16 years old when Egon Bahr and Michael Kohl signed the Basic Treaty in December 1972. He grew up with division and matured under conditions determined by the inter-German compromise. The GNV was as much a part of his adult life as the almost-impenetrable border. When he chose the indivisibility of the Eichsfeld as a mobilizing call and political tool, he knew that the Eichsfeld had been effectively divided since the late 1960s at least. But he also

[101] Sheffer, *Burned Bridge*, 240–2, for example, describes similar events and emotions in Neustadt and Sonneberg.
[102] Hermann Hillebrecht, 'Die Kuh ist nicht vom Eis', *Göttinger Tageblatt*, 15 November 1989; 'Vor 28 Jahre war es anders: bei Böseckendorf ging die Grenze für einen Tag auf', *Göttinger Tageblatt*, 18 December 1989; 'Und dann nach Worbis: CDU-Kreisverband feierte mit CDU-Freunden aus DDR', *Göttinger Tageblatt*, 18 December 1989.
[103] See a brief summary of Henning's campaign and its historical context at www.mdr.de/thueringen/thueringer-zeitgeschichte/aufbruch/artikel98450.html, accessed 18 August 2013. See also Thomas T. Müller, 'Der Abbau der Grenzsperranlagen und die Anfänge der grenzüberschreitenden Zusammenarbeit im Eichsfeld 1989/1990', in Grenzlandmuseum Eichsfeld e.V (ed.), *Grenze—mitten in Deutschland* (Teistungen: Cordier, 2001), 158; 'Zur Person Dr. Werner Henning', *Göttinger Tageblatt*, 15 December 1989.

knew that individual and kinship networks had been re-established since the mid-1970s through the GNV and the gradually expanding travel options. When he assumed office in November 1989, he probably realized that there was no realistic chance for a ceding of the Upper Eichsfeld to Lower Saxony. But he also could sense that utilizing this prospect might bring him popular back wind and political gains.

As this chapter has demonstrated, the final 17 years of the inter-German border were the years in which it earned its infamy and became a solid divide. Illegal crossing of the border became close to impossible in the mid-1970s. The inter-German compromise and international recognition of the GDR were crucial elements in this final solidification of spatial division of the territory. Local and regional administrations were entirely excluded from border-crossing coordination, and consequently lost touch with their counterparts across the border. After decades without meaningful contact since the early sixties at the latest, regional administrations along the border lost interest in border-crossing cooperation as a viable channel of administration.

The Basic Treaty created, for the first time, a mechanism for negotiating, demarcating, and regulating the border. The inter-German Border Committee met regularly throughout the period covered in this chapter. Its original mission, agreement on the exact path of the border, marking it on maps and on the ground, was completed by 1978. But during that time it had become indispensable to both states, as an arena for negotiating and regulating the myriad problems that the maintenance of a common border regularly gives rise to. Having eliminated local-level solutions, state agencies needed a permanent high-level body to deal with them.

At the same time, the opening of the inter-German border for flexible crossing by Western frontier residents, and especially the re-establishment of the border checkpoint, seemed to open a floodgate of civil communication in the Eichsfeld. Thousands of Western frontier residents crossed the border to the GDR every month, and thousands of East German pensioners made Duderstadt and Göttingen their primary destinations. Meetings multiplied, thanks to the Basic Treaty. Initially, the GNV and the opening of the checkpoints made the biggest impact; since the mid-eighties, compassionate leave added large numbers of visitors to the tally. In the GDR, conflicts about travel produced avalanche-like dynamics during the eighties. The SED leadership proved incapable of controlling this process, spelling the demise of the inter-German border even before the famous press conference of 9 November.

Conclusion

The period since 1990 has probably been the longest in modern history in which the majority of Germans accepted the existing borders of their country as stable and final. While the demarcation of 'where is Germany?' ceased to be contested, internal divisions between East and West continue to trouble German society. In a recent essay in *Der Spiegel*, Stefan Berg posited that it was time to bid farewell to this division:

> The end of a country is on the horizon, a country that never formally existed: East Germany. A demographic group that also never formally existed is coming to an end, as well: the East Germans. It's time for an obituary.[1]

The current German president, Joachim Gauk, is originally from East Germany, as is Chancellor Merkel; her party's victory in 2005 supposedly proved that Germany had finally overcome its division. But the dramatic narrative suggested by Berg, of a social division that developed primarily after unification and because of it, as he goes on to write, and disappeared via material investments and symbolic success stories, is misplaced. There was no single day in which division appeared, nor will it be possible to identify a single day when it will be completely undone. It would be much more constructive to document and analyse division and unification than to try and find the moment in which these long and inherently incoherent processes began or ended. In any case, an obituary is clearly premature at this point: the East–West divide refuses to die, as many measurable variables, annually quoted by the press towards the 'Day of Unity', demonstrate all too well.[2]

This book contributes to the understanding of the persistence of division by correcting the historical perception of how it came to be. In order to make sense of the process of division, an investigation of the development of the inter-German border is required. This book analyses connections between state-building and border formation and studies the effects of both processes on cross-border

---

[1] Stefan Berg, 'Goodbye Ossi: The Demise of Eastern German Identity', *Spiegel Online*, 30 August 2013, www.spiegel.de/international/germany/the-eastern-german-identity-has-disappeared-a-919110.html, accessed 1 September 2013.

[2] Lindsay M. Pettingill, 'Towards an Appreciation of German Disunity', *German Politics and Society* 97 (2010): 69–77; See some examples from recent years of the routinely repeating reports on the insistence of division to East and West in Germany: Justus Bender, 'Die Spaltung ist immer noch real', *Die Zeit*, 23 September 2008, www.zeit.de/campus/2008/05/ost-west-streit?page=1, accessed 9 November 2008; Alexandra Anders, 'Bilanz der Einheit', *Die Zeit*, 12 November 2010, www.zeit.de/wirtschaft/2009-11/ost-west-bilanz-karten?page=1, accessed 12 November 2010.

networks and regional communities. This analysis sheds light on the interrelations between the evolution of political borders and the dissolution and creation of communities and their boundaries. Rural conditions played a crucial role in shaping these processes. The inter-German borderlands were primarily rural areas; common practices of frontier residents revolved around agricultural work. Any change in land use or ownership was therefore of great consequence to these residents. Border formation required a thorough transformation of the political and social constructions that had for centuries developed on this land. It therefore required negotiation with frontier communities.

Border formation relied on negotiation and mobilization to a much greater degree than it relied on coercion. Both state-building projects faced great challenges in their efforts to win legitimacy, internally as well as externally, and their economic underpinnings were poor. Furthermore, state-building in West and East Germany took place amidst mutual competition and dependency. The competition between East and West limited communication across the divide between state organizations; their difficulties in attaining legitimacy increased significantly the leverage of frontier residents. The physical conditions of the rural borderlands further impeded border formation. Controlling movement across forested hills, open fields, and streams was a daunting task, consuming ever-growing resources on both sides. That the residents of these areas possessed an intimate knowledge of their environment made it even more complicated. Regulating movement of people and goods from the hinterland across this border proved a much easier task than imposing the same supervision on frontier residents. State agents negotiated land ownership, cultural cooperation, food supply, transportation, government aid, and more. Conflict and negotiation led to intensified interactions of peripheral rural populations with state agents. In the process, these people recognized the power and authority of state agencies and, over time, were forced to accept their priorities.

The inter-German border developed by way of a set of complicated processes, that culminated only between the late 1960s and mid-1970s in a stable division based on the strong effects of two separate states. The gradual shifts in the balance of power between state and non-state organizations and groups were palpable from the early 1950s. From the currency reform of June 1948 on, West Germany's concerns regarding central economic planning drove it to expand border regulation, and federal forces replaced local ones in enforcing these regulations. Frontier economy depended on lively exchange within networks which predated the inter-German border. State agencies redefined established practices and trade channels as criminal acts and tried to enforce an economic separation. Even before visible constructions appeared along most of the border, Western economic policy had endowed it with growing significance. East German state organizations, prioritizing effective coercion, transformed the conditions of border formation in 1952 with a wide-ranging policy change. In addition to violent deportation and mass emigration from the Eastern borderlands, the Eastern measures gave rise to prolonged conflicts over land.

Eventually, West German policy, more than East German violence, determined the conditions in which these conflicts played out. The battle over the recognition of the GDR, spurred by the Western claim to exclusive representation of the German people, dictated Eastern and Western state agencies' priorities. The strategies they applied in this conflict combined to undermine official cross-border contacts and coordination which were crucial for many aspects of life in the borderlands. Regional and local border-crossing networks were strong and effective in the early fifties and frontier communities fought to maintain them, but state-building priorities were threatened by such connections. By 1960, before physical barriers could disrupt cross-border networks and cooperation, the battles over recognition had completely eliminated them. East German state agencies again took the initiative in 1961, with another highly visible policy change and physical transformation of the border. Following the construction of the Berlin Wall, regulation of the rural border changed, ushering a second wave of deportations and many new restrictions. East German officials were instructed to avoid all contact with their Western colleagues. This instruction no longer made much difference as cross-border coordination had been in preceding years stripped of any practical value.

The implementation of the new East German border policy of 1961, erecting the Berlin Wall and ushering in a second wave of deportations, followed on the heels of the 'full collectivization' drive of 1959–60 in the Eastern borderlands. Both campaigns were billed as short and decisive; in actuality, both were drawn-out and riddled with conflict, and both ended in compromise. Together, they effected a wide-ranging transformation of land use in the rural frontier, usurping growing portions of land from frontier residents and turning them into controlled no man's lands. Despite different conditions, the Western borderlands experienced a similar transformation. Rapid economic expansion of the commercial and industrial centres of the West German hinterland drew the young and able away from the rural peripheries. Together with integration in the EEC, these processes rendered small-scale private agriculture, typical of many areas along the border, unprofitable. Frontier residents effectively resisted state-initiated consolidation of landholding. Nevertheless, many of them had to give up agriculture altogether or keep only low-maintenance crops. West German aid programmes to the borderlands further strengthened this trend. Along the inter-German border, the development of physical *distance* between former neighbours was unmistakable from the late 1950s. Frontier residents on both sides of the border were used to meeting, or at least passing in sight of, each other, but such opportunities became increasingly rare.

By the end of the 1960s and the beginning of the following decade, division took root in the fields along the inter-German border. Land ceased to be the subject of heated conflicts between frontier residents and state agencies. Cross-border networks existed, but their function was reduced to intermittent communication through mail, updates, and greetings on suitable occasions and rare visits. This contact was clearly marked by *difference*: the better-off Western relatives sent packages with goods to their poor Eastern kinfolk; in return they received home-knitted underwear, unavailable in their new shiny supermarkets. Both sides recognized the different expectations, opportunities, and concerns of the other.

Lip-service was paid to the existence of cross-border communities and loyalties, but they ceased to offer practical coordination.

Frontier residents and their networks no longer posed a threat to border formation and state-building by the end of the 1960s. In some sense, they became important agents in the production and representation of division. As guides for Western border tourists, they presented the backwardness of 'the East', pointed out its violence and repression, and directed Westerners' gaze towards coercion's most prominent physical expressions. As Eastern 'border helpers' (*Grenzhelfer*), they partook in securing border areas from the 'threats' of people from the hinterland who wanted to cross to the West. Frontier residents could still cross the border, but it became so risky and complicated that only young men tried it. Despite the high rate of success (up to 70 per cent of Eastern frontier residents in the Eichsfeld who attempted to cross to the West during the 1960s succeeded in doing so) fewer and fewer tried. The declining numbers reflected not only the danger, but also the fact that 'the West' had retreated from their immediate consciousness, receding from experience to a fantasy mitigated through forbidden media and memory.

A central pillar of Willy Brandt's *Ostpolitik* was the recognition of the GDR and the establishment of relations with it. This policy ended the long international isolation of the GDR, and in 1973 both German states were accepted to the United Nations. Western negotiators were able to salvage a semblance of de jure denial of division in the Basic Treaty of December 1972. But when it came to drawing a mutually recognized borderline, symbolic denial was not an option. The joint Border Committee reached agreements on the exact path of the border across over 90 per cent of its length. This compromise assumed a physical presence with uniform border stones and the 1978 official agreement between the governments.

Openly negotiating and delineating the border between them relieved both German governments of their long dependence on frontier residents to control the border. With broad international and domestic legitimacy, the inter-German border assumed new power. Following the Basic Treaty, it turned into the best-guarded border in the world, for the first time matching in real effectiveness the image it had in Western public relations. East German border construction and guarding, held back for two decades by the weight of non-recognition, now progressed apace. Elaborate constructions, deadly mechanisms, and area-consuming fortifications appeared or were spread and reinforced in the first half of the 1970s.

Maintaining a joint border required constant coordination. Local and regional administrations, not having been in contact with colleagues across the border for over a decade at that point, did not take the initiative to coordinate open issues as they had during the 1950s. Consequently, cross-border negotiations were monopolized by central state administrations. Some minor issues and incidents were sometimes solved through individual contacts that were fostered or enhanced through the new travel options introduced by the Basic Treaty.

Border-crossing travel became a major bone of contention between East German citizens and their government from the mid-1970s. Increasing travel options was one of the major goals of Brandt and Bahr's *Ostpolitik*. The travel agreement included in the Basic Treaty established several important new channels for legal cross-border travel. Most significant for the story of division were two such channels: the *Grenznahverkehr* (border area traffic, GNV), which allowed Western frontier residents to travel for short visits in GDR border districts; and the opening of new checkpoints, including the checkpoint on the road from Duderstadt to Worbis, for inter-German travel. These two changes combined to make cross-border interpersonal and kinship contacts a more viable option for Eichsfelder. Numbers suggest that they took greater advantage of this option than other groups of frontier residents: the Eichsfeld checkpoint saw the largest number of GNV travellers of any border checkpoint. Newly established or renewed contacts led to enhanced problem solving and a rekindling of regional networks, but it also led to an awareness of difference—almost foreignness—across the border.

East Germans clashed constantly with their government over travel during the 1980s. An element in the new travel arrangements agreed upon in the Basic Treaty negotiations—'compassionate leave'—allowed East German citizens to visit West German relatives on special occasions. Initially of negligible impact, tracking applications for 'compassionate leave' and emigration to the West in the 1980s shows that citizens gradually increased their demands and expectations in this area, and that the government reacted by continuously expanding the options for border-crossing travel. The changing international environment since Gorbachev was appointed Chairman of the Communist Party in the Soviet Union in 1985 further eroded East German state agencies' ability to restrain civil protests and migration pressures. The dramatic events of November 1989 were thus an important step on a journey already begun.

The Border Committee convened its ninety-first plenary meeting in Nürnberg on 6–7 December 1989. The atmosphere was giddy. Reports from the meeting recorded personal and informal exchanges, which historically had been refused by East Germans. The tone of the summary report is completely unlike that of similar reports from previous meetings. It is marked by open-endedness and uncertainty, not due to disagreements, but rather because the East German delegation openly conceded that it was unsure about its position on many of the issues raised. Leadership was in flux and a sense of instability characterized the delegation. Furthermore, in a quickly decentralizing power structure, GDR delegates were patently insecure about their ability to guarantee regional and local compliance.[3]

EPILOGUE: THE DEATH AND AFTER-LIFE OF THE INTER-GERMAN BORDER

On 18 November 1989 at 6 a.m., before the dawn of a frozen Saturday, the entire community of Ecklingerode, including babies and fragile elderly people, assembled

---

[3] '91. Sitzung der Grenzkommission am 6. und 7. Dezember in Nürnberg', 28 December 1989, NLA-HStAH, Nds. 380, Acc. 27/98, Nr. 73.

in front of the border fence, on the dirt road, which until 1952 connected them to the town of Duderstadt, less than two kilometers away. The thousand Ecklingeroder were received by an equally excited group of around 300 Duderstadt residents, including many relatives and local politicians. After East German border guards removed the fence, which had blocked this road for 37 years, both groups were led by their priests in a solemn procession, and the festive day opened with a joint church service. Breakfast at the Duderstadt priest's house followed. The hosts brought coffee and rolls and the guests brought their home-made *Wurst*. The joyous visit ended that evening with a party in Ecklingerode itself.[4] Similar events occurred throughout the Eichsfeld during those weeks. The border collapsed and gradually disappeared; barriers between old friends and relatives were gone. Hopes (and words) were high in the Eichsfeld for quick reassertion of regional unity. Quite soon, though, it became evident that coming together would not be easy. More starkly than the Cold War visits, the opening of the border laid bare a host of differences. Warm welcomes, emotional meetings, and generosity marked 1989–90. But as elsewhere in Germany, generosity was accompanied by a sort of benevolent paternalism, as West Germans sought to counsel and guide East Germans on how to do things the right way.[5] This was quite obvious in some of the meetings between local and regional officials.[6] Residents of the Eastern Eichsfeld were also taken aback when they found out that West German companies used the open border to secretly dump garbage in GDR dumps, thus avoiding strict regulations and high fees in the West.[7] Even before the unification of Germany in October 1990, then, the Eichsfeld experienced both the hopes and fears that this process brought with it to Germany at large.

The Eichsfeld is no longer a borderland. The new highway A-38, connecting Leipzig and Göttingen, crosses through the region, bringing it closer than it has ever been to all the major cities in Germany.[8] The longest tunnel along its route, undercutting the border between Lower Saxony and Thuringia, was named 'Tunnel of German Unity'. The marks of division are still etched into the terrain—the younger trees in the previous no man's land, the much larger fields in what used to be the collectivized East, the concrete slabs of the former patrol road that are still visible through the grass overgrowth in some areas, and the preserved, even reconstructed watchtowers and fences in border museums are still part of the

---

[4] Christina Hövener-Nolte, 'Grenzübergang Duderstadt/Ecklingerode geöffnet: Freudetränen und eichsfelder Wurst', *Hessisch Niedersächsische Allgemeine*, 18 November 1989, StAGö, Ztg. 910.

[5] This is the origin of the phrase 'besser-Wessis', which came to denote paternalistic West Germans who think they always 'know better'.

[6] See, for example, 'Grenzüberschreitende Kreiskonferenz', 12 January 1990, StAGö, Dez. I Oberstadtdirektor.

[7] 'Grenzkreise stimmen sich ab: Absage an Mülltourismus', *Hessisch Niedersächsische Allgemeine*, 8 November 1990, StAGö, Dez. I Oberstadtdirektor.

[8] This highway connects the eastern north–south highway A9 and the western north–south highway A7. Construction was completed in 2009 as both sides were connected in the Eichsfeld. See Heinz Hobrecht, 'Im Eichsfeld schließt sich die Lücke der Südharzautobahn ', *Göttinger Tageblatt*, 22 December 2009, http://beta.goettinger-tageblatt.de/Nachrichten/Duderstadt/Uebersicht/Im-Eichsfeld-schliesst-sich-die-Luecke-der-Suedharzautobahn, accessed 2 September 2010.

landscape of the Eichsfeld. Society in the Eichsfeld is also still divided into East and West in many ways; Eichsfelder still categorize each other, as many other Germans do, according to Cold War dichotomies.

In September 1990, the two German governments signed the Two plus Four peace treaty with the four Second World War Allies, which officially ended the war and re-established full German sovereignty based on the postwar borders.[9] No new state emerged in Germany in 1989–90 and no new legitimacy was sought by state organizations. Six old states (*Länder*), abolished by the GDR in 1952, were re-established only to join the existing Federal Republic, imitating their Western neighbours. No new borders emerged in Germany; old borders were ratified and then gradually faded in function, contributing to a diminishing presence of state agencies in the borderlands.[10]

The newly acquired territories of the FRG have become its frontier. The residents of the former GDR were excluded from most decisions about their own future in 1989–90. In the absence of vigorous state-building and border formation, the interaction of these new frontier residents with state agencies was not very intense. They had, by and large, minimal or non-existent leverage, and state agencies felt no need to compromise with them. In the 1950s, frontier residents held important bartering chips and used them in protracted, intense conflicts and negotiations with state agencies, which were anxious to achieve legitimacy. These negotiations contributed significantly to frontier residents' eventual integration into the divided Western and Eastern communities. After 1990, East Germans were treated as objects in their country's absorption by the larger, richer neighbour. Their marginalized position, and the resulting dearth of interaction with the state, stood in the way of their integration with the absorbing society.

The inter-German border was dismantled only in the physical and political sense. Barriers were taken down and the East German state hierarchy was dissolved. Legal cases were brought against those East Germans—officers of border-guarding forces, Stasi officials—perceived as responsible for violence against people who tried to escape to the West. The border had been reduced to its physical elements and the blood of its victims.

The absorption of East Germany into the FRG involved a denial of essential elements of the border. Ignored were changes of social and cultural structures, habits, relations, and orientations, and the division of society through the choices and actions of frontier populations. The role of West German state agencies and frontier residents in constructing the inter-German border remains the most denied

---

[9] The treaty entered into effect only in March 1991, five months after one of its signatories, the GDR, ceased to exist. For some details and the full text of the treaty see 'the Two plus Four Treaty', German Federal Foreign Office, www.auswaertiges-amt.de/EN/AAmt/PolitischesArchiv/EinblickeArchiv/ ZweiPlusVier_node.html, accessed 30 August 2013.

[10] In 1992, the FRG signed the Maastricht Treaty, greatly increasing the powers of the European Union. In 1995, the Schengen Treaty entered into power, abolishing border controls between the six original signatories, including Germany, and in 2000 the FRG gave up its cherished German Mark, the primary symbol of its success. Poland and the Czech Republic joined the EU in 2004 and the Schengen Treaty in 2007, reducing the entire length of Germany's borders to a minimal function of internal borders.

part of this border's history. The prevailing myth is that Western state organizations and Western frontier residents have always opposed this border and had no part in making it. For the second time in the same half-century, FRG state organizations are basing their policy on a denial of the reality of division. As in the 1950s and 1960s, so too in the 1990s and 2000s, denial has not led to the disappearance of division. To some extent, denial contributes to division as it did in the past, preserving and reproducing it.

The function of museums which sprang up along the inter-German border after 1990 exemplifies this phenomenon and marks a potentially significant change.[11] The border has been continuously reproduced in some of these museums, generating distance and difference between West and East. When I first visited the two border museums in the Eichsfeld, I was struck by the gap between instructors' knowledge and a sincere effort to educate visitors and the permanent exhibits, which largely reflected Western perceptions of the border—created and imposed by East German state agencies, dangerous, violent, and efficient. Such exhibitions were doubtless the consequence of the dependence of museums on attracting visitors and the popularity of such images. Few visitors want to hear complicated truths about the creation of the inter-German border. Border museums attracted almost exclusively Western visitors and school groups, who wanted to see uniforms, fences, bunkers, watchtowers, helicopters, and mines and hear about escapes and deaths. In recent years, there is a growing recognition of this problem and exhibitions are gradually changing. A major overhaul of the exhibition at the Border Museum Eichsfeld near Gerblingerode in 2011 has resulted in a much more diverse experience, presenting local events in a national and international context. The new exhibition, and especially the new texts which accompany it, set a much more balanced tone, fitting for a new course.

The history of the inter-German border was much more than just the better-known aspects of it. The more subtle elements in the processes of border formation and state-building were crucial in giving rise to a division that was much more resilient than the Berlin Wall. 'The wall in the head', as it had been termed, has its foundations not simply in divergent experience and expectations, but also, importantly, in the denial of certain experiences. Border museum visitors' expectations and interests reflect the dominance and inflexibility of the Western ethos and memory of division, excluding, by and large, conflicting experiences of frontier residents. Museum managers and instructors face the difficult task of recreating division as a multi-actor process of social division that all Germans can relate to as part of their shared history.

In the East and in the West, frontier residents were not simply faced with overbearing power but always had options and choices, and, initially, considerable influence as well. They found ways to circumvent or manipulate state agencies' regulations, especially during the first three postwar decades. They experienced the dividing effects of Western policies and practices. These experiences have thus far

---

[11] Maren Ullrich counted 13 institutions under the title 'border museums' along the inter-German border. See Ullrich, *Geteilte Ansichten*, 344–50.

found little expression in either public discussion or scholarship. The more recent memories of solidified divisions, severed social networks, and effective physical barriers are easier to retrieve; the events of 1989–90 have pushed earlier realities below the surface. But the perceptions, habits, and orientations to which these realities gave rise will not simply disappear, not before generations die out. Division will only be overcome when this history in all its complexity is acknowledged.

Bibliography

ARCHIVAL COLLECTIONS

Archiv des bischöfliches geistliches Kommissariat Heiligenstadt (ABGKH)
Archive of the Heiligenstadt Catholic Commissariat
E   Gottesdienste, Missionen, Gebete, Litaneien usw.
Hülfensberg
Community files

Bundesarchiv, Berlin (BArch-B)
German Federal Archive, Berlin
Abteilung DDR
DC 20 I/4   Präsidium des Ministerrates
DE1   Staatsplankommission
DK1   Ministerium für Land-, Forst- und Nahrungsgüterwirtschaft
DO1   Ministerium des Innern
DO4   Staatssekräter für Kirchenfragen

Stiftung Archiv der Parteien und Massenorganizationen der DDR
im Bundesarchiv (BArch-sapmo)
Archives of the parties and mass organizations of East Germany in
the Federal Archives
DY27   Kulturbund
DY30   Zentralkomittee der SED
DY30/IV 2/2   Beschlüsse des Politbüro
DY30/IV 2/12   Sicherheitsfragen
DY 30/IV A 2/12   Zollverwaltung
DY 30/IV A 2/14   Katholische Kirche
DY 30/IV B 2/20   Internationale Verbindungen
DY30/J IV 2/2   Sitzungen des Politbüro

Bundesarchiv Koblenz (BArch-K)
German Federal Archive, Koblenz
B102   Bundesministerium für Wirtschaft
B126   Bundesministerium der Finanzen
B136   Bundeskanzleramt
B137   Bundesministerium für gesamtdeutsche Fragen
B369   Deutsch-deutsche Grenzkommission, Vertretung der Bundes-
               grenzschutz
Z8   Verwaltung für Wirtschaft des Vereinigten
               Wirtschaftsgebietes/Zentralamt für Wirtschaft in der Britischen Zone
Z33   Chefinspektion des Zollgrenzschutzes britische Zone/Zollgrenzdirek-
               tion Nord und Zollgrenzdirektion Süd/Sonderbeauftragter für die
               Zonengrenze (Südteil) und Sonderbeauftragter für die Zonengrenze
               (Nordteil)

Bundesarchiv, Militärarchiv Freiburg (BArch-M)
German Federal Military Archive, Freiburg
DVH 27			Kommando der deutschen Grenzpolizei
DVH 29			Deutsche Grenzpolizei/Westgrenze
DVH 40			9. Grenzbrigade, Erfurt
DVH 52			Grenzkommando Süd
DVH 53–1			Grenzregiment 1, Geismar
DVH 53–3			Grenzregiment 4, Heiligenstadt

Bundesbeauftragte für die Unterlagen des Staatssicherheitsdienst, (BStU)
*The Commissioner for the records of the state security service of the
	former German Democratic Republic*
BV Erfurt, II
BV Erfurt, VI
BV Erfurt, XX			Staatsapparat
BV Erfurt, Kusch
BV Erfurt, SR
BV Suhl, III
BV Suhl, XII			Abwehrarbeit
BV Suhl, IX
BV Suhl, AKG			Auswertungs- und Kontrollgruppe
KD HIG			Kreisdienststelle Heiligenstadt
KD Lgs			Kreisdienststelle Langensalza
KD Mhl			Kreisdienststelle Mühlhausen
MfS BdL			Büro der Leitung

Hessisches Hauptstaatsarchiv, Wiesbaden (HeHStAW)
Hessian Central State Archive, Wiesbaden
502			Hessischer Ministerpräsident—Staatskanzlei
507			Hessisches Ministerium für Wirtschaft und Verkehr
531			Oberfinanzdirektion Frankfurt a.M.

Hessisches Staatsarchiv, Marburg (HeStAM)
Hessian State Archive, Marburg
401/11			Kommunalaufsicht
401/13			Polizei
610			Bundesgrenzschutzdirektion Mitte

Kreisarchiv Eichsfeld, Heiligenstadt (KrAEich)
Eichsfeld District Archive, Heiligenstadt
EA HIG			Rat des Kreises Heiligenstadt
EA WBS			Rat des Kreises Worbis
Community files from multiple communities

Landkreisarchiv Göttingen (KrAGö)
Rural District Archive of Göttingen, Göttingen
A32			Ordnungsamt
LK Dud			Landkreis Duderstadt
LK Gö			Landkreis Göttingen

Niedersächsisches Landesarchiv, Hauptstaatsarchiv Hanover (NLA-HStAH)
Lower Saxon Central State Archive, Hanover
Nds. 50   Staatskanzlei
Nds. 100   Ministerium des Innern
Nds. 120   Bezirk Hildesheim
Nds. 220   Oberfinanzdirektion
Nds. 380   Grenzkommission
Nds. 600   Ministerium für Ernährung, Landwirtschaft und Forsten
Nds. 950   Duderstadt
Nds. 1150   Grenzschutz Kommando Nord
Acc. 2000   Kleine Erwerbungen

Niedersächsisches Landesarchiv, Staatsarchiv Wolfenbüttel (NLA-StAW)
Lower Saxon State Archive, Wolfenbüttel
90N   Landkreis Blankenburg
4 nds.
12 neu 18   Braunschweig

Stadtarchiv Duderstadt (StADud)
Duderstadt Town Archive
Bro   Brochthausen
Fuhr   Fuhrbach
KEF   maps

Stadtarchiv Göttingen (StAGö)
Göttingen City Archive
A25   DDR
C9   Dezernat III
C14   Hauptamt
C46   Kulturamt
I A38   DDR
Ztg. 196   Göttinger Presse
Ztg. 203, 204   Göttinger Allgemeine
Ztg. 344–46   Göttinger Tageblatt
Ztg. 516, 910   Hessisch Niedersächsische Allgemeine

Stadtarchiv Heiligenstadt (StAHig)
Heiligenstadt Town Archive
I A   Stadtverwaltung
VIII A   Heimatmuseum

Stadtarchiv Witzenhausen (StAWitz)
Witzenhausen Town Archive
Zeitungen G12   Grenze bis 1987
Neuseesen
Werleshausen

Thüringisches Hauptstaatsarchiv, Weimar (ThHStAW)
Thuringian Central State Archive, Weimar
Bezirksbehörde der deutschen Volkspolizei Erfurt
Bezirksparteiarchiv der SED Erfurt
Büro des Ministerpräsidenten
Katasteramt Heiligenstadt
Landesbehörde der deutschen Volkspolizei Thüringen
Landesbodenkommission
Ministerium der Finanzen
Ministerium des Innern
Ministerium für Wirtschaft und Arbeit
Rat des Bezirkes Erfurt

United States National Archives and Records Administration, College Park, MD (NARA)
RG 59   State Department
RG 260   Records of U.S. Occupation Headquarters

OTHER PRIMARY SOURCES

Bundesanstalt für gesamtdeutsche Aufgaben. *Wo Deutschland noch geteilt ist: Beiderseits der innerdeutschen Grenze.* Bonn: Gesamtdeutsches Institut, 1985.
Bundesministerium des Innern. *6 Jahre Grenzkommission mit der DDR.* Bonn, 1979.
Bundesministerium für gesamtdeutsche Fragen. *Im Schatten der Zonengrenze.* Bonn, 1956.
Bundesministerium für innerdeutsche Beziehungen. *Die innerdeutsche Grenze.* Bonn: Gesamtdeutsches Institut, 1987.
März, Peter (ed.). *Dokumente zu Deutschalnd.* Munich: Olzog, 1996.
'Verordnung über die Überwachung des Verkehrs mit Vermögenswerten zwischen dem Gebiet der Bundesrepublik Deutschland und der sowjetisch besetzten Zone Deutschlands sowie dem Ostsektor von Berlin.' *Bundesgesetzblatt* Teil I, 1951, 439–42 (F.R.G.).
von Oppen, Beate Ruhm, (ed.). *Documents on Germany under Occupation, 1945–1954.* London: Oxford University Press, 1955.

NEWSPAPERS AND MAGAZINES

Die Zeit; Göttinger Allgemeine; Göttinger Presse; Göttinger Tageblatt; Hessisch Niedersächsische Allgemeine; Los Angeles Times; Thueringer Allgemeine Online Edition; Spiegel Online; Südhannoversche Volkszeitug; The Washington Post.

SECONDARY LITERATURE

Abelshauser, Werner. *Wirtschaftsgeschichte der Bundesrepublik Deutschland, 1945–1980.* Frankfurt am Main: Suhrkamp, 1983.
Adler, Peter and Katrin Völker. *Wir wollten nur noch raus!: Ein Dorf flieht in den Westen.* DVD. ARD, 10 August 2005.
Ahonen, Pertti. *Death at the Berlin Wall.* Oxford: Oxford University Press, 2011.

Anderson, James and Liam O'Dowd. 'Borders, Border Regions and Territoriality: Contradictory Meanings, Changing Significance.' *Regional Studies* 33 (1999): 593–604.

Anderson, Malcolm. *Frontiers: Territory and State Formation in the Modern World.* Cambridge: Polity Press, 1996.

Auerbach, Ludwig. 'Das ganze Deutschland soll es sein.' In *Adenauer und die Folgen*, edited by H. J. Netzer. München: Beck, 1965, 92–105.

Aufgebauer, Peter, 'Geschichte einer Grenzlandschaft.' In *Das Eichsfeld: Ein deutscher Grenzraum*, edited by Peter Aufgebauer et al. Duderstadt: Mecke, 2002, 66–74.

Baring, Arnulf. *Machtwechsel: Die Ära Brandt-Scheel.* Munich: DTV, 1984.

Bauerkämper, Arnd. *'Junkerland in Bauernhand?'*: *Durchführung, Auswirkungen und Stellenwert der Bodenreform in der sowjetischen Besatzungszone.* Stuttgart: F. Steiner, 1996.

Baumann, Ansbert. 'Thüringische Hessen und hessische Thüringer. Das Wanfrieder Abkommen vom 17. September 1945 wirkt bis heute nach.' *Deutschland-Archiv. Zeitschrift für das vereinigte Deutschland* 37 (2004): 1000–5.

Behrens, Petra. 'Regionale Identität und katholisches Milieu: die Eichsfelder Katholiken zwischen Kriegsende und Mauerbau.' In *Praktiken der Differenz: Diasporakulturen in der Zeitgeschichte*, edited by Miriam Rürup. Göttingen: Wallstein, 2009, 175–96.

Behrens, Petra. 'Regional Kultur und Regionalbewustsein im Eichsfeld 1920 bis 1990.' In *Regionalismus und Regionalisierung in Diktaturen und Demokratien des 20. Jahrhundert*, edited by Petra Behrens, Frank Hadler, Thomas Schaarschmidt, and Detlef Schmiechen-Ackermann. Leipzig: Leipziger Universitätsverlag, 2003, 32–46.

Bennewitz, Inge and Rainer Potratz. *Zwangsaussiedlungen an der innerdeutsche Grenze: Analysen und Dokumente.* Berlin: Links, 1997.

Berdahl, Daphne. *Where the World Ended: Re-Unification and Identity in the German Borderland.* Berkeley, CA: University of California Press, 1999.

Bessel, Richard and Ralph Jessen (eds). *Die Grenzen der Diktatur: Staat und Gesellschaft in der DDR.* Göttingen: Vandenhoeck & Ruprecht, 1996.

Booz, Rüdiger Marco. *'Hallsteinzeit': Deutsche Aussenpolitik 1955–1972.* Bonn: Bouvier Verlag, 1995.

Bothe, Hans-Günther. *Landwirtschaft und Flurbereinigung.* Stuttgart: Eugen Ulmer, 1963.

Buckler, Alois. *Grenzgänger: Erlebnisse aus den Jahren 1947–1961 an der inner-deutschen Grenze.* Leipzig: Thomas Verlag, 1991.

Clay, Lucius D. *Decision in Germany.* Garden City, NY: Doubleday and Company, 1950.

Diedrich, Torsten. 'Die Grenzpolizei der SBZ/DDR (1946–1961).' In *Im Dienste der Partei: Handbuch der bewaffneten Organe der DDR*, edited by Torsten Diedrich, Hans Ehlert, and Rüdiger Wenzke, 201–24. Berlin: Links, 1998.

Dierske, Ludwig. *Der Bundesgrenzschutz: geschichtliche Darstellung seiner Aufgabe und Entwicklung von der Aufstellung bis zum 31. März 1963.* Regensburg: Walhalla-und Praetoria-Verlag, 1967.

Dietzsch, Ina. *Grenzen Überschreiben: deutsch-deutsche Briefwechsel 1948–1989.* Cologne: Böhlau, 2004.

Eckert, Astrid. ' "Greetings from the Zonal Border": Tourism to the Iron Curtain in West Germany', *Zeithistorische Forschung/Studies in Contemporary History* 8 (2011): 9–36.

Eichsfeld Aktiv and URANIA-Bildungsgesellschaft Eichsfeld. *Die Entwicklung der Landwirtschaft des Landkreises Eichsfeld im Zeitraum von 1945 Bis 2000.* Worbis: S.N., 2003.

Eisenberg, Carolyn W. *Drawing the Line: The American Decision to Divide Germany 1944–1949.* Cambridge: Cambridge University Press, 1996.

Eyal, Gil. *The Disenchantment of the Orient: Expertise in Arab Affairs and the Israeli State.* Stanford, CA: Stanford University Press, 2006.

Farquharson, John E. *The Plough and the Swastika: The NSDAP and Agriculture in Germany, 1928–45.* London: Sage Publications, 1976.

Farquharson, John E. *The Western Allies and the Politics of Food: Agrarian Management in Postwar Germany.* Leamington Spa: Berg, 1985.

Fulbrook, Mary. *The People's State: East German Society from Hitler to Honecker.* New Haven, CT: Yale University Press, 2005.

Gavrilis, George. *The Dynamics of Interstate Boundaries.* Cambridge: Cambridge University Press, 2008.

Gavrilis, George. 'The Greek-Ottoman Boundary as Institution, Locality, and Process (1832–1882).' Paper presented at the Rethymno Conference in honour of Charles Tilly, University of Crete, Greece, 17–18 October 2003 (unpublished).

Geyer, Martin H. 'Der Kampf um nationale Representation. Deutsch-deutsche Sportbeziehungen und die "Hallstein Doktrin".' *Vierteljahrshefte für Zeitgeschichte* 44 (1996): 55–86.

Gleitze, Matthias O. 'Die Verteilung und Bedeutung der Betriebsgrössen in der Landwirtschaft des Kreises Duderstadt.' PhD diss., Rostock University, 1926.

Grafe, Roman (ed.). *Die Grenze durch Deutschland: Eine Chronik von 1945 bis 1990.* Berlin: Siedler, 2002.

Gray, William G. *Germany's Cold War: The Global Campaign to Isolate East Germany, 1949–1969.* Chapel Hill, NC: University of North Carolina Press, 2003.

Harrison, Hope M. *Driving the Soviets up the Wall: Soviet–East German Relations, 1953–1961.* Princeton: Princeton University Press, 2003.

Hartmann, Andreas and Sabine Doering-Manteuffel (eds). *Grenzgeschichten: Berichte aus dem deutschen Niemandsland.* Frankfurt am Main: S. Fischer, 1990.

Hertle, Hans-Hermann, Konrad H. Jarausch, and Christoph Kleßmann (eds). *Mauerbau und Mauerfall: Ursachen, Verlauf, Auswirkungen.* Berlin: Links, 2002.

Hohmann, Joachim S. and Gerhard Grischok (eds). *Grenzland Rhön: Geschichten und Bilder aus der Zeit der Teilung.* Hünfeld: Rhön Verlag, 1997.

Hussong, Ulrich. 'Die Teilung des Eichsfeldes im Jahre 1815.' *Eichsfeld Jahrbuch* (1993): 5–92.

Jessen, Ralph. 'Partei, Staat und "Bündnispartner": Die Herrschaftsmechanismen der SED-Diktatur.' In *DDR—Geschichte in Dokumenten*, edited by Matthias Judt. Berlin: Links, 1997, 27–43.

Johnson, Jason B. 'Dividing Mödlareuth: The Incorporation of Half a German Village into the GDR Regime, 1945–1989.' PhD diss., Evanston, IL: Northwestern University, 2011.

Joossens, Luk and Martin Raw. 'Smuggling and Cross Border Shopping of Tobacco in Europe.' *British Medical Journal* 310 (1995): 1393–7.

Judt, Matthias. 'Aufstieg und Niedergang der "Trabi-Wirtschaft".' In *DDR—Geschichte in Dokumenten*, edited by Matthias Judt. Berlin: Links, 1997, 87–102.

Kilian, Werner. *Die Hallstein-Doktrin: Der diplomatische Krieg zwischen der BRD und der DDR 1955–1973.* Berlin: Duncker und Humblot, 2001.

Kleßmann, Christoph. *Die doppelte Staatsgründung: deutsche Geschichte 1945–1955.* Göttingen: Vandenhoeck und Ruprecht, 1982.

Kleßmann, Christoph and Georg Wagner (eds). *Das gespaltene Land: Leben in Deutschland 1945–1990.* Munich: C. H. Beck, 1993.

Kleindienst, Jürgen (ed.). *Von hier nach drüben: Grenzgänge, Fluchten und Reisen im kalten Krieg 1945–1961*. Berlin: Zeitgut Verlag, 2001.

Klinge, Astrid. 'Anmerkungen zur Durchführung der "demokratischen Bodenreform" 1945 im sowjetsich besetzten Eichsfeld.' *Eichsfeld-Jahrbuch* 13 (2005): 167–92.

Kramer, Alan. *The West German Economy, 1945–1955*. New York: Berg, 1991.

Kriedte, Peter, Hans Medick, and Jürgen Schlumbohm. *Industrialization before Industrialization: Rural Industry in the Genesis of Capitalism*. Cambridge: Cambridge University Press, 1981.

Krüsemann, Markus. 'Struktur und Entwicklung der regionalen Wirtschaft seit dem Zweiten Weltkrieg.' In *Das Eichsfeld: Ein deutscher Grenzraum*, edited by Peter Aufgebauer and Dietrich Denecke. Duderstadt: Mecke, 2002, 80–108.

Kuklick, Bruce. *American Policy and the Division of Germany: The Clash with Russia over Reparations*. Ithaca, NY: Cornell University Press, 1972.

Künzel, Arthur. 'Das Wanfrieder Abkommen vom 17.9.1945.' *Schriften des Werratalvereins Witzenhausen* 4 (1981): 28–36.

Langenhan, Dagmar. '"Halte dich fern von den Kommunisten, die wollen nicht arbeiten!" Kollektivierung der Landwirtschaft und bäuerlicher Eigen-Sinn am Beispiel Niederlausitzer Dörfer (1952 bis Mitte der sechziger Jahre).' In *Herrschaft und Eigen-Sinn in der Diktatur*, edited by Thomas Lindenberger. Cologne: Böhlau, 1999, 119–65.

Lapp, Peter Joachim. *Gefechtsdienst im Frieden—Das Grenzregime der DDR*. Bonn: Bernard and Grafe, 1999.

Last, George. *After the 'Socialist Spring': Collectivisation and Economic Transformation in the GDR*. New York: Berghahn Books, 2009.

Lindenberger, Thomas. 'Die Diktatur der Grenzen: Zur Einleitung.' In *Herrschaft und Eigen-Sinn in der Diktatur:Studien zur Gesellschaftgeschichte der DDR*, edited by Thomas Lindenberger, Cologne: Böhlau Verlag, 1999, 13–44.

Lindenberger, Thomas. 'Diktatur der Grenze(n). Die eingemauerte Gesellschaft und ihre Feinde.' In *Mauerbau und Mauerfall: Ursachen, Verlauf, Auswirkungen*, edited by Hans-Herman Hertle et al. (Berlin: Links, 2002), 203–13.

Lindenberger, Thomas. '"Zonenrand", "Sperrgebiet" und "Westberlin"—Deutschland als Grenzregion des Kalten Kriegs.' In *Teilung und Integration: Die doppelte deutsche Nachkriegsgeschichte als wissenschaftliches und didaktisches Problem*, edited by Christoph Kleßmann and Peter Lautzas. Bonn: BpB, 2005.

Loth, Wilfrid. *Die Sovjetunion und die deutsche Frage: Studien zur sowjetischen Deutschlandpolitik von Stalin bis Chruschtschow*. Göttingen: Vandenhoeck & Ruprecht, 2007.

Lüdtke, Alf. *Eigen-Sinn: Fabrikalltag, Arbeitserfahrungen und Politik vom Kaiserreich bis in den Faschismus*. Hamburg: Ergebnisse Verlag, 1993.

Major, Patrick. *Behind the Berlin Wall: East Germany and the Frontiers of Power*. Oxford: Oxford University Press, 2010.

Major, Patrick. 'Going West: The Open Border and the Problem of Republikflucht.' In *The Workers' and Peasants' State: Communism and Society in East Germany under Ulbricht 1945–71*, edited by Patrick Major and Jonathan Osmond. Manchester: Manchester University Press, 2002, 190–208.

Mestrup, Heinz. *Die SED: ideologischer Anspruch, Herrschaftspraxis und Konflikte im Bezirk Erfurt (1971–1989)*. Rudolstadt: Hain, 2000.

Migdal, Joel S. (ed.). *Boundaries and Belonging: States and Societies in the Struggle to Shape Identities and Local Practices*. Cambridge: Cambridge University Press, 2004.

Mitchell, Timothy. 'The Limits of the State: Beyond Statist Approaches and Their Critics.' *American Political Science Review* 85 (1991): 77–96.

Moeller, Robert G. *German Peasants and Agrarian Politics, 1914–1924: The Rhineland and Westphalia*. Chapel Hill, NC: University of North Carolina Press, 1986.

Möller, Gerhard. '"Keine Gebietsänderung verlief aber so dramatisch . . ." Wie Bad Sachsa und Tettenborn "in den Westen" gelangten.' *Beiträge zur Geschichte aus Stadt und Kreis Nordhausen* 30 (2005): 121–49.

Müller, Thomas T. 'Der Abbau der Grenzsperranlagen und die Anfänge der grenzüberschreitenden Zusammenarbeit im Eichsfeld 1989/1990.' In *Grenze—mitten in Deutschland*, edited by Grenzlandmuseum Eichsfeld e.V., 157–62. Teistungen: Cordier, 2001.

Münkel, Daniela (ed.). *Der lange Abschied vom Agrarland: Agrarpolitik, Landwirtschaft und ländliche Gesellschaft zwischen Weimar und Bonn*. Göttingen: Wallstein, 2000.

Murdock, Caitlin E. *Changing Places: Society, Culture and Territory in the Saxon-Bohemian Borderlands, 1870–1946*. Ann Arbor, MI: University of Michigan Press, 2010.

Murdock, Caitlin E. '"The leaky boundaries of Man-Made States": National Identity, State Policy and Everyday Life in the Saxon-Bohemian Border Lands 1870–1938.' PhD diss., Stanford, CA: Stanford University, 2003.

Naimark, Norman. *The Russians in Germany: A History of the Soviet Zone of Occupation, 1945–1949*. Cambridge, MA: Belknap Press, 1995.

Nass, Klaus Otto. *Die Vermessung des Eisernen Vorhangs: deutsch-deutsche Grenzkommission und DDR-Staatssicherheit*. Freiburg: Centaurus, 2010.

Newman, David. 'Borders and Bordering: Towards an Interdisciplinary Dialogue.' *European Journal of Social Theory* 9 (2006): 171–86.

Osmond, Jonathan. 'Kontinuität in der Landwirtschaft der SBZ/DDR zur Zeit der Bodenreform und der Vergenossenschaftlichung 1945–1961.' In *Die Grenzen der Diktatur*, edited by Richarch Bessel and Ralph Jessen. Göttingen: Vandenhoeck & Ruprecht, 1996, 137–69.

Palmowski, Jan. *Inventing a Socialist Nation: Heimat and the Politics of Everyday Life in the GDR, 1945–90*. Cambridge: Cambridge University Press, 2009.

Patel, Kiran. *Europäisierung wider Willen: Die Bundesrepublik Deutschland in der Agrarintegration der EWG 1955–1973*. Munich: R. Oldenburg Verlag, 2009.

Pettingill, Lindsay M. 'Towards an Appreciation of German Disunity.' *German Politics and Society* 97 (2010): 69–77.

Port, Andrew I. *Conflict and Stability in the German Democratic Republic*. Cambridge: Cambridge University Press, 2007.

Potratz, Rainer. 'Zwangsaussiedlungen aus dem Grenzgebiet der DDR zur Bundesrepublik Deutschland im Mai/Juni 1952.' In *Grenzland: Beiträge zur Geschichte der deutsch-deutschen Grenze*, edited by Bernd Weisbrod. Hanover: Hahnsche Buchhandlung, 1993, 57–69.

Ritter, Jürgen and Peter Joachim Lapp. *Die Grenze: Ein deutsches Bauwerk*. Berlin: Links, 2006.

Roggenbuch, Frank. *Das Berliner Grenzgängerproblem*. Berlin: Walter de Gruyter, 2008.

Röhlke, Cornelia (ed.). *Erzählunge von der deutsch-deutsche Grenze*. Erfurt: Sutton Verlag, 2001.

Ross, Corey. *Constructing Socialism at the Grass-Roots: The Transformations of East Germany, 1945–1965*. New York: St. Martin's Press, 2000.

Ross, Corey. 'East Germans and the Berlin Wall: Popular Opinion and Social Change before and after the Border Closure of August 1961.' *Journal of Contemporary History* 39 (2004): 25–43.

Sahlins, Peter. *Boundaries: The Making of France and Spain in the Pyrenees*. Berkeley, CA: University of California Press, 1989.

Sälter, Gerhard. *Grenzpolizisten: Konformität, Verweigerung und Repression in der Grenzpolizei und den Grenztruppen der DDR 1952 bis 1961*. Berlin: Links, 2009.

Sarotte, M. E. *Dealing with the Devil: East Germany, Détente, and Ostpolitik, 1969–1973*. Chapel Hill, NC: University of North Carolina Press, 2001.

Sauer, Josef Hans (ed.). *Die Rhön: Grenzland im Herzen Deutschland*. Fulda: Verlag Parzeller and Co., 1967.

Schaefer, Sagi. 'Border Land: Property Rights, Kinship, and the Emergence of the Inter-German Border in the Eichsfeld.' In *Praktiken der Differenz: Diasporakulturen in der Zeitgeschichte*, edited by Miriam Rürup. Göttingen: Wallstein, 2009, 197–214.

Schaefer, Sagi. 'Hidden behind the Wall: West German State-Building and the Division of Germany.' *Central European History* 44 (2011): 506–35.

Schaefer, Sagi. 'Re-Creation: Iron Curtain Tourism and the Production of "East" and "West" in Cold War Rural Germany.' *Tel Aviver Jahrbuch für deutsche Geschichte* 40 (2012): 116–31.

Schier, Barbara. 'Die Ablieferungsgemeinschaft der merxlebener Neubauern als Klassenkampfinstrument? Ein Thüringisches Dorf auf dem Weg zur Kollektivierung.' In *Zwischen Bodenreform und Kollektivierung: Vor- und Frühgeschichte der 'sozialistischen Landwirtschaft' in der SBZ/DDR vom Kriegsende bis in die fünfziger Jahre*, edited by Ulrich Kluge, Winfrid Halder, and Katja Schlenker. Stuttgart: Franz Steiner, 2001, 213–28.

Schnier, Detlef and Sabine Schulz-Greve. *Wanderarbeiter aus dem Eichsfeld: Zur Wirtschafts- und Sozialgeschichte des Ober- und Untereichsfeldes seit Mitte des 19. Jahrhunderts*. Duderstadt: Mecke, 1990.

Schwark, Thomas, Detlef Schmiechen-Ackermann and Carl-Hans Hauptmeyer (eds). *Grenzziehungen—Grenzerfahrungen—Grenzüberschreitungen: Die innerdeutsche Grenze 1945–1990*. Darmstadt: WBG, 2011.

Shears, David. *The Ugly Frontier*. New York: Knopf, 1970.

Sheffer, Edith. *Burned Bridge: How East and West Germans Made the Iron Curtain*. Oxford: Oxford University Press, 2011.

Sheffer, Edith. 'On Edge: Building the Border in East and West Germany'. *Central European History* 40 (2007): 307–39.

Sheffer, Edith. 'The Foundations of the Wall: Building a "Special Regime" in the Borderland.' Paper presented at the German Studies Association annual conference. Pittsburg, PA, 30 September 2006.

Smith, Joshua M. *Borderland Smuggling: Patriots, Loyalists, and Illicit Trade in the Northeast, 1783–1820*. Gainsville, FL: University Press of Florida, 2006.

Sowden, J. K. *The German Question 1945–1975*. London: Bradford University Press, 1975.

Stadt Duderstadt. *Die Grenze im Eichsfeld: Leid, Hoffnung, Freude*. Göttignen: Verlag Göttinger Tageblatt, 1991.

Steege, Paul. *Black Market, Cold War: Everyday Life in Berlin, 1946–1949*. Cambridge: Cambridge University Press, 2007.

Steiner, André. 'Wirtschaftsgeschichte der DDR.' In *Bilanz und Perspektiven der DDR-Forschung*, edited by Rainer Eppelmann, Bernd Faulenbach, and Ulrich Mählert. Paderborn: Ferdinand Schöningh, 2003, 229–38.

Steininger, Rolf. *Eine vertane Chance: Die Stalin-Note Vom 10. März 1952 und die Wiedervereinigung*. Berlin: J. H. W. Dietz Nachf., 1985.

Tilly, Charles. *Identities, Boundaries, and Social Ties*. Boulder, CO: Paradigm Publishers, 2005.

Tompkins, David. 'Orchestrating Identity: Concerts for the Masses and the Shaping of East German Society.' *German History* 30 (2012): 412–28.

Trittel, Günter J. *Die Bodenreform in der britischen Zone 1945–1949.* Stuttgart: Deutsche Verlags-Anstalt, 1975.

Uhl, Matthias. *Die Teilung Deutschlands: Niederlage, Ost-West-Spaltung und Wiederaufbau 1945–49.* Berlin: be.bra, 2009.

Ullrich, Maren. *Geteilte Ansichten: Erinnerungslandschaft deutsch-deutsche Grenze.* Berlin: Aufbau Verlag, 2006.

von Christen, Frieda. 'Die sowjetische Besatzungszeit in Werleshausen und Neuseesen (Juli bis September 1945).' *Schriften des Werratalvereins Witzenhausen* 4 (1981): 15–27.

Weiß, Erich. *Zur Entwicklung des Flurbereinigungsgesetzes der Bundesrepublik Deutschland in den Vergangenen 6 Jahrzehnten.* Butjadingen-Stollhamm: Agricola, 2009.

Weinreb, Alice. 'Matters of Taste: The Politics of Food and Hunger in Divided Germany.' PhD diss., Ann Arbor, MI: University of Michigan, 2009.

Wettig, Gerhard. 'Stalin and German Reunification: Archival Evidence on Soviet Foreign Policy in Spring 1952.' *Historical Journal* 37 (1994): 411–19.

Wilson, Thomas M. and Hastings Donnan. 'Nation, State and Identity at International Borders.' In *Border Identities: Nation and State at International Frontiers*, edited by Thomas M. Wilson and Hastings Donnan. Cambridge: Cambridge University Press, 1998, 1–30.

Wolfrum, Edgar. *Die Mauer: Geschichte einer Teilung.* Munich: C. H. Beck, 2009.

Index